THIS IS OHIO

ALSO BY JACK SHULER

The Thirteenth Turn: A History of the Noose

Blood & Bone: Truth and Reconciliation in a Southern Town

*Calling Out Liberty: The Stono Slave Rebellion
and the Universal Struggle for Human Rights*

The Overdose Crisis and the
Front Lines of a New America

Jack Shuler

COUNTERPOINT
Berkeley, California

Library of Congress Cataloging-in-Publication Data
Names: Shuler, Jack, author.
Title: This is Ohio : the overdose crisis and the front lines of a new America / Jack Shuler.
Description: First hardcover edition. | Berkeley, California : Counterpoint, 2020.
Identifiers: LCCN 2019058614 | ISBN 9781640093553 (hardcover) | ISBN 9781640093560 (ebook)
Subjects: LCSH: Opioid abuse—Ohio.
Classification: LCC RC568.O45 S525 2020 | DDC 362.29/309771—dc23
LC record available at https://lccn.loc.gov/2019058614

Jacket design by Jaya Miceli
Jacket photograph by Doug Swift
Book design by Jordan Koluch

COUNTERPOINT
2560 Ninth Street, Suite 318
Berkeley, CA 94710
www.counterpointpress.com

Printed in the United States of America

10 9 8 7 6 5 4 3 2 1

TO THE ONES WHO KEEP SHOWING UP

The axe doesn't have to have the last word. We have the last word.

—CLIFF HOUSTON

Contents

Part 3: Nothing About Us Without Us
Spring–Summer 2019

Author's Note

Please note that I have changed or not disclosed the names of some people mentioned in this book to protect their identities and their privacy. I have obscured some locations for this purpose as well. I recognize that this is a story of a small piece of the social services landscape in central Ohio. There are other organizations and people working to combat the overdose crisis who are not mentioned and who do not always get the light they deserve. My intention in this book is to show how a group of people in one place—people who have often been absent from our public conversations about this ongoing tragedy—have experienced the overdose crisis. I have also provided extensive research and resources in the endnotes, especially concerning the drug war and substance use disorder. I urge readers to take advantage of them.

Finally, I have tried to use person-first language when writing. In dialogue in which people are speaking to one another or to me, I stayed true to the language they used. Person-first language is an important intervention for combating the stigma associated with substance use disorder. Health in Justice at the Northeastern University School of Law has produced an excellent resource called "Changing the Narrative" (changingthenarrative.news) not only for understanding person-first language but also for addressing some of the inaccuracies in reporting and public perception of drug use and the overdose crisis. I admit that in the past I failed on this point on many occasions in my own writing, and I am now appreciative of the people who created this resource.

The Corner

Early August 2019. A busy summer morning in a grassy corner lot at East Main and Buena Vista Streets in Newark, Ohio, a small city about forty-five minutes east of Columbus and the county seat of Licking County, named after the river and the salt licks that once attracted deer and buffalo to the area. Storms rolled through last week, and the worst of the summer heat has been kept at bay. Today: low humidity, blue sky with scraps of clouds wandering through. A tent is set up in the shade of a sprawling mulberry tree; a scrawny hackberry and a silver maple linger just behind. Some folks call these trash trees, but they are resilient wonders, pushing up through hardscrabble urban dirt and concrete, willing themselves into existence.

These trees give ample respite to the unsheltered who gather at this corner, where a group of mostly women have set up this tent every Saturday for about a year and a half now. The group members offer food—always hot dogs, sometimes fried bologna sandwiches, chips, cookies, fruit when available—and clothing, which hangs on portable racks, lies folded neatly on tables, or is stuffed helter-skelter in bags below. They also offer brown paper bags—

harm-reduction kits—containing sterile syringes and the drug naloxone (also known by its trade name Narcan), used to reverse opioid overdoses.[1]

Every Saturday, between seventy-five and one hundred people who are homeless and underserved in this community come to this empty corner lot, which muds up in the spring and is now overgrown with crabgrass and knee-high weeds in the corners. The group under the tent is Newark Homeless Outreach, the brainchild of Trish Perry and Jen Kanagy, two fiercely independent and engaged women who saw a gap and raced to fill it. Jen is a nurse by trade, and Trish works as a transportation manager at one of the many local distribution centers, though her real passion is advocating for people with substance use disorder. Every Saturday they're here at the corner, despite the vagaries of Ohio weather.

The corner also attracts many local grassroots activists and organizers. People like Eric Lee, an activist and addiction recovery advocate who drops in sometimes to connect with friends and help people who, like him, have served time and are trying to navigate reentry from prison or jail; Chris Gargus, a deeply religious organizer for an abstinence-based addiction treatment group called the Champions Network; and Tresa Jewell, a former nurse who served in a mobile army surgical hospital (MASH) in Vietnam and who now runs a small nonprofit called John's Helping Hands and delivers food to people who are homeless and living in camps around central Ohio.

Most men and women and some children, the town's nomadic poor, come here by foot or bicycle. Most are white, like 92 percent of Newark and like Trish and most of the folks who serve them, though some are not. In the summer, some are shirtless or in jeans and cutoff T-shirts, weighed down with backpacks and shopping bags. Some are people who use drugs. Some have mental health issues. Some have been convicted of felonies. Some work minimum-wage jobs and struggle to raise their children. And some are just wandering. They are hungry or food insecure.[2] They are unhoused or underhoused. And, in most places, they feel unwelcome.

A dozen people walk around the tables picking up donated snacks or riffling through stacks of used clothes, boxes of shoes, and a bin full of zip-lock bags jammed with basic toiletries. Volunteers mostly stand back; they help people when needed, but they rarely limit folks, as there's enough to go around. Someone grabbing three sandwiches instead of one probably needs them or plans on sharing.

Today a bungee cord on the coolers keeps people from dipping their hands in. There has been a rise in hepatitis A cases, and intravenous drug users are a particularly vulnerable population—the health department will be here next week to give hep A vaccinations.[3]

Many folks seem down, the bad mood raw and palpable. Peggy Ruton's son was just sent to prison for two years, and Trish's son Billy McCall has just been sentenced to eleven months because of a probation violation. And there are rumors of an uptick in overdoses. But the work must go on.

Trish walks over when she sees me and, before saying hello, launches into a report about the overdoses and the hep A and complains about the lack of a syringe exchange in Licking County. As if on cue, a young woman in a black ball cap walks over, her body shaking despite itself, her words slurring a bit, and she asks if Trish has any harm-reduction kits. Two men perk up and walk over to hear Trish's response.

"Nope. All out. I was out in thirty minutes today." She turns to me and says, "Gave out forty."

"Okay, thank you," the woman says, shaking and walking away.

"Come early next week," Trish responds. "See? And the health board, they don't see this stuff."

Trish is interrupted by a woman, maybe in her sixties, hair askew and wearing glasses that barely hide the tears welling up in her eyes. In almost a whisper she asks Trish if she's "the woman who runs this thing."

Trish says, "Yes."

The woman replies, "It's my daughter."

Trish puts her arm around her, and the woman whispers about her daughter's drug use. I catch pieces of their conversation.

"I don't have anyone to talk to. I wish I could get her some help," she tells Trish. "I wish I could do something."

Trish knows how it feels to have a child you cannot save, one you worry over at three in the morning. So Trish is here, looking after others, providing a space where people feel safe—she's doing the thing that she wishes she could have done for her son Billy. In this moment, as she consoles this frustrated mother, she is thinking about that woman's needs, but Trish is also, she will readily admit, thinking about her own.

I step away to give them space when C.J. Wills—a local advocate who, like many here, has been in prison and who always seems ready to help others—rolls up, parks his car, and gets out. He is shirtless, his many tattoos on display, including the handprints of his son when he was a toddler, hugging his waist.

"What happened to your shirt?" I joke.

"It's too damn hot," he says, a wad of chew under one cheek.

C.J. is carrying a pallet of chicken-flavored ramen noodles that he takes over to the table. He has been homeless more than once and knows that when you're camping or sleeping in a car, you need quick, portable calories. He gives what he has even when he has little. But C.J. just had surgery on his back—doctors found a cyst the size of a softball.

"That's why my back was hurting." He should be resting at home, he says.

"Why aren't you?" I ask.

"I will."

I walk to the shade, where I meet a woman who tells me there aren't many places where she feels safe, but this is one of them. She's in her early fifties with dark hair and bright eyes, and is, she says, harboring a lot of pain—physical and mental. Her child died in a car accident, one sibling died from an overdose, and another is dying from cancer. And her own body is hurting, she says, but it's hard to make appointments with counselors or doctors when you don't know where you'll be sleeping next. "I'm tired. I'm tired every day, but I just keep moving," she says. She lived out west years ago—California, Arizona. "I left my soul in Lake Havasu," she says a few times, romanticizing a place and a time better than the unstable present. Occasionally, she says, she has a couch to sleep on. But mostly she doesn't. When she sleeps outside she uses her backpack as a pillow and tries to stay with or near other people—she tries to never be alone. While we're talking, a woman in jeans and a T-shirt sits down about ten feet away from us next to three men who have been chatting and eating, one of them fixing a flat tire on his red mountain bike. The woman has a severe look as she plops down. She's just been released from the jail, which is catty-corner to where we are. She walked out the door and came straight over. The woman looks tired, sad, maybe even angry.

Trish walks over to me with another woman. I've seen her before but can't remember where. It turns out that years ago she was involved in the Newark Think Tank on Poverty, a local organization committed to supporting the voices of people who are poor and treating them as experts. But before we get very far in the conversation, I hear the woman who just got out of jail shout, "I'm trying the best I can," and then she's standing up and pushing the man who was sitting next to her.

Trish jumps in quickly. "Y'all need to leave now. We can't have this here."

Conflicts like this at the corner aren't common. In over a year and a half of coming here most Saturdays, it is the first I've seen. But the sun is high, and people are stressed out.

The woman from the Think Tank keeps talking, barely batting an eye at the pushing and shoving. She says she had been living in a building with cheap apartments. The building's owner believed that no one should be left behind and rented to folks who couldn't find anywhere else to go. He hired her to help keep the place safe. She felt good about being there, about helping people have a dry place to sleep. To be honest, she says, she thought a lot about the Think Tank and what it stood for. But then the city came along and issued multiple violations, and everyone was sent packing. She wonders out loud where they expect people to go.

"How about the Basket?" she says, answering her own question. "Think about how many people we can get in there."

The Basket is a seven-story, 185,000-square-foot building sitting empty along Highway 16 east of town.

"It wouldn't work. It's too far from jobs," someone interjects.

"Yeah, well, the local government would be tickled pink to get us out of downtown."

I walk back to Trish, who's talking with a young man who wants to get into treatment. He's wearing a gray sweatshirt, thin as a rail, and looks exhausted as he holds up two backpacks. He says he's been sleeping under a bridge for a few days.

"All I want to do is get high when I'm on the street. I have no stability, and then I use. With stability, I'd be okay."

Last night, he says, he walked into the police station at eleven and tried to go through the Newark Addiction Recovery Initiative (NARI), a police-run program that lets people turn in their drugs in exchange for help finding a treatment program. It was a desperate move—ordinarily, he wouldn't walk into a police department, hand over the drugs he was carrying, and ask to go into treatment. But last night he'd done just that. An officer showed up in his street clothes, did an intake, and tested the meth the young man was carrying; it turned up positive for the synthetic opioid fentanyl. Another officer drove him to the hospital, where he was seen by a nurse and then a doctor. So far, things were going as they should. But then, at four in the morning, he was released from the hospital and given a business card for the Ohio Addiction Recovery Center in Columbus, a reference guide for local food pantries and crisis resources, and a list of mental health and recovery providers in Licking County and neighboring Knox County. His discharge papers, which he shows me, indicate a diagnosis of "polysubstance abuse" and instruct him to stay hydrated, return to the emergency room if his condition worsens, and follow up with his primary care physician. He doesn't have one, he tells me.

"Until it's their kids," he says, "they aren't going to do anything." He says he wasn't sure what to do, so he walked here to speak to Trish.

I look at my phone. Only thirty minutes have passed since I arrived at the corner. A week before, *The Newark Advocate*, the local paper, announced above the fold that Newark would be named one of Ohio's "Best Hometowns" by *Ohio Magazine*, in recognition of a downtown renaissance—a renovated courthouse, the preservation of a Louis Sullivan–designed building, new restaurants and stores, an outdoor market space, gorgeous music and arts venues, and a new state-of-the-art skate park.[4] Mayor Jeff Hall was quoted as saying, "We've accomplished quite a bit, with public and private collaboration, to turn this into a destination, and also a place people living here don't have to drive very far to have a nice night out."

Many of the folks on this corner don't see these renovations in the same light, don't get to go out to the new restaurants, don't understand or care what a public-private collaboration is or means. There is too much to contend with. For one, the overdose crisis is relentless. It is digging, grating, kicking, and pushing. It is again and again and again. For those caught up in the crisis, these women on the corner are the helpers running to the fire, not away from it. They are not sending prayers—they are organizing.

A few months earlier, I was sitting among a few holdouts from an addiction and poverty conference at Wilson Middle School off Church Street in Newark.[5] We were listening to Kim Kehl, the trauma-informed care coordinator for Ohio Mental Health and Addiction Services, as he spoke about how people in the helping professions must recognize not only the trauma their clients face but even more so, if the work is to be sustainable, the trauma they themselves face while helping. Kehl pulls up a photo on the overhead of a bathtub, filled to the brim. He says it feels like an appropriate metaphor for helping people understand trauma: their bathtubs are full and they try to bail them out, but they just keep filling. This is disconcerting because, for people who have experienced trauma and adversity, their body's alarm systems are chronically on. Kehl tells the story of a first responder who was dispatched to a homicide and discovered three adults who had overdosed and a two-year-old lying on top of their mother, crying. How can anyone be prepared for a scene like that? he asks. Then, almost in passing, Kehl clicks to a slide on which is written the term *community trauma*. He points out that sometimes whole communities endure a life-altering traumatic experience—say a tornado, a mass shooting. At some point, he says, that community may need to address that experience.

Kehl pauses, then asks, "Any questions?"

Allen Schwartz and I raise our hands at the exact same moment. Allen, a gray-bearded community organizer, is one of the founders of the Newark Think Tank on Poverty, which he helped start with his wife, Lesha Farias, in 2014. They have come a long way since then, from mobilizing focused campaigns and lobbying office holders to organizing this conference, asking local leaders to attend. I think I know what Allen is going to say.

"You go," I say.

"No, you can," he replies, a midwestern gesture from a guy raised on the East Coast.

"Well," I ask, "I wonder if this community was traumatized?"

"Right," Allen says, jumping in. "I would say this town *was* traumatized. It was traumatized first by deindustrialization, and it had the heart ripped out of it." And now this—the overdose crisis. The bathtub is overflowing, he says, so we need to stop bailing and turn off the spigot.

In a 2018 article, psychologist and group therapy coordinator Jeff Brand argues that the opioid crisis is a form of collective trauma on par with the HIV/AIDS crisis.[6] Some communities may be resilient, though it would be hard to find one that has sidestepped the trauma. Brand writes that trauma fosters the dialectics of "fragmentation versus integration," "violation versus security," "disconnection versus connection, alienation versus belonging, and loss of meaning versus meaning/purpose."[7] Brand links his argument to sociologist Kai Erikson, who used the term *collective trauma* to describe "how communities beset by disaster qualitatively change."[8] Collective trauma disrupts the ways communities work—changing patterns of organization and leadership and other "cascading consequences," which may contribute to people feeling "devalued, helpless, and hopeless."[9] Brand notes that we in the United States have seen this trauma before with crack cocaine and the ramping up of the war on drugs—and that we should not make that mistake again.[10] There is a way forward, though. Communities must work to "tell a shared story about 'what happened'" and how they are addressing it.[11] A shared story "can act as a counterweight to the sense of fragmentation and alienation. The narrative becomes the basis for shared meaning, flexible thinking, reestablishing mastery, building self-efficacy, and much more."[12] This is how people move from being victims to being agents of change.

In a way, the Newark Think Tank on Poverty is trying to do that. It is an intervention, attempting to give people a sense of control and to help them create meaning. Its members seek to show that the situation is not hopeless, that resilience is real. They are, like many people in this community and across this country, writing a new story, a story about connection and rebuilding—about what comes next. They are writing a story about people creating something across differences—about good, old-fashioned, sloppy grassroots community organizing, which is also the story of this book. Not the political organizing on the left that came in the wake of Donald Trump's election as president. A different kind. A kind of organizing that had been bubbling up across the so-called Rust Belt and Appalachia for some time, in part a response to the overdose crisis but also an acknowledgment of an ever-widening gap between those who have and those who do not—or who are just barely holding on to what little they do have.

The organizers like those in Newark know how to address overdose and substance use disorder in this country because they have learned from one another and taught themselves, and because many of them have lived experience. They know that there are evidence-based interventions, and they know, too, that many of those interventions are not being used—or used enough. Many of them support harm reduction, which is both a public health philosophy and a set of approaches for reducing the harms that come with drug use and drug policies.[13] One of the basic tenets of harm reduction is that we have to meet people "where they're at" but not leave them there.

Yet it will take more than harm reduction and evidence-based treatment to address the overdose crisis—it will take a shift toward thinking of addiction and overdose as a social justice problem, a human rights crisis affecting mostly poor people, in rural areas and the Rust Belt as well as in underserved communities from Baltimore to Bellingham. And as anyone who spends any time at the corner of East Main and Buena Vista in Newark, Ohio, will tell you, the overdose crisis especially affects those caught in our criminal justice system and those failed by our health-care system. These activists in places like Newark know that fear, stigma, and a lack of resources get in the way. Indeed, they know that many types of people— those who use drugs, who have been in prison, who have mental health struggles, who are poor, or who are not white, straight, or cisgendered—are stigmatized. They know that this can feel like an intractable problem. Many of them know this because at some point they, too, have been marginalized. For that reason, they are also the people who know the most and can, if decision-makers will listen to them, help us find a way forward. In doing so, they might show the rest of us something profoundly disturbing about our culture as well as something profoundly hopeful.

During the summer of 2016, in the run-up to the presidential election, I had planned to report on and write about the ways people on the margins in my own community were experiencing politics. Neither candidate was talking about poverty in the ways I knew it existed in Appalachian Ohio and the rest of the Rust Belt. Instead, one candidate focused on blaming immigrants while the other candidate focused on criticizing her opponent. That summer, Lesha Farias became a community guide for me, teaching me about the unhoused and poorly housed in Newark and introducing me to many of my neighbors. I learned about people in my community living in train cars, sleeping in tents, and staying in low-budget motels, sometimes for weeks and months at a time. In some of these cases, homelessness, poverty, mental health, and substance use disorder combined to form a seemingly toxic and impenetrable mix. It did not appear to me that either candidate for president was speaking to these people in my community in the swing state of Ohio.

Of course, Donald Trump was elected, and that same year 63,632 Americans died from unintentional drug overdoses.[14] The number shot up to 70,237 in 2017.[15] In 2018, the death rate dropped to 68,557 (the first drop since 1990)—still a staggering and unnecessary loss.[16] By way of comparison, around 50,000 people died from HIV/AIDS in the United States in 1995, the most to die in one year from that disease.[17]

The hundreds of thousands of human beings who have died in the overdose crisis smoked, swallowed, injected, or snorted legal and/or illegal drugs—many that contained a powerful opioid called fentanyl—for myriad reasons, one being that it made them feel better temporarily. And after the drugs were in their systems, their breathing slowed, became irregular, and stopped. Their skin grew clammy. They began suffocating. They became limp and unresponsive. They fell off toilets in bathroom stalls. Slumped over in cars. Fell asleep on their beds and never woke up.[18]

To anyone paying attention, something deeply unnerving is happening in the United States. Mothers are losing sons. Daughters are losing fathers. Communities are watching voids open wide, revealing chasms of loss and despair. This overdose crisis is widely felt—it touches the lives of first responders, social workers, teachers, pastors, clerks, and warehouse workers. It even shows up in the work of the college students I teach, who bravely write about loved ones who have overdosed or who struggle with substance use disorder. It weighs heavy on them. It should weigh heavy on us all.

Since 2000, the accidental overdose rate in Ohio has more than tripled, and overdose deaths are the leading cause of injury death, surpassing car crashes, for Ohioans under the age of fifty-five.[19] One study found that opioid overdose alone accounts for over half a million years of life lost in Ohio between 2010 and 2016.[20] Ohio's Licking County is, in some ways, just another victim. Save for Newark, most of the county is rural, even though it's in the orbit of the Columbus metropolitan area. Unemployment is low, and there's an energy in the community as it shakes off its Rust Belt moniker and attracts industry, including new Amazon and Facebook facilities on its western edge.

But like most other places in this state, Licking County has experienced its share of overdose deaths. The county coroner reports that in 2016 there were eighteen deaths; in 2017, thirty-five; in 2018, forty-two; and in 2019, thirty-six, the majority including some form of opioid.[21] Even so, we don't have it as bad as many other places in the state. From 2012 to 2017, the age-adjusted overdose death rate per 100,000 people was 14.9 in Licking County versus, for example, 56.5 in Montgomery County, home of Dayton, and 40.6 in Scioto County, down south and home of Portsmouth.[22]

Despite the popular narrative that the overdose crisis is being treated as a health crisis, we in Ohio (and throughout the United States) have responded primarily through the criminal justice system; the response is therefore punitive—to people who use drugs, to their families, and, indirectly, to ourselves. Thus, the long-term economic and social impacts of the crisis on Ohio are stark. According to a report from the C. William Swank Program in Rural-Urban Policy, a think tank at The Ohio State University, the costs associated with treatment, criminal justice, and lost productivity in 2015 alone were between $2.8 billion and $5 billion.[23] The long-term effects of this catastrophe will include disrupted families, strained social services, and thousands of people burdened with drug charges. In Licking County, for example, the number of children in foster care has nearly doubled in recent years, the overwhelming majority of child removals due to parents' substance use disorder. At the beginning of 2017, for example, there were 360 children in foster care in the county; as of March 2018, there were 530. In 2017, 86 percent of children in foster care in the county came from homes where there was substance use disorder.[24]

There are numerous interventions for addressing substance use disorder, of course, but it never feels like there are enough. The Swank Program notes that "in the best-case scenario, Ohio likely only has the capacity to treat 20-percent to 40-percent of the population abusing or dependent on opioids."[25] There aren't always spots for withdrawal management (a.k.a. detox), not enough beds for inpatient treatment, not enough sober living facilities, not enough intensive outpatient programs, not enough medically assisted treatment options.[26]

And though it may seem this way as viewed from the outside, opioids are not the only street drug in town. Indeed, most overdoses involve more than one substance, and methamphetamine use appears to be on the rise. In 2018, crystal meth was the second-most-common drug used by overdose victims in Licking County—involved in thirteen of forty-two cases— behind only fentanyl and its analogs.[27] If methamphetamine (addiction to which cannot yet be treated medically) competes with opioids as the most used illicit drug, then that means places like Licking County need more intensive outpatient options with supportive housing, more sober living facilities, more long-term recovery beds.[28] It also means that we need to stop using the term *opioid epidemic* and instead speak in terms of the overall overdose crisis. At a November 15, 2019, hearing for the New York State Senate Joint Senate Task Force on Opioids, Addiction & Overdose Prevention, Keith Brown, director of health and harm reduction at the Katal Center for Health, Equity, and Justice, said it quite clearly: "Opioid deaths and other drug fatalities are the symptom, not the disease . . . This is really important about how we address this moving forward because we can't keep playing a whack-a-mole game with substances when that's not actually the issue." Most overdose deaths, Brown said, are actually polysubstance related and are deaths of despair. What we're really seeing, he added, is a "crisis of housing" and a "crisis of health care." He concluded, "These are the chickens coming home to roost from the drug war that has been largely impacting black and brown people and poor people since it was started."[29]

At times, though, from where I sit, it feels like the public has lost interest—like a disaster has happened, requisite attention been given, and the public has moved on. The news seems more focused on sensational-death stories like terrorism rather than the individuals who die unnecessary deaths across this country every day. Indeed, overdoses continue, fueled in part by synthetic opioids that have tainted the illicit drug supply. The trauma accumulates.

In a piece titled "Notes Left Over," the poet Walt Whitman writes of the United States, "I like well our polyglot construction-stamp, and the retention thereof, in the broad, the tolerating, the many-sided, the collective."[30] I think what Whitman saw, in his optimistic view of this country, was a nation of democratic craftspeople who *could* work together to create something great. But we are not so great that we cannot fail, and in many ways the overdose crisis is a sign that we have failed—indeed, we lead the world in drug use.[31] The overdose crisis is a human rights crisis that exposes the deeply troubling consequences of bad policies and cultural failings. We do not give people who use drugs basic dignity. We treat their substance use as a moral failing. This is, in fact, *our own* moral failing. If we continue down this path and cannot save lives, then this crisis is more than just policy failure; it is a failure of imagination.

And yet there are people imagining other possible worlds and doing the work to address this crisis, people who are interested in more than simply bailing out the bathtub. This book tells the story of a grassroots movement begun by people who use or have used drugs or who have lost someone to overdose as well as their allies, people agitating for change or just doing it themselves. This is a story of ordinary people doing extraordinary things. It is admittedly focused on the lives and experiences of a group of people in one small corner of the United States, the one I reside in. However, the struggles and actions of people in this corner, I believe, resonate with those around this country and beyond—because they are not the only people working to address this crisis. At the end of this story is not death, but rather a gorgeous reminder of what we could be if, as my friend Gordon Casey notes, we used our collective imaginations for the good of both the person standing next to us and the person we do not see.

Part 1

THE HEART OF IT ALL

Spring 2016–Summer 2017

Show a people as one thing, as only one thing, over and over again, and that is what they become . . . The consequence of the single story is this: it robs people of dignity. It makes our recognition of our equal humanity difficult. It emphasizes how we are different rather than how we are similar.

—CHIMAMANDA NGOZI ADICHIE

1

Rusted Belts and Think Tanks

Newark, Ohio, is a red city in a red county, in the orbit of ever-growing Columbus but also on the edge of Appalachia.[1] In its twenty-one square miles live fifty thousand people. One of its claims to fame is an enormous building in the shape of a basket, just off Highway 16.[2] Beginning in 1997, the Basket served as an office space for the Longaberger basket-making company. In 2000, the company had over $1 billion in assets. Layoffs led the company to move staff out of the building to another site. And then, eventually, the last remaining employees left in July 2016, just as I began the reporting that led to this book. The basket-making company, which once employed over 8,200 people, many from Licking County, closed. The property owed over $700,000 to Licking County, which was set to seize the building in 2017 before a private buyer materialized at the last minute.[3]

But if you head west on Highway 16 and exit at Hudson Avenue, you can drive down the newly paved blacktop to North Third toward the courthouse square, where gorgeous nineteenth-century buildings surround an imposing limestone courthouse, centered on a green town square peppered with giant hardwoods. On the west side of the square is a nineteenth-century shopping arcade complete with terrazzo floors and skylights. On the same block, on the corner of North Third and Main, sits "The Old Home," once owned by the Home Building Association Company and one of a handful of "jewel box" buildings designed by architect Louis Sullivan.[4] Its mosaics of teal and blue and green and ornate stone face the recently paved streets. Keep driving down West Main, pass the Licking County Library, and turn left on Union near the empty lot where workers at Wehrle once made stoves. Farther down, you can see the former home of Rockwell International (later Meritor), which made heavy-duty truck axles.

Just across the street from that empty building and overgrown parking lot is one of the earliest examples of building and making and doing in Licking County—the Great Circle Earthworks, part of the Newark Earthworks, some of the largest intact earthworks in North America and the largest geometric set of earthworks built in Ohio.[5] Long before Europeans showed up in these parts, people gathered at nearby Flint Ridge, a place where, if you haven't guessed, flint was readily available and could be used to make valuable tools. Some of these people may have built these incredible monuments, including the nearby Newark Earthworks, comprised of both the Octagon and the Great Circle, which many hope will receive UNESCO World Heritage status. The Octagon earthworks are a kind of lunar observatory—every 18.6 years, the structure's center aligns with the northernmost point of the moon's cycle. And on any given day, the middle of the Great Circle Earthworks off Highway 79 is an inner sanctum, a place apart. The grassy interior is home to walnut, oak, and maple trees, whose bright red leaves shake in the breeze every autumn, the cars on the highway just audible. Because the people who settled here after European colonization found other uses for the Great Circle Earthworks—as a fairground and a military muster point—it remained intact as the industrial Midwest developed all around it.

A crossroads for canals and railroads, Newark became an industrial powerhouse in the region over the course of the nineteenth century. The Baltimore and Ohio Railroad operated a roundhouse here—and later the National Road, U.S. Highway 40, ran just six miles south of town. Surrounded by farm country and with abundant natural gas in the county and coal just south of it, Newark was in an excellent position for industry. About ten thousand people lived in Newark in 1880, and nearly triple that many by 1930. People, especially immigrants from Eastern Europe and from Germany, were lured to Newark by manufacturing jobs. There were German church services and even a German newspaper. They came to work at Wehrle, a foundry that became the nation's largest stove manufacturer and lasted until 1970 (the name had changed to Roper by the time it closed); at Heisey Glass, which produced tableware and decorative figurines; at the Jewett Car Company, which made interurban train cars; or at the American Bottle Company, the largest bottle plant in the nation, which made bottles for Adolphus Busch—by 1900, it was producing up to eighty tons of bottles every day. Later they worked for Rockwell, Holophane, or Longaberger. A number of these companies were lured to Newark by its Board of Trade, which offered incentives for relocation like free land and bonuses, as it did for the J. T. Rugg company, which made rope and halters for horses, and later lawn mowers for Sears, Roebuck, and Company and J. C. Penney. Rugg merged with a company in Columbus, and in 1973 the company closed the Newark plant as a tax write-off.

As with the Rugg closure, there was no singular dramatic moment of industrial loss like you might see in a steel or coal town. Instead there was a steady decline—new technologies supplanting old, locally owned businesses being bought out by larger ones, factories shuttering via cutbacks and layoffs. The story of Newark is the same as in many places—as the world became more connected, local companies were gobbled up by bigger ones. Having agriculture and being close to Columbus has always given Newark a base, has always helped support this place. But now farmland is also disappearing at a rapid clip in Licking County as Columbus moves in this direction.

In ten years, Newark could be part of a central Ohio megalopolis, but I suspect it will retain its scrappy, no-nonsense identity, rooted firmly in its manufacturing past. Blocks from the county courthouse is The Works, an interactive museum focused primarily on the history of industry in Licking County. On the second floor, in addition to the giant bones of a mastodon, you'll find cases full of things that people in this community once made—stoves, glass bowls and plates, and so on. The display is at once a paean and a dirge.

There's a photo in one case of the employees of Wehrle Stove Company from around 1892. Maybe eighty men stand in front of a brick building with two large windows; some are propped up on the sills. They are dressed in filthy work clothes: light cotton shirts and pants, covered in sweat and dirt. Some wear no shirts at all—only suspenders. Lots of mustaches, folded arms, serious faces. One man looks off to his right; the man next to him, with massive biceps, looks directly into the camera. Here and there, if you look closely, you can see a few children. And down in the front row, just off center, a man with his head cocked to the left, with a slight grin. This is not a past that I want to romanticize: their work was hard, hot, and dangerous. These men made things: They built stoves that people cooked on and fed their families with, and during World War II, Wehrle completely switched over to making artillery shells. These were not objects that you conjured into being, but objects that you crafted into existence.

Jeff Gill has a boiler problem. It's early spring, and the nights and mornings can still be pretty chilly here in Ohio. When he walked into the sanctuary of Newark's Central Christian Church yesterday, it was 62 degrees. Jeff, a tall, earnest Midwesterner, had to preach and didn't have time to figure out what was going on. One member up in the balcony had his coat on. Jeff says that man kept giving him the fisheye during the service. So we walk down to the basement of the sixty-nine-year-old church to look for the source of the problem. In the boiler room—cement floor, gray walls, shelves with storage boxes, seasonal ornaments, and some random snow skis stashed in a corner—he checks the pumps to make sure everything is running correctly. He turns everything off and on.

He wonders if it's the coupler in the motor's pump, a cheap part that breaks all the time. Maybe that's the weak point in the system. Sometimes when it breaks, he says, it makes an awful noise but persists. But then, after he flips a switch in the fuse box, the pumps hum again. Easy enough.

First problem of the day solved. Now he needs to see if his associate pastor has any other problems. It's a hectic Monday. The church runs a medical loan closet, so a volunteer is moving wheelchairs and walkers down a hallway. The custodian is on vacation, so three other church members are cleaning: running a vacuum across the sanctuary's red carpet, wiping down the pews. These people keep this church community thriving, and yet, Jeff says, like a lot of mainline Protestant churches in the age of the megachurch, his church is handicapped by the fact that many folks are thinking about "the glory days" when these churches were bigger, when the lines for Easter service wrapped around the block. At reasonably successful events someone will say to him, "Well, we used to get more folks here."

He chuckles. "It's like you never have a victory." That feeling of never being as great as we used to be, Jeff thinks, has been a burden on this generation.

But he's seen bigger problems than boilers or empty pews. When he's not managing this church, Jeff works for the Licking County Municipal Courts as a mediator, and that means confronting poverty in this community. The United Way reports that in Newark proper, 56 percent of families are either living below the poverty line or living at "the bare-minimum economic survival level."[6] Many people struggle to find affordable or subsidized housing—and there's a long list for housing vouchers.[7] And when housing is available, it's not always livable.[8] In recent years, this has made homelessness visible in Newark—people standing at highway exits asking for money, people sleeping on the courthouse steps.

Jeff sees a parallel between the changes in his church and the economic changes facing the Rust Belt as a whole. When he moved to Newark, he says, the community was just beginning to absorb the first round of major industrial closings. He'd come from West Virginia, where he says he heard the coal-mining version of the same story—we're down, but it's going to come back.

"It is not coming back. The old way of manufacturing—it's just not coming back," Jeff declares. Only recently, he says, have local leaders begun talking about what's next—but that hasn't infiltrated the folks in the pews quite yet. Jeff says it used to be possible to go through life being a bit of a jerk and a hard drinker, and getting fired every five to eight years. "You could still put food on the table, own a car, and maybe even take your family on vacation. You were a solid citizen. You could get away with that." It's not the same anymore. If you fail a drug test, get convicted of a felony, or punch your boss, you're blackballed. Now jobs require more skills, and many people are stuck working temporary jobs or getting paid off the books, he says. And when people fall out of that economy, they end up on the street. As of late, it seems there are more of those people.

Jeff would be the first to tell you it's not all doom and gloom here. Some would argue there has been a renewal in this community. There are plenty of jobs—the county unemployment rate was 3.7 percent in October 2019— but the jobs available often do not pay enough to sustain people, especially those with children.[9] Amazon has opened a major distribution center in the county, about thirty minutes from downtown Newark, with over four thousand employees.[10] There's still some manufacturing, and Boeing, Owens Corning, and a host of smaller manufacturers all have a presence in the county. The Rust Belt moniker does not fit so easily. But it is still not like it used to be. Many jobs have moved closer to I-70, farther away from downtown Newark and the neighborhoods that struggle the most. And someone who in the past may have worked in a high-paying manufacturing job keeps it together on much less these days.

Fadhel Kaboub, an economist at Denison University (where I teach) and president of the Global Institute for Sustainable Prosperity, says that Newark is a microcosm of the U.S. economy—a once-prosperous industrial city that has felt the effects of neoliberal free-trade policies. In a sense, it's not unlike many other cities around this part of the Midwest. It has taken some time for people to recognize that this change is permanent, that this is a different economy, requiring a different set of skills—not just in Newark, of course, but globally. In the Rust Belt, it means education and training. Amid the overdose crisis, this can mean life or death. According to one study, people with only a high school diploma overdose at a rate "over 4.5 times higher than those with even just some college."[11] In 2018, almost two-thirds of those who died from a drug overdose in Licking County had a high school diploma or less.[12]

According to Kaboub, in towns like Newark there are many people who have looked for work for a very long time but are not technically counted as unemployed. The Bureau of Labor Statistics calls these people "discouraged workers." For the whole state of Ohio, if you add in those numbers, and the number of involuntary part-time workers, the unemployment number almost doubles from 4.5 percent to 8.3 percent (per data from 2018).[13] Even that number, Kaboub says, does not include people who aren't working because of long-term illnesses, a lack of adequate child or elder care, or a lack of transportation. "So," he says, "you can just imagine the extent of the true cost to society."

Part of the current economic recalibration is the people in a community figuring out how to address the damage done by the economic system and trying to fill the gaps. One narrative in this community is focused on growth. Indeed, the community improvement corporation, focused on attracting business, is called Grow Licking County. But what happens when the growth stops? And is growth the only viable solution for economic sustainability? Are there alternatives? Kaboub points to an Edward Abbey quote: "Growth for the sake of growth is the ideology of the cancer cell." We must think about creating sustainable communities. Citing economic anthropologist Karl Polanyi, Kaboub says the creation of free markets is not natural—that they benefit those with power. In the wake of the damage produced by neoliberal policies like free trade and deregulated financial markets, resistance is inevitable.[14] Sometimes, he says, that resistance comes from nongovernmental organizations (NGOs). Sometimes it comes in the form of labor activism. And sometimes what happens is a political movement.

From where Lesha Farias and Allen Schwartz are sitting in a booth at the Sparta, a diner in downtown Newark that hires formerly incarcerated people as well as people in recovery, it looks like progress all around. The street in front of the Sparta is being ripped up as part of a $22 million streetscape renewal project to meet Environmental Protection Agency storm-water regulations but also to renovate downtown.[15] The project brought new traffic patterns and lighting to the square. A block away from the Sparta, the courthouse is also undergoing a multimillion-dollar renovation.[16] In turn, new restaurants, yoga studios, and loft apartments are popping up around the courthouse square. It feels like good things are happening here.

"If you look out the window from where we are," Lesha says, "it's all glorious."

But the reality for most working-class people is more complicated. She notes that the businesses coming to downtown Newark are mostly providing services the working class, or the 20.5 percent of the community living in poverty, can't utilize.[17]

The working class and the middle class live in two different worlds—

even in a small town like Newark. Most middle-class people are sealed off from working-class poverty and avoid seeing it firsthand. Official employment numbers may be up, but the industrial or distribution center jobs that do exist, Allen says, don't always offer the best working conditions and can be unstable—and besides, the possibility of those jobs being replaced by technology like artificial intelligence looms large.

"The norm is people working more than one job with unstable schedules," Allen says. "People are treated as expendable, and then they begin to *feel* expendable."

Responses to an article about the new Amazon distribution facility in *The Newark Advocate* underscore Allen's assertions, as well as the trouble with employment in the community. Facebook comments from former Amazon employees mention the sporadic hours and the fact that while some people would love to work with the company, they lack transportation.[18] Indeed, there are no fixed public-transportation routes in the county.

Addressing all these issues has been made even more difficult for Newark because of budget cuts and tax changes made under Ohio governor John Kasich. On the campaign trail, the onetime presidential candidate claimed he had solved Ohio's budget issues even as municipalities around the state, including Newark, struggled to pave streets and pay for public safety. *The Plain Dealer* estimated in 2016 that Newark had lost almost $1.7 million in state funding since 2011.[19] Over seventy cities across Ohio have lost more than $1 million.

Both Lesha and Allen are seasoned community organizers who, a few years ago, grew frustrated with how poverty was being addressed in Newark. There were many charity organizations doing important work offering immediate and much-needed assistance. But charity, they say, only stanches wounds. It doesn't fundamentally change the system or promote justice. They felt that in order for systemic change to happen, people who were struggling should actually become the decision-makers—they should have seats at the table when it came to how poverty would be addressed in their town. In 2014, they started the Think Tank, a group made up of people who are currently struggling with poverty or who have struggled in the past. The group's goal is to have their voices heard by people who make decisions.[20] They wanted people to feel a part of something but, more than that, to feel like their knowledge and experience, their stories, mattered and could be a part of something that effected change.

Allen wears a faded and well-worn orange ball cap that rarely comes off. Like Lesha, he speaks with determination and intention.

"Poverty is the big invisible in the U.S.," Allen says. "We try to ignore it by saying things like 'This is the land of promise' or 'If you really want to work, there's no reason you shouldn't' or 'If you're poor, it's your own damn fault.'"

They want to change that narrative. Of course, what they are saying about Newark and about the Rust Belt is nothing new: industries decline, communities become dislocated, people feel disempowered. But what if things were different?

Lesha says that the first meeting of the Think Tank was empowering: "For people to come together who share the same struggles, the same stories—there was a sense of belonging."

The group received a grant from the Catholic Campaign for Human Development (though the Think Tank has no religious affiliation) and used it to pay attendees for their time as consultants. They held their first listening session at the county library and wrote down on a large dry-erase board all the issues that people in poverty in Newark face. The three issues that rose to the top were (1) discrimination against people with criminal—especially felony—records, (2) a lack of living-wage jobs, and (3) gaps in services for people with mental health or substance use issues.

The Think Tank moved quickly to address the problem of finding employment when you have a criminal record by advocating for new policies. About one in eleven Ohioans has been convicted of a felony, and one in three has a criminal record of some kind.[21] The Ban the Box movement—

aimed at removing from job applications the check box that asks if applicants have a criminal record—was gaining traction in Ohio, and the group made it their issue. Working within a larger coalition, coordinated by the Ohio Organizing Collaborative and the Ohio Justice & Policy Center, they lobbied state representatives to pass the Ohio Fair Hiring Act in 2015, a bill banning questions about criminal histories on initial applications for public employment, and then encouraged their local city council members to ban the box in Newark.[22] Ultimately, both efforts succeeded. After that, they helped organize a coalition to support Licking County's returning citizens (that is, formerly incarcerated people returning to their communities).

These were concrete victories, but now the Think Tank is trying to build a platform for addressing systemic concerns. Rather than being an issue-specific movement, the group aims to become an integral part of community decision-making, something that they train for in their own monthly meetings. On a gorgeous July day, there's a big crowd gathered for a Think Tank open meeting at the Licking County Library. There are several dozen Think Tank members, as well as a handful of people from local nonprofits who are starting to pay attention to what the Think Tank is doing.

Lesha calls the meeting to order; then a Think Tank member stands up to talk about the history of working-class activism and union organizing in the United States. "People who are in the struggle," he says, "have to come together to tell these stories and to reenergize spiritually and to get ready to go back out there. Otherwise, it's so lonely. We have to acknowledge the current hopelessness and then organize for a better fight."

Next there are reports about having criminal records expunged, the local farmers' market, and a group addressing predatory lending. Trish Perry announces an upcoming overdose awareness rally. At the end of the meeting, there's a request from a local transportation advocate for the Think Tank to consider advocating for fixed-route transit, such as regular bus routes. The power of the Think Tank is that its members have experienced poverty, and so their recommendations come with an understanding that many policymakers lack. The Think Tank is reviving democracy in a place where participation has come to mean, for some, voting for elites every two or four years. Here, these activists want seats at the table.

When someone talks about a forthcoming report from a state legislative committee on recommendations for streamlining criminal justice statutes that would bring about some major changes to the state's criminal justice code, Allen immediately asks: "Are there any returning citizens on that committee?"

Everyone in the room knows the answer.

2

The Cavalry's Not Coming

n April 2019, federal prosecutors charged sixty health professionals with illegally prescribing pain medications; some of those charged were doctors accused of having traded sex for pills.[1] This was the largest pill mill bust in U.S. history. Around the same time came an announcement that, in Cleveland, U.S. district judge Dan Aaron Polster was sorting through hundreds of city, county, and state lawsuits aimed at both opioid manufacturers and distributors. Those suits targeted the companies that, plaintiffs say, created an unprecedented health crisis over the course of twenty years.[2] But there have been plenty of other doctors, other pain clinics, other so-called pill mills. The model for a pill mill is straightforward. All you need is a prescriber (typically the only person with any kind of medical background in a given clinic), an office, some prescription pads, a few pens, and a cash box. People who use prescription opioids like Purdue Pharma's effective time-release painkiller OxyContin (the brand name of the generic drug oxycodone) can sometimes visit multiple clinics in a day—there is plenty of cash to be made. It's a story that has been told by intrepid reporters like Beth Macy, who focused on southwest Virginia in her book *Dopesick*, and by Sam Quinones, who focused, in part, on Portsmouth, Ohio, in *Dreamland*.[3] To understand the rest of Ohio, it helps to understand what happened in Portsmouth. At one point, Scioto County and its roughly seventy-five thousand inhabitants had half a dozen clinics.[4] Most were based in Portsmouth, but some were in nearby Wheelersburg and across the Ohio River in South Shore, Kentucky, a point Quinones underscores in his book.

Portsmouth is about two hours south of Newark. According to a 2019 *Washington Post* analysis of Drug Enforcement Agency (DEA) numbers, from 2006 to 2012, about 76 billion oxycodone and hydrocodone pills were shipped out in the United States, and 68.5 pills were prescribed per person in Scioto County (compared to 33.1 in Licking County).[5] In 2010 alone, at least 9.7 million doses of opiates were dispensed in Portsmouth's Scioto County—123 doses each for every person in the community, child and adult alike, more than any other county in Ohio.[6] In early 2011, Lisa Roberts, a nurse for the Portsmouth Health Department, got a call from a Purdue Pharma representative.

"We might have a PR problem," Lisa remembers him saying. (The representative did not respond to requests for verification.)

The "PR problem" was a public health crisis created, in large part, by health care, or the lack thereof.[7] And Portsmouth felt like ground zero, where pills—oxycodone being the most popular—were being sold on the illicit market with an incredible street value. Pill mill doctors made money, but so did the underemployed people in this part of Appalachia, those eking out a life through Supplemental Security Income (SSI) and a reformed federal welfare system. For many, selling and taking Oxy were adaptations for survival—but adaptations that came with great risks, as many overdosed.

"It's more than a problem," Lisa replied. "It's a nightmare."

The Purdue rep told her he was coming down for a meeting with a group of local officials.

Lisa is a slight woman with dark hair and eyes, and an Appalachian accent. Charming but uncompromising and tough—and intensely smart.

Before she hung up the phone she added, "If I were you, I wouldn't mark my car in any way, because half the people will kill you because they think you've got the product and the other half will kill you because you made it."

Portsmouth feels at once both Appalachia and Rust Belt. Perched on a bluff above the Ohio River, looking out over the dramatic cliffs of Kentucky on the other side, the area was once home to a steel mill—shut down for good in the 1980s—and once burned the coal buried in those hills. The small city lies at a crossroads for trains, rivers, and highways. In its heyday, it was a manufacturing behemoth, making everything from bricks to steel to shoes to golf clubs. For decades, Shelby Shoe and Empire-Detroit Steel each employed thousands. The shocks of deindustrialization have resonated throughout the community. Portsmouth's population peaked at 42,560 in 1930. It's about half that today, and about 35.1 percent of its citizens live below the poverty line. People who would have worked in those steel mills now have limited options, coupled with the stress of being poor. Opioids are useful because they make people feel better and offer an escape—and, perhaps, help them bury deeper issues.

Portsmouth's prime real estate in the region, a driver for industry, also made it easier for people using pain medication to get more. The city is just across a bridge from Kentucky and about forty miles to the West Virginia border, making it easy for people to get multiple prescriptions in multiple states within hours. This is where the opioid crisis percolated, a place where OxyContin was marketed, a place that many believe was targeted.[8] In 2018, Scioto County ranked first in the state for overdose deaths.[9]

Lisa says the Purdue rep drove down to Portsmouth—in an unmarked car—to attend a meeting at the health department with the prosecutor, the head of a recovery center, and the police chief. The prosecutor brought along a stack of newspaper stories highlighting the effects of the legal and illegal trade in prescription pain medicine in the community dating back to 2001. It was a contentious meeting, to put it mildly, Lisa says.

"I felt a little bit bad for the guy," she says with a grin, "because we had not been very good hosts."

After the meeting, Lisa walked her guest over to a storefront a few blocks away. Members from a grassroots organization called Surviving Our Loss and Continuing Everyday (SOLACE) had been filling up the large glass window of the old Marting's Department Store with photos of loved ones who'd died in the pill epidemic. Lisa recalls that the rep was speechless; all the people, young and old, all the lives lost. He responded, Lisa remembers, by saying simply, "I understand." And then he left. Purdue followed up with a letter explaining that it was working to better track prescriptions and drugstore robberies and to educate the public. Lisa was unimpressed. None of that would help her community, she thought. It was too little, too late.

She realized then, she says, "The cavalry's not coming."

For years, people like Lisa Roberts had been putting out fires, trying to figure out how to combat this crisis on their own. She says that the story of how people in power outside of Portsmouth responded to this crisis is really just the story of Appalachia. People want timber, so they build roads and trains to take it out. They want coal. They take that. They want steel. Same thing. Every time, she says, industry comes in, extracts, and leaves without having to deal with the outcomes—that becomes the responsibility of the people living there. The pills were no different.

The pharmaceutical companies had an army of reps and, as Lisa tells it, they had flooded the Appalachian region—a place just ready to soak up what they had to offer. It was a place with numerous manual laborers whose bodies were wracked by pain and injury, men and women who lacked access to sophisticated hospitals that may have instead treated pain with physical therapy, massage, acupuncture, or surgery, which insurance companies might not have paid for anyway.[10] Instead, these people with chronic pain or injuries would go to their primary care physicians, many of whom had been visited by those drug reps and been convinced that there was no need to fear prescription opioids. There was so much driving all of this—a confluence of pain, pills, poverty, and people looking the other way. Certainly corporate greed played no small part. But the crisis was also fueled by lax federal oversight. Writing for *The New Republic*, Zachary Siegel points out that "nearly every step of the pharmaceutical supply chain is implicated in the soaring death rate," that many are responsible for the "obscene quantities" of pills sent to towns around America—this includes the manufacturers and distributors as well as regulatory bodies.[11] Siegel notes that more pills were being manufactured and more were being shipped, steps that require DEA approval.[12]

It would be easy to blame the DEA, Big Pharma, and the pill mill doctors for their roles in what happened in places like Portsmouth, but that wouldn't completely explain why so many people are overdosing now, nor would it explain how opioids caught on so quickly or why they continue to appeal to people in the United States or why opioid use disorder is a thing. It's not the drug itself—the majority of people who use opioids will not become addicted.[13] For many people, the pain relief from opioids can be life-changing and life-improving. So what is happening? Canadian physician Gabor Maté argues, "We can never understand addiction if we look for its sources exclusively in the actions of chemicals, no matter how powerful they are . . . Mere exposure to a stimulant or narcotic or to any mood-altering chemical does not make a person susceptible. If she becomes an addict, it's because she's already at risk."[14]

In some cases, addiction can be situational. Probably one of the more relevant examples involves American soldiers in Vietnam.[15] In May 1971, U.S. congressmen visiting Vietnam were alarmed by the widespread use of heroin among soldiers. A follow-up study by Lee Robins, a professor at Washington University in St. Louis, revealed that over 90 percent of returning veterans who had been addicted in Vietnam were not addicted once they returned to the United States to their families or communities and were distanced from the stress and death of war. It would seem, then, that their heroin use in Vietnam was a response to a unique and dangerous situation, and that people can grow out of problematic use. Robins's study counters much of what popular culture purports to be true about drug use and addiction: that the drug itself is the culprit and that once addicted, always addicted.

But to be sure, *addiction* is not a term about which everyone agrees. The most recent edition of the American Psychiatric Association's *Diagnostic and Statistical Manual of Mental Disorders* (DSM-5) asserts that "substance use disorder is a chronic, relapsing brain disease characterized by compulsive drug seeking and use, despite harmful consequences."[16] In September 2019, the board of directors of the American Society of Addiction Medicine adopted its own new, updated definition, which reads:

> Addiction is a treatable, chronic medical disease involving complex interactions among brain circuits, genetics, the environment, and an individual's life experiences. People with addiction use substances or engage in behaviors that become compulsive and often continue despite harmful consequences. Prevention efforts and treatment approaches for addiction are generally as successful as those for other chronic diseases.[17]

As these definitions show, addictions are associated with negative consequences and are generally believed to be shaped by genes, behavior, and/or environmental factors, and are described as distinct from the symptoms that imply a physiological transformation, or dependence on a substance.[18] In other words, a person may experience withdrawal symptoms without being addicted to a given substance per se.

Thinking about addiction as a disease is convenient—and certainly this concept is central to many self-help and abstinence-based traditions, in part because it combats the idea that addiction is somehow a moral failing. But in her book *Unbroken Brain*, Maia Szalavitz writes that "the term 'brain disease' is both vague and stigmatizing. It doesn't capture the critical role of learning in addiction."[19] And research shows, too, that framing addiction as a disease can make people feel like their situation is a fixed state.[20] Szalavitz, one of the most important writers covering addiction and health care in America today, defines *addiction* as a learning disorder—a person learns to associate use of a drug, for example, with pleasure or respite. This "compulsive behavior despite negative consequences" is learned over time—and you come to believe that it can solve problems.[21] People who are in difficult situations (e.g., unemployed, without proper health care, homeless) can face even more harms because they will likely seek out the thing they've learned will give them comfort. Thus, a person transitions from needing to wanting, or as neuroscientist Marc Lewis writes, desiring.[22] Much as it does in learning a new skill, the brain adapts; it's a maladaptation for sure, but an adaption to circumstances nonetheless. Indeed, stress[23] or trauma[24] can produce the circumstances for addictive behavior to be cultivated. Szalavitz writes, "Addiction isn't just taking drugs. It is a pattern of learned behavior. It only develops when vulnerable people interact with potentially addictive experiences at the wrong time, in the wrong places, and in the wrong pattern for them."[25] And some places are especially wrong; certain environments make people more susceptible to addiction and overdose.

For many years, what Canadian psychologist Bruce K. Alexander calls the "Myth of the Demon Drug"—that drugs themselves inevitably cause addiction—held sway, and still does given our policies of prohibition and the ongoing drug war.[26] Alexander questioned this myth, which he said was based on early experiments with rats held in isolated cages. Through a series of studies in the late 1970s and early 1980s, he demonstrated that rats housed in isolated laboratory cages are more likely to drink a morphine solution than are rats living in a more social and natural environment (a structure he created and dubbed "Rat Park").[27] Alexander's "Rat Park" studies underscore the importance of environments in mitigating behaviors or fostering dependence on substances.[28] More recently, in his 2008 book, *The Globalization of Addiction*, Alexander argues that "dislocation" is the root of addiction in the twenty-first century, that humans are social beings for whom interdependence and connection are necessary, and that we have created a world that seems to undermine both.[29] This concept is rooted in the work of Erik Erikson and Karl Polanyi, but Alexander says it can also be found in the writing of thinkers as diverse as Plato and Charles Darwin and can be called "alienation" or "disconnection." Dislocation comes from a lack of "psychosocial integration," which is a "profound interdependence between individual and society that normally grows and develops throughout each person's lifespan."[30] Alexander suggests that this dislocation is a kind of "poverty of the spirit."[31] A lack of psychosocial integration is deeply problematic for an individual and his or her community.

Alexander defines *addiction* in multiple ways, but the one most relevant to this book is that addiction "is overwhelming involvement with any pursuit whatsoever that is harmful to the addictive person and his or her society."[32] He makes it clear that he is concerned with addictions writ large, not solely those that entail drug use. For Alexander, addiction is not a disease without cure but an *adaptation* to the overwhelming sense of dislocation in the modern world—it's a response to that dislocation. To that end, he argues that addiction is not a medical or criminal problem but, in his words, "a political problem."[33]

Alexander writes, "Along with dazzling benefits in innovation and productivity, globalization of free market society has produced an unprecedented, worldwide collapse in psychosocial integration."[34] In such a society "virtually every aspect of human existence is embedded within, and shaped by, minimally regulated competitive markets. This sort of social system would have been inconceivable a few centuries ago, but it is fast becoming a planetary standard." The effects of this system are seen in persistent homelessness, mass shootings, environmental destruction, and entrenched poverty, but we are all affected by this "free market society," as Alexander calls it, because every aspect of our lives is framed by it. Within this cultural and economic milieu, he writes, dislocated people "struggle valiantly to establish or restore psychosocial integration—to somehow 'get a life' to 'figure out who they are' or to build community."[35] Many are successful, but others adapt to the dislocation and become known by such names as "junky, miser, shopaholic, workaholic, crackhead, alcoholic, religious zealot, anorexic, bulimic, etc."[36]

Alexander's assessment is clear and brutal when he writes, "As psychosocial integration is a fundamental human need, and free market society, by its nature, produces mass dislocation at all times (not just during times of collapse), and as addiction is the predominant way of adapting to dislocation, addiction is endemic and spreading fast."[37] We have two options, Alexander declares: transform society or live with the "poverty of spirit" that dislocation produces.

Central to this book is the idea that addiction is a political problem. I will try to describe those behaviors that, when coupled with illicit substances, can degrade a person's health and well-being and can lead to increased risk of overdose. Through this lens, addiction can be viewed as a response to socioeconomic conditions. This is not to say there are no other contributing factors. Addiction is complex, and there are many risk factors in addition to socioeconomic realities: genetics, a history of trauma, and mental health struggles, for example. Effective treatment should also consider these things, which in general as a country we have not created political policies to do. Journalist Zachary Siegel writes elsewhere that "treating addiction with medicine and compassion, not tough love, is what works best. We know that stigma, alienation, and incarceration make things worse."[38] Currently, we do not have a political framework that truly supports a treatment approach combining medicine and compassion—and this is the problem.

The concept of dislocation incorporates and privileges many of the experiences of the people I have been following for the past few years—not only those who have experienced substance use disorder but also those who seek to reduce its harms. These people are responding to a deep sense of dislocation in our modern world. For that reason, Alexander's research is especially important in the Rust Belt and in Appalachia, where this dislocation feels especially acute.[39] Pennsylvania State University sociologist Katherine McLean studies the environmental, or contextual, factors that exacerbate the overdose crisis in the Rust Belt area of Monongahela Valley, Pennsylvania.[40] She discovered that social isolation, poor housing stock, lack of transportation, and, in general, lack of opportunity were driving heroin use in McKeesport, a deindustrialized city near Pittsburgh. In a sense, overdose was a political problem. "While state and county efforts to ameliorate overdose mortality have focused upon creating an open market in naloxone," writes McLean, "this study suggests the need for interventions that address the poverty and social isolation of opiate users in the post-industrial periphery."[41] She points out that most media coverage of the present overdose epidemic has been focused on the middle class but that "the links between disadvantage and drug risk" are largely absent.[42] In the part of the country where she does research, environment and history are significant risk factors for addiction and overdose. She writes that those she interviewed "forced a consistent connection between overdose, drug use, and poverty. On the one hand, a widespread lack of jobs and money was seen as increasing the local lure of drug use . . . The dearth of legitimate employment opportunities was a theme reiterated across multiple interviewees who inevitably compare the current economic plight with the city's midcentury heyday."[43]

Brooklyn College sociologist Alex S. Vitale writes succinctly, "There is no way to reduce the widespread use of drugs without dealing with profound economic inequality and a growing sense of hopelessness."[44] The research is clear that the most poor and marginalized in our communities are the most vulnerable to overdose and are also the most susceptible to substance use disorder.[45] And if addiction is a dislocation problem, as Bruce Alexander posits, we have bigger things to deal with. But Big Pharma shouldn't get off easy here. Purdue still pumped OxyContin into the region, exploiting underlying problems. It and other companies still marketed their drugs as an easy fix to pain. They still sent emails that revealed their intentions: "Just like Doritos, keep eating. We'll make more," they wrote. "Keep 'em comin'!" they urged. "Flyin' out of there. It's like people are addicted to these things. Oh, wait, people are . . . ," they joked.[46] According to allegations in a March 2019 lawsuit, Purdue's president, Richard Sackler, wrote in a company memo that he opposed "criminal addicts . . . being glorified as some sort of populist victim."[47] Portsmouth, along with most of Appalachia, was likely targeted because it faced economic challenges, because it was a place where people were struggling. In a sense, capitalism targeted its own victims, buzzards surrounding a wounded animal.

But Portsmouth is decidedly not dead; it never was. It fought back. The community let the so-called pain clinics know that they were no longer welcome. Activists, many of them connected to SOLACE, began picketing the clinics, organizing town halls, and pushing the state and federal government to act. Portsmouth's city council passed an ordinance in late March 2011 that said pain clinics must register with the state pharmacy board, be affiliated with a hospital or university, have malpractice insurance, and be subject to random inspections.[48] When the ordinance was challenged in court, a group of women sat in the front row wearing teal-green SOLACE shirts, Lisa Roberts among them, looking on.[49] The judge ruled in the city's favor, and afterward a reporter from the Ohio News Network asked Lisa for a comment. Eyes wide, face beaming, she replied, "Today was a victory. An important victory."

Around the same time in 2011, every Thursday for seven weeks, a group of churches marched while holding signs, blowing shofars, and calling on the God who brought down the walls of Jericho. On the seventh march, a miracle occurred: It rained hard, and then a double rainbow appeared. It seemed like the flood was over. In that same week, the DEA conducted mass raids and House Bill 93, known as the Pill Mill Bill, passed unanimously.[50] When Governor Kasich signed it into law, a group of women from SOLACE were standing behind him. The law closed many legal loopholes and required Ohio's board of pharmacy to license physicians and distributors of dangerous drugs. As a result of these measures, Scioto County saw a dramatic reduction in prescription opioid use.

However, one recent study "found no effects of pill mill laws on prescription opioid, heroin, or synthetic opioid overdose deaths in Ohio."[51] And, Lisa Roberts says, "Contrary to many people's beliefs, opioid-addicted people don't just go away when the supply goes away." It didn't take long for people to find other opioids—first heroin, then synthetic opioids like fentanyl—and now more methamphetamine.[52] There was a boom in intravenous drug use, and that was when Lisa pushed for a syringe exchange. Overdose deaths involving fentanyl began to rise dramatically around Ohio and West Virginia, and police and journalists ramped up fear around this new scourge.[53] Police claimed that if your skin came in contact with these drugs, you could overdose (which is extremely unlikely and has led to media panic and lawmakers pushing harmful policies).[54] Nonetheless, people were dying; there was real danger. What was happening in Portsmouth and elsewhere in Ohio had moved well beyond pills. By 2016, only 13.9 percent of overdoses in Ohio involved prescription opioids, while 58.1 percent involved fentanyl or another closely related synthetic opioid.[55]

Overdoses involving synthetic opioids can't be addressed by lawsuits. In Portsmouth, solutions are both immediate and long term, effective and otherwise. Those solutions include protests outside pill mills, syringe exchange, and rallies for addiction recovery. The activists and organizers haven't done it all on their own. Lisa Roberts points out that they have had some help—Senator Rob Portman has listened to them, the DEA has helped raid the pill mills, and the state has sued Big Pharma—but the socioeconomic struggles that make opioids an attractive choice ultimately feel like a burden that places like Portsmouth will carry on their own. Prescription opioids kicked off a series of what Lisa calls "plagues" for Portsmouth—and for all of Ohio: first heroin, then fentanyl and all the overdoses, and now (because of the rising intravenous drug use) rising hepatitis C rates, cases of endocarditis, abscesses, and infections.

Lisa takes the long view and says she knows this is not a sprint. She is excited about the growing advocacy coming from people in recovery. "First it was the parents and caregivers, and now it's the people they saved who are helping other people," she says. "No one's going to save us from this; we're going to have to save ourselves. It really is about figuring out what your community needs are, working really hard together, to make sure you're doing what you can, minimizing the damages to people who became addicted."

But Lisa says she would not turn down any money that comes to her community as a result of the lawsuits against pharmaceutical companies. The cost of all of this has fallen on the public sector. "We've all paid for this," she says. "And they've been on the receiving end and have not had to pay for this catastrophe that they made." Social services, emergency medical services, police, jails, prisons, foster care, treatment—the list is long. But Lisa says you have to be creative with a problem of this magnitude. It will take many systems working together to address the overdose crisis. "I wish that the heartland could have an economic boom because that is probably the only thing that's going to fix this," she says. "Drugs are a symptom, really."[56]

Lisa speaks of her community health work matter-of-factly; she continues, like a bulldog, and snubs the patina of sadness that surrounds it. "I don't have a choice, somebody has to do it," she explains. "Even though we've had a lot of deaths, we've had way more that don't die. Last year, we know that one hundred fifty-five of the people that we trained to give naloxone used it and they lived."

She has been a trendsetter in Ohio. She helped start Project DAWN (Deaths Avoided with Naloxone), the first public naloxone distribution program in Ohio. She also runs a syringe exchange, a monumental accomplishment in a conservative stronghold, and advocates for medication-assisted treatment (MAT), which uses methadone, Vivitrol/naltrexone, or buprenorphine to treat opioid use disorder.[57] Because of her work in Portsmouth, Lisa has become a resource for researchers from around the country—researchers from Yale to The Ohio State University come calling. And Lisa tells anyone who will listen that naloxone should be cheaper and more readily available, as should MAT, especially in rural America. (Curiously, dispensing buprenorphine requires additional training for physicians, whereas dispensing OxyContin did not.)[58] Right now, she says, these responses are over-regulated. Ohio lists naloxone as a dangerous drug and therefore requires a license to distribute it, which makes it more difficult to get to the people who use it and need it the most.[59]

Because she can distribute through her health department, Lisa gets naloxone into the hands of as many people as she can. "If you want to do the Lord's work, carry naloxone!" is one of her favorite slogans. Every Friday, about two hundred folks from the community take advantage of the health department syringe exchange, started as a response to soaring hepatitis C cases in the county. On one Friday I watch as person after person files through the health department's conference room. Pop music plays while clients and workers chat and catch up with one another like old friends.

Abby Spears, a longtime health department employee, is responsible for counting the used syringes brought in. Abby tells me that, when not helping with the exchange, she is using data and geomapping to identify health disparities in Portsmouth.[60] The concept of a "food desert" is well-known, she explains, but there are also "resource deserts." She mapped overdoses on top of blighted and abandoned properties and discovered some clear patterns: that where there is poverty, there are more overdoses, and that where the social determinants of health lag—"the conditions in which people are born, grow, live, work, and age that shape health" like education, neighborhood, and socioeconomic status—there are more overdoses.[61] Now that she knows where the greatest needs are, she can work to get resources to people living in those places.

Today, Abby greets everyone warmly, counts what they have, and ushers them to one of the three or so intake workers who give them new works. She tells me that despite all of Portsmouth's troubles, she could never imagine leaving. "It's something that lives in your bones," she says. And so she appreciates the work she is engaged in at the health department—she feels like she's building the place up rather than bringing it down. But it's difficult work, she says, because the struggles that this community faces have existed for a long time and because both unspoken nihilism and stress run deep here. In some ways, she says, that stress is rooted in trauma and has been ramped up in the past decade as so many people have died.

"I've lost . . ." She pauses. "I've truly never counted." And then she adds, "Every time there is a loss, the desire to fix this becomes profound. I've been here thirty-seven years, so most of my life has been spent in a place that has been defined by the opioid epidemic."

"Were you traumatized by this or are you just especially resilient?" I ask her.

"The two aren't mutually exclusive," she responds.

Hope Shot

Eric Lee rolls his eyes. He's heard this talk about rehabs before. *This one's the best; it's going to save me if I can just get there.* Now he's hearing it from Johnathon, another person who is struggling, another person he's trying to save.

Johnathon sits on the edge of the bed at the Budget Inn in Newark flipping a cigarette in his hands. Eric stands by the door, hand resting on a wood-paneled table. He's been in the room for almost an hour, and he has yet to sit down as Johnathon tells his story.

A decade earlier Johnathon was making good money, had savings, and owned his home. But after he suffered a workplace injury, a doctor prescribed opioids and eventually he became addicted. Now he's here and, he says, he doesn't want to go through the withdrawal anymore.

"You want it as soon as your eyeballs open," Johnathon says. "As soon as your brain starts running, your main concern is getting well. That's what they call it, 'getting well,' because you're in withdrawal. You're physically sick. Your body hurts. Your muscles contract. You puke and you shit."

Eric, broad-shouldered with a receding hairline and a two-inch Afro, listens with patience. He himself spent twenty years in and out of prison, in and out of treatment, and is now in recovery going on seventeen years. When not taking classes in substance abuse counseling, Eric mentors others. On Tuesday nights, he leads a support group for people on judicial release; on Wednesday nights, he plays a central role in a recovery group; and in his free time he sponsors, formally and informally, dozens.

He finds them, or they find him—smoking cigarettes after recovery meetings, eating lunch at the Salvation Army, or hanging out at The Main Place, a mental health day program and resource center. Because of this, Eric has an important vantage point for understanding the addiction crisis—he sees it from above and from within, and no one is paying him to do it.

Today, Johnathon thinks he's won the lottery—a spot in The Refuge, one of the best treatment programs around, he says. A week from now, someone is going to drive him the two hours down to Vinton County and check him in. But between this moment and that, he has to stay sober because the rehab does not offer withdrawal management. This means he has to avoid the temptations just outside the door of his motel room, the dealers who hang out in the neighborhood, the other people who use drugs and crash here. Before getting a room at the Budget Inn, Johnathon slept for weeks in a dirty old recliner wedged between two buildings in downtown Newark, covering himself with a faded blue moving blanket. Now the St. Vincent de Paul charity is covering the fifty dollars a night he needs to keep a roof over his head until he gets into treatment.

"None of that shit matters," Eric sighs, "if you don't want to do it."

"Well, everyone says it's a good program," Johnathon says, his voice rising in frustration before he stands up, brushes past Eric, and walks to the door, cigarette in hand. He cracks open the door, lights the cigarette, and drags deep.

Johnathon is a slender, boyish forty-year-old with a close-shaved head and a little stubble on his face. His eyes grow big for emphasis and shut tight when his dimples emerge. He looks tired. A blue ball cap hides his eyes as he gazes across a wet parking lot and smokes. It's a gloomy October day, and Johnathon's mood fits nicely. He finishes his cigarette, tossing it into a puddle. He comes back inside and sits back down on the bed just as Eric turns to leave.

"The concept of one day at a time," Eric says, "that's what matters to a recovering addict. That's the one thing you have control over. You can't go back and change anything in the past. You can't change your future. The reality of the here and now is where you need to live and stay. Right now you got freedom from active addiction. The only thing that will change that is if you pick up some dope. I don't give a shit how much rehab you get, how much you learn about the disease of addiction. You know enough to know this—every time you pick up, you fuck up."

Eric gets that there are so many pressures complicating things for people who use drugs—trauma, family, work, mental health—but he's telling Johnathon that he still has agency.

"I do hear what you're saying," he says.

"I'll be checking on you," Eric says.

When we leave Johnathon's motel room, Eric asks me for a ride from the Budget Inn to The Main Place. It has a reputation of being a safe space not only for people with mental health concerns but also for people who use drugs and for the unhoused—sometimes all those categories intersect. His car is parked next to my truck, but, he says, he needs to conserve his gas. "I put a couple dollars in this morning," Eric says, then adds, in passing, that he's in between jobs and just trying to finish up his degree—he's working on a master's in nonprofit management. Times are tight.

"My daughter's car's not working right now. I might just have to siphon some gas out of hers so I can get around later," he tells me as we drive. Eric is tall and broad; his knees are pulled close in the tiny cab of my old Ford Ranger.

"This is the worst I've seen it," Eric says as we drive. "They call 'em zombies, the walking dead. It's not far from it. All the backpacks. The homeless camps."

It's not clear why we're going to this meeting—it's just a couple having a hard time. At The Main Place, I follow Eric inside and we go into a small room with the couple. They explain that they're sleeping in a tent down by the river, and it's starting to get cold. He's working but having a hard time. Eric gives them some suggestions, people they can talk to, and offers some words of encouragement.

When we leave The Main Place, Eric suggests we get lunch at Sally Ann's, a.k.a. the Salvation Army. We wait in a line that stretches to the back of the room. Eric starts chatting with a young man, recently released from jail, who is not sure about his next move.

Eric moves through this world of poverty and addiction with finesse, from one place to the next, one connection to the next. He doesn't carry a planner or seem to keep records or times in his phone. He just "has to go talk to a guy somewhere." And people know him. He's greeted wherever we go like he's the mayor. He gets hugs and pats on the backs. People tell him how they are doing. How long they have been sober. And sometimes, in one of these check-ins, it will turn out the person is struggling. And that's when Eric engages, laser-like, and his whole world is the person struggling in front of him. This happens again and again.

At Sally Ann's we tuck into Styrofoam plates of rice and some vegetable casserole with cheese, cups of weak coffee. Eric is deep into the young man's story. He's lost in his problems. One problem: he has a job but no way to get there. We finish and go outside. Eric shares a cigarette with him, pulls out his phone, and makes a call. He speaks for a few minutes, grabs a piece of paper and a pencil, and writes a name and number down on it. He hands it to the young man.

"This man is gonna pick you up in the morning. Five a.m. You be ready."

"Thank you, brother," the young man says.

"You're welcome. You can do this."

We walk back to my truck.

"That was amazing," I tell him as I'm cranking the engine, admittedly in awe.

"Well . . ." Eric sighs and gets quiet and quickly changes the subject. "You can just drive me back to my car. I need to see about getting some gas. I got some hose back at my place. That should work."

That Eric has become the connector he has might surprise some who knew him back in the day. But his time in prison, his time of active using, and his other struggles have made him into the person he is now. He grew up in Newark, one of nine children. When his youngest brother was born, his father left his mother for a woman who had only six children. So Eric grew up in poverty and had to get scrappy at a young age. He remembers asking his mother for new shoes when he was eight years old—a pair of Chuck Taylors he had seen at a shoe store downtown. She told him he would have to earn the money to pay for them. So he stole some rags, polish, and brushes from Grant's Department Store, made his own shoeshine kit, and shined shoes in all the bars downtown. It took him a long time to earn the fifteen dollars he needed to buy those shoes, but he did it—one quarter at a time. That experience was the beginning of many things for Eric Lee. It was when he learned about the world. It was also when he learned how to drink.

He would go out back by the trash cans at bars, where they stacked up all the empty cases, and he'd pour all the little bits left in beer bottles until he had a full one. If he got lucky, he would find some whiskey, too. Later he started smoking weed, then he found pills, and eventually he encountered crack in the 1990s. The drugs made him feel better, he says. Until he was doing too much, and they didn't anymore.

The first time Eric was in prison was in 1974, four months before his eighteenth birthday. He was sent an hour and a half north of Newark to Mansfield Reformatory, the *Shawshank Redemption* prison. But there were no wise elders or daring midnight escapes. He spent the first few months in the juvenile wing and then on his birthday had an assessment and was sent across the yard to adult prison.

Eric told me once that he was "a pretty bad operator in those days." He spent much of his time on the streets in Newark and Columbus, shot dice, and hung out with some people who were a little radical and affiliated with local black nationalists. When he would end up in prison, people would assume he was just a country boy from Licking County, but he would show them. He was never scared.

"The label 'angry black man' fit me. It fit me. I was angry and, obviously, I'm black. But I was a little angrier than most people. I was more angry than hurt, let's put it like that."

"What were you angry with? The system?"

"How long do you have? We don't want to dredge all that up, but since you asked, it's just the way I was raised. To be so poor and to be so street, living in the streets, stealing to survive." And also, he says, how he was treated by some of the teachers in school.

When his mother died, Eric was twenty-seven and serving time in Ohio's London Correctional Institution. He was granted a leave and made the trek back to Newark accompanied by two armed guards. At the funeral, he walked into Shiloh Baptist Church, a place central to the African American community in Newark, in chains, a jacket covering his shoulders, a guard holding his arm. In that moment, he says, he felt a deep shame.[1] But the reality is that Eric's life has corresponded with one of the most dramatic spikes in incarcerated people in human history. Over the course of the 1980s and '90s, under Republican and Democratic administrations, the number of incarcerated people in the United States grew from under 300,000 to over 2 million, plus another 4.5 million in some sort of community control—parole, probation. Michelle Alexander, a professor of law, has famously called this "the new Jim Crow."[2] In her groundbreaking 2010 book, Alexander explores how our current incarceration system targets marginalized Americans—especially black people—and how it exacerbates already entrenched poverty and racism; indeed, it institutionalizes them.[3] This has been especially obvious with the drug war as well as the overall response to crack versus opioids.[4] The patterns are stark and the numbers clear. In 2017 (the most recent year for which data is available), African Americans made up 33 percent of those incarcerated in the United States, despite being just 12 percent of the population.[5] In Ohio in 2010, according to the Prison Policy Initiative, African Americans made up only 13 percent of the state's population but 43 percent of people in its jails and prisons. By comparison, in that same year, 81.9 percent of Ohioans were white, but whites made up only 53 percent of those in Ohio's jails and prisons.[6]

Eric's time was for assault, robbery, and once for selling a rock of crack cocaine. He got three to ten, he remembers, and he told the judge, "'Man, look man, I'm no drug dealer. I was just doing that to support my habit, as you well know. I just need help with this addiction.' You know what he said? 'I'm going to help you all right, I'm going to send you right down to London Prison. I know they got some programs you can get into to get you some help.' But you see what it cost me and what it cost the state? What it cost me, it cost the state even more."

As we drive back to his car, Eric tells me that the couple we just visited needs to find housing before they can even consider being sober. Despite his deep connections to recovery groups, and despite how he "got tough" with Johnathon earlier, this strikes me as practical and nonjudgmental.

"I sat in the judgment seat one time," Eric says. "The record I left behind, people judged me harshly, and I know how it feels to be ostracized, and marginalized, and all those feelings of being pretty much on the bottom—and that's not a time to tell a person, here's what you need to do." In the right situation, he says, they could find another way out. "What they need is a hope shot."

It's the opposite, I guess, of a dope shot, and it undergirds his work. I have seen him do it again and again. His take on addiction, rooted as it is in his embrace of Narcotics Anonymous, might strike some as "unscientific" or not "evidence-based." Indeed, the research findings on twelve-step groups, like Akron, Ohio–born Alcoholics Anonymous (AA), are mixed. A 2006 Cochrane Review concluded, "No experimental studies unequivocally demonstrated the effectiveness of AA or [other twelve-step facilitation] approaches for reducing alcohol dependence or problems."[7] More recently, psychiatrist Lance Dodes told a National Public Radio reporter that the success rate for AA is between 5 and 10 percent.[8] He added:

> The reason that the 5 to 10 percent do well in AA actually doesn't have to do with the 12 steps themselves; it has to do with the camaraderie. It's a supportive organization with people who are on the whole kind to you, and it gives you a structure. Some people can make a lot of use of that. And to its credit, AA describes itself as a brotherhood rather than a treatment.[9]

AA is not for everyone, Dodes points out, and for some people it can be harmful. He says, "It's harmful to the 90 percent who don't do well. And it's harmful for several important reasons. One of them is that everyone believes that AA is the right treatment. AA is never wrong, according to AA. If you fail in AA, it's you that's failed."[10] Maia Szalavitz writes that "the idea of powerlessness and the claim that the steps are the only way . . . can actively interfere with recovery if taken to heart."[11] She also notes a potentially troubling link between twelve-step programs and the criminal justice system; some drug courts, for example, require participation in them.[12] (Drug courts are a diversion program whereby courts work with social services and treatment care workers to help people with substance use disorder.) And some twelve-step groups disparage medication-assisted treatment, which can be particularly challenging.[13]

But for some people, the practical wisdom and the camaraderie of the twelve-step group are appealing. In a 2016 article, researchers Annette Mendola and Richard L. Gibson write that even though they do not exactly provide a treatment, twelve-step groups "do have something important to offer people who are attempting to quit an addiction: they provide a social network that supports recovery; they emphasize both the powerfully compulsive nature of addiction *and* the importance of harnessing an individual addict's personal responsibility; there are no dues or fees for members; there are no requirements, pledges, or oaths to become a member; meetings are available in many places and at many times of the day and night; and they are compatible with other measures."[14] For people with few resources, these things matter.[15]

For Eric, recovery or sobriety is more than science or practical wisdom; it is deeply felt reality, and it brings form and function to his life. When he first felt it, he was at Camp O'Bannon, a yearly gathering of recovery folks, and he remembers being in that crowd and having a deep sense of peace, like he knew he could live his life in a different way if he was connected to these people—a true sense of mutual aid, as it were. That feeling can happen to anyone, Eric tells me again and again. "Your shit is never as bad or as good as you think it is," he says. "For a lot of people, you have to come to the end of the road before you make a decision to move forward. In the end you come out looking better. All it takes is time. Time heals all wounds. If you can put some clean time together, you'll feel better. We know that. All you have to do is sit still. You don't have to be profound. You don't have to know all this shit. You don't have to know all this literature. You don't have to have a recovery program. You have to not use, and gradually your body will start to heal."

Eric is clear about one thing, though: while recovery might begin with an individual, it can't remain that way. He had to get out of his own space, his own issues, and go out into the world to help others—like Johnathon, that couple, the man at the Salvation Army. And he became an activist in the parking lot of the same church where he had to be accompanied by a guard in order to attend his mother's funeral. He listened to some folks from the Ohio Organizing Collaborative on a bus tour talk about the problem of mass incarceration in Ohio and the school-to-prison pipeline—that was something he knew a lot about.

"I'm sitting there like, damn, shit sound familiar, that was my experience coming up in school," Eric says. He remembers feeling criminalized in school, and he can see where that led him. They asked him to say something. All he can remember saying is that, before, he had been a part of the problems in his community but now he wanted to be a part of the solutions. So he and his son got on board the bus and traveled around the state, even attending a rally in Cincinnati at which they were confronted by some neo-Nazis. That activist experience made him hunger for more. When he showed up at his first Newark Think Tank on Poverty meeting, there was a conversation about obstacles faced by people in poverty—folks there seemed to agree that issues related to felony convictions should be high on the list. Eric understood that, because he had experienced the struggles of trying to find a job and housing, of trying to get his life back together after prison. But now, with the Think Tank, he could do something to make things better for others.

When Eric testified in front of an Ohio state senate committee about Ban the Box, he told those in power why the issue meant so much to him, how having a felony conviction held him back. He was standing with other members of the Think Tank. The collective energy was palpable, he says. He felt empowered, sharing that story, sharing his truth, his life. He was the expert. He told me once that it felt like they were all beating a drum together. When he spoke, he said:

I have been impacted negatively by background checks from prospective employers. Today, I am a 60 year old grandfather far removed from those behaviors that would be an issue with any employer. The question on the application, "have you ever been convicted of a felony" has for years been used to disqualify me based on actions in the past that do not reflect the qualities of my character today. I work with recovering drug addicts and returning citizens. I encourage them to not let the mistakes of their past determine their future . . . I applied for a pick-and-pack job through a temp service at $10.00 per hour. After running my background check, I was informed they would have to call the corporate office to "see if they would be willing to take a chance on me." My application shows a solid work history with impeccable references, yet once again my background check had been an unfair barrier to my employment. It was humiliating.[16]

He told the state senators that not only do formerly incarcerated people need jobs, they need jobs that pay well. He told them he works forty hours a week and still qualifies for the Supplemental Nutrition Assistance Program (SNAP). He told them that he is trying to do the best he can for himself and his community. That he is going to school. He said, "We need to do more to unburden people who have moved on with their lives. Once we pay our debt to society, we should be able to get a fresh start."

The Think Tank might give Eric some purpose, but his voice and the voices of others with lived experience of poverty and addiction give purpose to the Think Tank. It's central to the ethos of the organization. But this idea that social change comes best when advocated for by the people most affected by the problem is not new. It has been a core value for the disability rights movement, with its mantra of "nothing about us without us," which was, in a sense, a central value of the activism of HIV/AIDS activists in the 1980s and '90s, especially groups like the AIDS Coalition to Unleash Power (ACT UP).[17]

In the rural and Rust Belt areas of the United States, there is a nascent movement, led by people with lived experience, that argues we are not in the midst of an opioid or addiction crisis; we are in the midst of a human rights crisis. The war on drugs, overcrowded prisons, and the continued rise in overdoses come back to one thing—an inability to treat people who use drugs with human dignity. And, those in this movement say, nothing can be done about us without us. While efforts to address the crisis have been intended to improve conditions for people who use drugs and their families, those people have not necessarily had seats at the table. This is changing.

Johnathon didn't stay long at The Refuge. He wasn't ready for treatment, he said after the fact. He wanted to leave after just twenty-four hours. A few days later, he asked to leave and was driven to the parking lot of a Walmart in nearby Athens, about an hour and half southeast of Newark. From there, he caught a ride to Newark, where he was back on the street and back in the trap houses, places where illicit drugs are sold. By early November, weeks after he left The Refuge, he was spending some of his nights sleeping under a bridge.

One night, he gazed into the darkness of the low-running water of Raccoon Creek, shivering. He could hear the trickle of water, the rumble of cars overhead, and the occasional whistle as trains crossed a trestle a few hundred yards away. It's a peaceful place; trees of heaven and birch trees line the banks, and in warmer weather fish jump. But it is not without its ghosts. One time, Johnathon says, he cooked up two grams of heroin with the intent of taking his life. He says the memory of what happened next is foggy: he thinks a guy who was fishing found him passed out on the muddy bank of the creek. But, he says, he didn't want to go that way that night. Johnathon called Colleen Richards, a mother and volunteer for NARI.

The next morning, Colleen and Trish Perry waited for Johnathon to meet them in front of the county library. When Johnathon finally arrived, he was carrying a plastic shopping bag with toiletries. Johnathon is fastidious. Even though he had slept outside, he was clean, with just a slight five-o'clock shadow. They took him to McDonald's and told him how the program works. He was nervous about willingly walking into a police station, but eventually they convinced him to give it a try. Before he could go there, he told them, he needed to get well. As they walked out together, Johnathon handed his leftover fries and burger to a woman who was homeless.

Colleen and Trish waited more than an hour in front of the police station. Eventually, Johnathon came walking down Fourth Street smoking a cigarette and wearing a camouflage jacket and jeans, his grocery bag of toiletries over his shoulder. He was hesitant. His eyes were squinting.

Colleen introduced him to an officer who would help get Johnathon into the program. Trish handed him a care bag with some snacks, socks, and extra clothes.

"Do you need anything else?" Colleen asked.

"No," Johnathon replied. "You know what I really want? Pumpkin ice cream. I love that stuff. They have it at the United Dairy Farmers in October."

"Well, we don't have that, but we can try to get you clean," the officer answered.

But after several days in withdrawal management, and no possibility of a bed in a long-term treatment facility, Johnathon had nowhere to go. So he called Think Tank member C.J. Wills, a friend of Eric Lee's, someone also in recovery. C.J. helped Johnathon get a place at a local men's shelter.

A few weeks later, in December, Eric, C.J., and I are in a coffee shop across from the courthouse in downtown Newark. "Feliz Navidad" plays on the radio more than once, and a woman across from us is sipping something with cinnamon and whipped cream. The conversation turns to Johnathon.

"I'mma tell you this right now," Eric says. "Until he's ready, all we can do is pray for him. We don't look him up. We don't chase him down."

C.J. says, "When I picked him up at Shepherd Hill, I said, 'Are you done? What are you gonna do different this time?' He said he was gonna start going to meetings. He went to one meeting with me."

Eric says he worries that there are trap houses around town and Johnathon will have to steer clear. But they can't hold his hand.

Eric leans in toward C.J. "The true testament of man's character is what he'll do when no one's looking or there's no PO or judge, when it's just your decision. That's when it's an impactful moment, you make that decision to turn it over to the will of God, that's when people move it forward."

If Eric sounds like a preacher, it's because he is, in a way, preaching his gospel of recovery. When he stopped using at age forty-seven, Eric says, it was a personal decision he made in the presence of a supportive and affirming recovery community, a community that abounds in Licking County. There are meetings every day with names like Journey Home, First Things First, and Club Serenity. One of the bright sides, if that's even possible, of the addiction crisis around this country is that it has pushed people into community who lacked it before.

"For me," C.J. says, "rehab was getting locked up. I prepared myself inside. And you always think you got it. But when I came out and real life kicked in, I didn't have it."

He had the desire to change, C.J. says, but he didn't change the "people, places, and things" that had led him to use in the first place. He says he needed a new community, a new support network.

"I can tell you this," Eric jumps in. "You might not think you had it, just like Johnathon, but I really truly believe that he already has everything he needs. He's got it in him; he just don't know it. The disease erases everything. You feel like you have to learn it all over again." He looks over at C.J. "You already have it. You don't need me."

C.J. laughs loudly.

Eric presses. "You already had everything you needed to stay clean for twenty-four hours. This is all about staying clean for one day. This is not about staying clean for the rest of your life . . . And if you sat in the jail cell, you know it ain't gonna kill you to stay clean. That's because we do what we want to do deep down inside. And if you wanna still use, if you wanna get high, you gonna get high. I don't give a shit what nobody say."

Eric's turning point was when a judge told him that it looked like he cared more about the drugs than about his kids. His life had never been presented to him in such stark terms.

"That was where I had a moment of clarity. Everything up to that point, in that moment—he was right."

It was March 22, 2004, and Eric says that he was so humiliated in that courtroom that he "sort of got sober out of spite."

It's not that Eric has given up on Johnathon or that C.J. has picked up the mantle; it's that Eric sets the bar high. Even for himself.

"It's hard to recover alone and without our community," Eric says.

This is something that C.J. knows all too well. In a very real way, it was his community that saved him.

C.J. grew up in Newark and had a hard life. There was addiction and abuse in his home. As a teenager he got caught up in a gang, and was drinking and smoking too much. He eventually found his way to meth and, like Eric, to jail and eventually to prison. His last stint was for four years, and when he got out, he found himself doing the things that he'd been doing before prison—and he was getting the same results. But he desperately wanted to get control of his life and visitation rights with his son, Maddox, whose name is tattooed on his arm and whose childhood handprints are tattooed on his back, a sort of perpetual embrace.

It wasn't one thing that transformed C.J. One night he took twenty hits of acid, smoked some meth, and overdosed in the middle of a street. He woke up to the blinding lights of a hospital emergency room with no clothes and no plans. He wandered the city until he reached a bench on the courthouse square. He says he prayed, after which his first thought was to go see Scott Fulton, head of adult probation and someone C.J. trusted. Fulton made C.J. his special case, meeting with him once a week and working through a reentry workbook. Fulton also encouraged C.J. to connect with the Newark Think Tank on Poverty. Lesha and Allen embraced C.J., and the meetings and commitments of the organization gave him purpose. But he still struggled. One cold night, he got into an argument with his mother, who kicked him out. C.J. had nowhere to go. He pulled his truck over into a parking lot, covered himself in some old coats, and fell asleep. When C.J. woke up, he realized he was in the parking lot of a church. He drove over to a trap house to get warm, and he called Eric, who told him to come over immediately.

When C.J. got there, the two men drank coffee in the early-morning hours and made plans. He spent a night or two with friends, a couple of nights at the Budget Inn, and finally landed in an efficiency apartment.

C.J. has relapsed several times since then, but he has also begun to reorganize his life with the help of people like Eric and a growing community. Now, if he does relapse, he has people to lean on. He doesn't have one recovery group; instead, he seems to surround himself with a community of support. He has participated in court-mandated programs like Bridges Out of Poverty, Triple P Parenting, and Father Factor. Somehow, someway, C.J. has cobbled together this network for his own recovery. That he has managed to do this befits his scrappy look—shaved head, goatee, tattoos. And for a working-class man in this county, a self-assembled network is sometimes the best and only option.

But he wants more. C.J. needs a stable job. He's working construction—it's not steady enough. He's trying to scrape together enough money to give his son a Christmas. He wants to provide for him, to be there for him. He dreams of one day having a small house on the edge of town, one with a yard where he can throw the football around with Maddox. He desperately wants stability.

"The book [the Narcotics Anonymous Basic Text] says we did many people harm, but the most harm we did to ourselves," Eric says. "I didn't feel shit when I was using up all the money, going, and coming back." His kids, especially, he says, suffered. "They suffered a lot more than I did." There was a time when Job and Family Services said they had given Eric enough chances—that they were done with him. "No one thought I could do it," he says, "a middle-aged black man. People judge you as an addict!"

He says he's tried lots of treatment—but that treatment was not the solution for him. He had to come to a place where he was ready. "I just think, with all the information, with all the treatment they give you, it's still a decision you make in a moment of desperation."

And now C.J. and Eric are here together, connecting over war stories and battle scars.

"I'm still learning," C.J. says. "I'm still learning."

4

Semicolons

In 2016–2017, the numbers were getting worse and health officials across the state were starting to notice a rise in overdoses involving fentanyl as well as some other illicit substances like cocaine or meth. It wasn't clear if people were buying meth, cocaine, or opioids. But the overall numbers were clear.

Writing in *The Plain Dealer*, Dennis Cauchon of Harm Reduction Ohio, an organization based in Licking County, notes that fentanyl is a serious public threat because it is now killing people who use cocaine: "Far more Ohioans use cocaine than use heroin . . . In the 3,480 Ohio overdose autopsies reported to the state as of this writing, 757 of the fatalities were for cocaine and fentanyl versus 476 for heroin and fentanyl." In discussing how to prevent fentanyl overdoses, Dennis advocates for the use of drug-testing strips so that people will know what's in their drugs.[1]

When I spoke to Dennis, I used the term *addiction crisis*.

"No," he said, "it's an overdose crisis."

For Eric, the overdose crisis began almost two decades ago when his sister died from an overdose of crack cocaine, just after he got out of prison. C.J. recently lost a childhood friend.

Johnathon says he's overdosed over a dozen times. When his friend Chance died of an overdose last March, he made sure he went to the funeral. He wanted to pay his respects, but he also needed the reminder of just how close he could have been. In June he went to court; he had a drug charge from right around the time he had been at the Budget Inn in October. Johnathon got probation and had to participate in the Licking County Alcoholism Prevention Program (LAPP), through which he began seeing a counselor and attending group meetings.

After Johnathon signed a waiver, his counselor let me sit in on a session, during which they talked at length about how far Johnathon has come. His counselor wants him to start thinking about what will replace his opioid use disorder. He's not sure he's found that yet, but he has found connection. He has found a way in and is doing very well. He has an apartment and sobriety. He told his story on the local television news and at a NARI fundraiser, speaking clearly to the dozens who came, thanking the people who have helped him. But he keeps photos of some of the places where he used to sleep on his phone—abandoned houses, park benches, underneath the Wilson Street Bridge—reminders of the path he was on that keep him grateful for the people who helped him get off it.

Those helpers, women like Trish Perry, are part of a new wave. Call them activists, organizers, citizens. Call them warriors. They are on the ground, on the phone, on social media. They are fighting this overdose crisis. They counsel people who use drugs, helping them get into treatment, and they advocate for them. They sit in hospital ERs with people awaiting withdrawal management. They distribute naloxone to anyone who'll take it.

They are, and this is important, mostly mothers. I have met many fathers who care for and advocate for their sons and daughters with substance use disorder, but mothers seem to make up the majority of those people on the front lines, the ones starting organizations, lobbying legislators, counseling others. In Licking County, Trish especially has gained a reputation, for better or worse, as a mother not to be messed with, a mother who will go to the mat for her child. Sometimes she can piss people off—online and in person. She is honest to a fault, fueled by righteous anger at some times and sweet, nonjudgmental love at others.

Right now she is frazzled. A slow-moving life crisis is shifting into high gear. Her son Billy is not doing well and has decided that today he wants to go into treatment. On top of that, she's trying to get custody of her grandson. She took the day off work for a meeting with the judge, but for some reason it has been rescheduled.

Her phone beeps three times. She looks down. It's her grandson, Ethan.

"I can't make no plans," Trish sighs. "When your son is an addict, you just . . ." She trails off and looks down at her phone. She's trying to go out of town on vacation, but now even that is up in the air. She just wants a break from this place and wonders aloud what it would be like to be carefree.

Trish brushes her hair, brunette with blond tips, away from her eyes and smiles a bright but slightly crooked smile. Her skin and face glow, but her eyes are tired. She's waiting for Billy to call or text to tell her he has found a treatment facility that will admit him. It's a big deal that he's asking to go into treatment, that he's even reaching out. He's tried three times before.

And maybe that's the reason Trish is having a hard time talking about the day she helped Johnathon. I've been asking her questions for about fifteen minutes but can't get much out of her. She'll only talk about that day in generalities, and she manages to change the topic more than once. But then she fixates on a moment.

"I guess I have more of an emotional connection, you know, because to see someone who just shot up dope, it was hard for me to sit there as they were filling out the paperwork," she explains haltingly. "All I saw was Billy." What she remembers most, she says, is the way one of the nurses treated Johnathon in the emergency room. She stops for a second and wipes her eyes. "He just was working him over. Couldn't find a vein. And he was treating him like an addict and not like a person." She'd been there before, she says, with Billy. The same hospital. The same ER. Billy's veins were so blown out that the nurse was flummoxed. "And I remember feeling ashamed," she says, and starts crying.

Trish has learned, though, not to be ashamed. On the top of her right arm is a tattoo, a Christmas gift from Billy, with "Blessed never give up;" over a background of pastels—green, red, and purple, with seagulls flying above. The semicolon is there to separate one story from the next story yet to be written, one tragedy from one triumph, one collapse from one recovery.[2]

She shows it off with pride because getting people's attention about addiction and overdose is her life's work. In addition to working forty hours a week at a pet store, she is taking classes to earn her bachelor's degree, helping to raise her grandson, and caring for her father, who has cancer. She wakes up every morning at four to check her email, to schedule posts for a Facebook support group she runs, to write cards to prisoners and folks in treatment, and to read up on addiction and pending legislation. In the past year, she has hosted three naloxone trainings, spoken to two Ohio House committees, and organized an overdose awareness rally in Newark.

Every day, she says, she's in the fight.

"People don't want to admit that it's here, and it's not going anywhere," she says. "Just yesterday there were three overdoses in this county."

Trish has had a life of ups and downs—and maybe it's the experience of those downs that makes her so deeply empathetic with people living on the margins in this community. She was born in Portsmouth, Ohio, and much of her family is from southern Ohio. Her father managed pig farms, a career that moved the family all over the country and eventually down to Oklahoma. That's where Trish met an enrolled member of the Cherokee Nation, married him, and had two sons; the first was Joe and the second was Billy, who was born in Woody Guthrie's hometown, Okemah, Oklahoma. After Billy was born, Trish and her husband moved apart; eventually they divorced. Her ex-husband's family kept Joe, while Billy went with her. After a brief stint in California, Trish moved to Texas.

There she was in a relationship with a man who was trafficking meth. She got caught up in it and was charged as well. He went to prison, but she got probation because her record was clean. By the early 1990s, though, she was sick of Texas and left before finishing her probation. Her mother was dying, and she wanted to move back to her hometown of Portsmouth—bringing Billy with her. They drove there in the winter in a car with no heat, she remembers, little Billy holding a bucket on his lap with his pet salamander in it all the way there. Once they arrived, the salamander escaped and Trish got a job managing a restaurant. She was eventually relocated to Kentucky, where one day fate would have it that she would get pulled over. Texas wanted her back. In Texas, she got eight years and ended up doing three and a half. While she was in prison, her mother died and Billy, living with her father, grew up.

In some ways, she says, all of this had an effect on Billy. The moves. Her absences. The fact that he's never met his father. And Trish says that Billy never understood why his father's family wanted Joe, the eldest of the two sons, and not him. She thinks that's where a lot of Billy's issues stem from—he always felt less important. On the one hand, she says, he has this important heritage through his father, but on the other hand it links him to that hard family history.

Billy began to struggle as a teenager, was arrested for selling pills at one point, and never finished school. Then, ten years ago on Labor Day, Trish learned that her son was shooting heroin. She knew he had used drugs recreationally, but she had never seen evidence of heroin in her house. In addition to running a successful DJ business, Billy had a construction job, a home, a girlfriend, and custody of his son. He lost all of that quickly. At the time, Billy wanted to go out to Oklahoma, to reconnect with his family there, thinking that might help him. But, Trish says, they didn't want him. Again he felt rejected. Trish tried to find help for him but could not. She says she was kicked out of places for being too loud and for asking too many questions.

In desperation, Trish wrote a letter to the editor of the local newspaper, *The Newark Advocate*:

> Hello. I just want to make it known that there is not adequate help in Licking County for drug addicts. I know someone who has been trying for months to get help and trying to get in a detox program, but the ultimate reality is if you don't have a medical card where the state can pay your bill or a lot of cash, you will not get in . . . Again: No money, no insurance, just an addict who is in need of help.[3]

That someone who needed help was Billy, of course. He still needs it.

"I'm trying to not let it totally control my life," Trish says. "But with all the activist work, if it saves one life . . . there might be another mom out there who saves Billy."

Trish's phone rings.

"Yeah," Trish answers. "Yeah? And they cut the water off? And where is he?"

It's a friend of Billy's. She can't find him. Trish's mood turns.

"Okay. I'm coming." Trish hangs up. "I guess I'll go try and find my son. It's never good when he doesn't answer his calls. Another eventful day."

It's not even noon.

Part 2

MOVEMENT

Fall 2017–Spring 2019

Pray for the dead and fight like hell for the living.
—MARY HARRIS "MOTHER" JONES

5

Swimming Upstream

In an innocuous meeting room on the south side of Newark, about twenty people, members of the Newark Think Tank on Poverty's leadership team, are gathered on a Sunday afternoon in late October 2017. They are deciding on a new campaign, and Eric Lee is hoping it will focus on addiction—hoping that, as an organization, the Think Tank will begin to advocate for equal treatment for all people who use drugs, whether their drug of choice is opioids or methamphetamine. Allen Schwartz is running the meeting. Methamphetamine, he says, is viewed mostly as a "poor man's" drug. That means only half of the crisis is being addressed.

There's a lot of skepticism here. Some wonder if state and federal grant money is earmarked specifically to combat opioid use or if it can be used in the fight against meth. Some wonder if there's going to be enough money at all. And some wonder if the people who need resources will actually gain access to them.

The crisis has become a political issue—talks of funding a response have percolated all summer long. At the end of May 2017, Ohio's attorney general, Mike DeWine, announced a lawsuit against five opioid-producing pharmaceutical companies.[1] President Donald Trump announced that the "opioid epidemic" was a national public health emergency, though not a national disaster, as some had expected.[2] Still, the problem of opioid addiction had been pushed into the national conversation and, apparently, federal dollars would follow.

In the fall of 2017, as part of his gubernatorial campaign, DeWine unveiled "Recovery Ohio," a twelve-point plan to deal with the substance abuse crisis in Ohio.[3] Going beyond the target of opioid use, it focuses on building greater capacity for treatment and prevention. At the same time, there's talk of cutting Medicaid expansion, a move that would send many into a spiral.[4]

But here in this room, talk is of this community, of people with names and familiar faces, of family members, of loved ones.

Eric sits directly across from Allen. He's quiet, contemplative, a little uneasy. Eric's strength is the "one-on-one" and the outreach—what he was doing with C.J. and Johnathon almost exactly one year before. He's not into deliberative processes.

Following the Ban the Box campaign, the Think Tank placed its members on the boards of a number of groups throughout the county, but they've struggled to find the energy that earlier movement generated. Now there's a clear problem to address, one that many members, especially Eric and C.J., have direct experience with—how hard it is to get treatment for substance use disorder if you're poor. They also feel like meth use is being overshadowed by opioids because there's no medication-assisted treatment for it, no clear "cure." Meth is clearly present, members of the Think Tank say. Local law enforcement agrees. Over the summer, three men, allegedly tied to the Mexico-based Sinaloa Cartel, were arrested after a traffic stop.[5] A search of their hotel room uncovered twelve pounds of meth and fifteen thousand dollars in cash.

The Think Tank members vote to advocate for fair treatment of all people who use drugs who are struggling; they vote to raise public consciousness.

Eric speaks up. "I'm happy with the vote, but I'm hoping we can fold in housing and public transit. We have to remember that what we're really talking about is poverty."

"We're not going to be crazy about not doing other things," Allen responds, "but we're saying for the next six to twelve months we're going to own this campaign. Current title: Equal Treatment for Addiction Epidemics." Allen says that they want to make the point that, compared with opioid use, methamphetamine use is higher around here and that people who use meth are treated poorly. He points out that they've talked both to local experts and to their in-house experts like C.J. who can speak to the stigma that people who use meth face when they seek help.

"This is not my line of work," Allen says. "I've learned ten thousand times more about addiction since I started working with the Think Tank. But I have a niece who died from an overdose, and another who is now addicted to opioids." He admits that until recently he never put these things together.

Eric speaks up again. "The only other thing that I wanted to say was, you're leaving out taking this message to the street just like with Ban the Box . . . We went out, we got people it affected directly, and we had them tell our stories," he says. "The last thing I'd want to see," he says, concluding, "is us making all these plans, and we leave the addicts out, we leave the stories out."

So the Think Tank begins the work of gathering stories and sharing their agenda with people in positions of power.

C.J., Allen, and five others meet one evening with municipal court judge David Stansbury, who runs a drug court. They explain their advocacy plan, how they want to make sure that people who use meth are being treated fairly in Licking County, looking for feedback.

Judge Stansbury agrees that methamphetamine use is significant here and that it is not getting enough attention. But, he tells them, "You know you're swimming upstream, because once the national media gets ahold of something, it's hard to reframe the conversation."

Allen responds, "We're used to swimming upstream."

C.J., wearing a gray hoodie and a Cleveland Browns hat with a shiny helmet logo—his Browns haven't won a game yet this year—smiles and nods his head. He asks the judge how often people come into his court and say they've tried to get help but nothing has been offered.

Stansbury says it happens from time to time.

The perception on the street, Allen says, is that you will be treated differently if you are using meth—that you can't get into treatment centers. C.J. adds that it's hard to get help. Drawing on his experience, he says, "The only way for the hospital to accept you is to pretty much say you're going to harm yourself."

But as Eric says, the most important thing for the group is to listen to people with drug use experience, to learn directly from them.

On a Saturday afternoon, the Think Tank gathers for a general meeting in downtown Newark. C.J. and Eric are there.

Allen opens it up and explains what will be happening at this meeting, that today they will only be listening. "It is by raising our voices that we will not be disappeared," he says, explaining that this is what happens in some countries to people who speak up about political issues.

In this case, he means that if we want structural change, the people who have been most affected by the gaps in the system must be heard and not have their voices erased from the public conversation.

"That's what the Think Tank is about," Allen continues. "Using our experience and our voices to push those lessons out onto the people who have power so that we can get a system change. We don't have the resources that some service providers have, but we're here to change the system. That's why we want to focus attention on the meth addiction problem."

Allen then asks the invited experts, people with lived experience with substance use disorder, to help the Think Tank better understand the obstacles people trying to go into treatment face. One woman talks about the despair and lack of self-worth she felt when she was using, and how that hampered her efforts to seek help. Some people talk about transportation—the lack of fixed-route vans or buses makes it hard to get to any appointments. Others talk about the criminal justice system. People who use drugs, they say, often end up in jail over petty crimes or possession charges. When they get out, many don't know what to do next. One man explains that when he got out of jail there was a trap house right in front of him, and he ended up in jail again.

It's an important moment for the Think Tank. They have their own experts, people who understand these very circumstances, people like Eric and C.J., but on this day, they opened the doors a bit wider. The stories flowed, peppered not only with the language of personal responsibility of self-help and recovery but also with the frustrations of the justice system's interventions into the lives of people who use drugs, this war on drugs.

Alex S. Vitale notes in *The End of Policing* that it's true that illegal and legal drugs can produce many harms—to people who use them, to families, to communities—like overdoses and the spread of disease. "But there is a mountain of evidence that shows that most users suffer no significant harm," he continues, "and that harms that do occur could be reduced by ending, not expanding, the War on Drugs."[6]

A term I've heard folks in the Think Tank use at their meetings, time and again, is *dominant narrative*. Allen defines it as "the stories, images, judgments (values) used by the culture to justify/rationalize the system as it is, including the class structure and power relationships." He says they call it that because "it dominates other narratives and it serves the dominant class." The dominant narrative is that poor people and people who use drugs are somehow morally deficient. The dominant narrative is that they should be pitied and helped but not called upon to lead. The Think Tank is upending that narrative.

Days later, they meet with Scott Fulton, C.J.'s mentor and the head of adult probation in Licking County. They meet in an old warehouse that once housed a tech start-up and is the future home of the county's new adult probation day reporting program. Rather than visiting a probation officer once a week for a urine screen and a check-in, adults on probation will come here every day for workshops, GED classes, and supervision. The hope is to reduce recidivism rates while helping adults with substance use disorder.

Allen tells the tired-looking probation officer that they have been talking to people and that they're hoping he can provide them with data and a picture from his vantage point about treatment options in Licking County. The Think Tank is concerned, Allen says, that people are not getting the treatment they need.

Scott agrees that it's important for people who want treatment to be taken care of. But he also says that most people need to be ready for treatment. "You got to change your environment, your friends, everything in your life," he says, "because all of that keeps driving what you're going to do and it's easy to blame the program. It's not the program." He thinks it's up to the individual, that it doesn't matter where someone travels to, that they can get the exact same treatment here in Licking County that they could get at a place like the well-known, Minnesota-based Hazelden.

Allen wonders, "Will money coming down be just for opiates? That would be a big issue for us."

Scott says that's what his perception is, adding, "The thing is, there's no magic wand. The person going in there is going to have to do the work . . . They have to listen and do the work. It's not easy getting clean. It's not easy staying clean. Basically, you have to change everything in your life. Right?" Scott looks at C.J., and C.J. nods.

Allen presses. "Where the rubber hits the road, because we're going to have to come up with a list of demands, but if I was a TV reporter and I came up to you and said, 'Mr. Fulton, what would you want? We're being told that the response to the meth crisis is not adequate, what would you suggest?'"

"I don't know how to answer that yet. You have to get that conversation going." Scott pauses. "I don't know if saying meth . . . It's addiction. That's what upsets me about this whole opiate thing. It's not opiates. It's about addiction. It's about people having issues and problems and dealing with them. It's not about the substance."

"It is to the system," Allen says.

"You already know why that is," Scott says. "It's class. Middle-class, upper-class white people—the banker's son, the senator's son living on the cul-de-sac that are hooked on this and dying, not the person working at Universal Veneer living in the East End."

Lesha Farias speaks up. "I don't think it's just meth. We just don't have an adequate number of addiction facilities whether it's inpatient or outpatient."

"And I'm sad to say," Scott replies, "that [for some people] they have to be involved in the criminal justice system to get help."

"I'm trying to get at the frame of our campaign," Allen says, guiding them back on track. "We could frame this as seeking adequate addiction services for all. The frame that we've chosen, though, is that at least half of the addiction community in Licking County is not getting served. We have to choose one or the other."

Lesha responds, "Can you look at it as 'Can we look at the real addiction problem in Licking County?' Then you can look at meth and you're not limiting yourself . . . Our education piece is 'What is the real addiction problem in Licking County?' And then we bring out the statistics because we're educating people. We don't want to go to another one of these meetings where we hear about the problem but nobody has any idea for a solution. I can't sit through another one of those."

Throughout the conversation, C.J. has been mostly quiet, at times holding his head in his hands, scratching a pen on a pad. He's the guy who has the experience, more than anyone in this room. They are talking about his struggles because it was his story of not being able to get into treatment that lit this fire. But he trusts them with his story. In some ways, these are the people he trusts the most.

He suddenly turns to me and asks if my recorder is off. It is. And then he tells a story, one whose full details I've agreed not to share but that even in outline helps explain C.J. in ways that, until now, I've not been able to. C.J. says that he was abused as a child, and he has run from it most of his life. Meth was one way out. And now, right now, he can't hold back the tears. This man with his tattooed body. This tough, strong, resilient man.

The room is quiet after he speaks. No one knows where to begin.

Lesha says, "You are so strong for sharing that with us."

"It's been on my mind," C.J. says. He pauses, then adds, "I guess it's the talk about trauma."

C.J. is deeply intuitive and self-reflective, almost to a fault. He struggles still to find meaning in the complications of his life and says often that his favorite book of the Bible is Job because he can relate. Every time he has a success, something presses back. But Job is also a story about a relentlessly hopeful man. C.J. has now uncovered something that begins to explain his life and could help him move forward. Gabor Maté—the Canadian physician—argues that underlying some addictions is untreated trauma. In his book *In the Realm of Hungry Ghosts*, he writes that deprivation, physical or emotional, can be traumatic for a child and can negatively affect brain development.[7] If abuse happens, if you don't feel connection, especially at a young age, then a drug can become that "warm, soft hug" that may have been absent for you. He writes, too, "A sense of deficient emptiness pervades our entire culture. The drug addict is more painfully conscious of this void than most people and has limited means of escaping it."[8] That may have described the C.J. of a decade ago. But now, in different circumstances, with different means and supports, he can see a way out.

After his revelation, the rest of the conversation about addiction doesn't matter—which substance is more prevalent in Licking County, what the grant dollars must be used for. What matters is this one man who is coming to terms with his childhood, who is building a new life before their eyes.

6

Systems of Care

In late November 2017, C.J. goes to an "addiction awareness" rally outside the Licking County Courthouse wearing his big smile, a blue Think Tank shirt, and his beloved Cleveland Browns ball cap. He hands out the first issue of *Justice*, the Think Tank's newsletter, with a headline that reads "We Want Real Treatment for Meth Addiction Recovery." C.J.'s life is improving. He has a car. He has regular visitations with his son and a steady maintenance job. One popular American narrative is that poor people are lazy, that they're not trying hard enough. But C.J. is full of "try hard" and then some. He says he wishes he could tell his story to people running for office. He'd tell them "straight up" that when he got out of prison, he couldn't get a job. That's when he went back to using. It's that simple. "If you don't have hope, you lose all will," he says.

C.J.'s friends in the Think Tank say that he's a born organizer. He's not afraid to speak to anyone—he just walks right up to passersby and shares his story, starts building connections. Allen Schwartz told me once that the Think Tank is about helping people like C.J. find a community and a place where they won't be judged. "If that's all we do," he said, "then we will have done something."

They already have done something. Now C.J. is committed to sharing his story and the Think Tank is providing a platform. A reporter from ABC 6 News hears C.J. speak up at the rally and asks him for an interview.[1] He tells her about how he was treated when he went to a hospital seeking help for his meth addiction. He tells her this is an addiction crisis, not an opioid crisis. He tells her that he's fighting for all who are suffering.

But that fight is a day-to-day thing, and for people in recovery it's about rebuilding and reimagining the world, about finding a supportive community to help them through adversity, and about tapping into their own resiliencies. For the working poor, this process is doubly difficult because the smallest things can throw them off course. Out of the blue, C.J. gets a bill from the parole board for "unpaid fees." The bill is for $640. He's not sure how he's going to pay for it, and he spirals. Despite all the good things that have been happening for him, he's depressed, he's lonely, he's frustrated.

"I feel like I'm doing everything right," he says as we sit down in a booth at a Bob Evans, "and now this."

C.J. and I are meeting up before going to a church meeting about "opioid addiction." Allen texted me beforehand and asked if he could join us. We order coffee and burgers just as Allen arrives and gets straight to the point—he wants to help C.J. with those "unpaid fees." He wants to figure out how they can handle this problem together. In this moment of crisis, C.J.'s community encircles him.

In the addiction research community, what is happening here, some might say, is part of a model of addiction recovery called recovery-oriented systems of care (ROSC).[2] It's an approach to addressing addiction that seeks to move beyond pathologizing someone as an "addict," forever marred by that designation. This begins with prevention and, hopefully, ends with holistic continued care that focuses on building people up so they attain and sustain long-term recovery.

Michael T. Flaherty, a Pittsburgh-based clinical psychologist and consultant in ROSC, says that recovery-focused care should be about building on strengths, increasing "recovery capital." This can mean using less or abstaining, but it can also mean finding better housing, employment, education, emotional and family health, physical health, better relationships, ways to serve others, and, in general, a meaningful life.[3] By increasing one person's "recovery capital," he points out, the entire community grows. And as this resilience grows, the ability to address an addiction crisis grows. Bruce K. Alexander supports this model when he writes, "Although personal strength and courage are absolutely necessary, the way out is not simply suppressing an addictive habit with iron will-power, for this often precipitates other kinds of social problems or different addictions, which can be worse ... The best way out of addiction is overcoming dislocation by finding a secure place in a real community."[4]

Finding your way into a stable and supportive community is very often the key to recovery. But it's a challenge to build such recovery capital in a place that has its own social and economic challenges—and Newark, like many places, has them. And yet it can be a matter of life and death. Princeton economists Angus Deaton and Anne Case have noted the increasing death rates for working-class whites across the nation, so-called deaths of despair—deaths by drugs, alcohol, and suicide that are the result of economic and social issues that create a perfect storm of disconnection.[5] The numbers are especially high in Ohio. This crisis is hitting poor and working-class people the hardest because they feel the economic struggle the most. They feel despair, hardship, suffering, sorrow, hopelessness.

Despite those challenges, people like C.J. are becoming resilient. C.J. is being embraced by his community, and he's building a new one.

"There's no cookbook," Flaherty says. "It's highly individualistic. It's understanding the illness first as an illness, and then accepting that there's some way you can get over it, and then meeting others you connect to, so it strengthens your sense of self-esteem."

Then he adds, in a turn of phrase that resonates, "It's a positive moving."

In C.J.'s life there is certainly a positive moving.

It's 8:30 p.m. in November, and Newark's assistant fire chief, David Decker, sits at his desk doing paperwork. Suddenly, a red light flashes in the hallway; a voice comes over the intercom indicating an EMT run. A possible drug overdose. Within seconds, Decker is in his department-issued SUV, racing through downtown Newark, passing the courthouse, lights flashing and siren wailing as he careens over the train tracks and down Main Street.

He's the first to arrive at the house. When he enters, he finds a woman lying motionless on the floor, anxious kids circled around her. Spotting the woman's partner in the house, Decker shouts to him: "Can you get these kids upstairs? They don't need to see this."

Decker deftly administers Narcan, and soon the woman comes to. An EMT transports her to the nearby hospital.

Decker returns to the firehouse and sits back down at his desk. Soon enough, the red light blinks again. It's the same address. The same emergency. He races back over. This time it is the woman's partner—the man he'd just seen.

There is, Decker says, nothing irregular about tonight.

"In my first fifteen or twenty years of service, I bet I didn't administer Narcan no more than a dozen times," says Decker, who is now in his twenty-ninth year as a firefighter. "In the last two and a half or three years we've probably given one hundred doses of Narcan on runs I've been on."

Decker takes a holistic view of the problems facing his city. The addiction crisis, he says, is largely a poverty problem.

Decker doesn't need a study to tell him about what he sees every day. Addiction, he says, can start with a dead car battery. It's that simple. "A guy's car breaks down. He can't make it to work. They terminate him," he explains. "So now he starts into stealing. Which leads to drug abuse. Which leads to kids being removed. So on and so forth."

What he's describing, really, are daily problems and the inability to address them or cope with them, especially for people with limited means. And then a person adapting to those problems—addiction as a learned behavior.

And then, he says, because it's mainly the poor who are overdosing, no one seems to care.

"Do you see any rich politician's kids dying of a heroin overdose?" he asks.

While some politicians have dealt with personal tragedy of their own, research confirms that the overdose crisis has indeed hit low-income communities harder than well-off ones. For example, a 2017 report from researchers at The Ohio State University's Swank Institute found that "an Ohio county's unemployment rate in 2010 is positively correlated with overdose deaths in 2015 . . . Counties with a higher poverty rate have a higher overdose rate."[6]

Decker's firehouse services some economically challenged neighborhoods, so it's not hard to find the source of his perspective.[7] This also happens to be the part of town where Decker grew up.

Decker's clean-cut look, flat tone, and no-nonsense demeanor is almost cliché first responder, but beneath that exterior lies a man who cares deeply, and who finds himself frustrated often. He struggles to understand why people judge people who use drugs, why people would call for a limit on the use of naloxone or become frustrated by repeated calls to the same house for the same person.

"Some of the patients that we bring up are remorseful. Even tearful and ashamed," Decker says. "I'm guessing all these people didn't have a longing to become addicted to anything."

In many ways, the overdose crisis is magnifying deeper issues for nonusers as well. In Newark, as elsewhere, there's a growing sense that the pressures of being a first responder are causing mental stress and post-traumatic syndrome. And county social services, especially the foster care system, are struggling to keep up. For his own part, Decker and his wife decided to foster a child. One less kid, they figured, left bouncing around a congested foster care system.

"We talked about how overwhelmed the system was because of the drug crisis," Decker says. His own intervention in his foster child's life has convinced Decker that what's really needed to address the addiction crisis is better support for social service agencies and for struggling families.

Invoking almost the exact same metaphor that Kim Kehl invoked, Decker opines, "Let's say you're drowning in the deep end of a swimming pool and someone throws you a bucket and says, 'Start emptying that pool out.' Now, you're doing all you can just to keep your head above water. You don't have an arm free to fill up the bucket so we can get this pool empty."

It's a moral issue, Decker says. People need to be decent to one another. "We have a responsibility to do the right thing," he continues. "If you're arrested and tried for a crime, a jury of your peers will ask, 'Did he do the right thing or the wrong thing?' And I think that runs through everything in life."

Our conversation is interrupted once more when an enormous flat-screen panel, situated in the middle of the fire station's common area, starts blinking red. He calmly but swiftly throws his jacket over his shoulders and heads for the SUV.

There's no shortage of people like Decker who are trying. People who are trying to help and to build stronger systems of care, so to speak. This community is overwhelmed by people who want to help, not just the usual suspects. The guerrilla warriors of this community—counselors, judges, community organizers, probation officers, firefighters, and a host of grass-roots mothers and fathers and people in recovery packing naloxone and a prayer. Local agencies are being joined in the struggle by people who are looking for new ways to address the problem. Groups like the Think Tank and OhioCAN (Change Addiction Now), the organization Trish Perry affiliates with—as well as groups like the Licking County Champions Network, the Crossroads Crusaders, and John's Helping Hands—directly and indirectly support parents and friends and people who use drugs themselves. The health department has created an online Narcan training system. And the county's addiction task force brings people from law enforcement to the health department to the same table every couple of months. And yet, they'll all agree, it doesn't seem like enough.

Early January 2018. The temperature on the corner bank's electronic display reads single digits. Eric is waiting in front of the First Presbyterian Church on North Third Street in downtown Newark with his five-year-old granddaughter, Kortni. She's bouncing around wearing a pink-and-purple winter coat pulled tight, her pink backpack bobbing up and down. Eric's wearing only a black beanie and a thin coat. It's not enough for this cold. He tells me he's been in some pain as of late and winces as we climb the stairs to a second-floor meeting room. He has an enlarged prostate and he's been off work for a couple of weeks. He's just glad there's nothing cancerous this time.

For over three years, Eric has been running a group here for people on judicial release. They meet every Tuesday evening in this old meeting room with its peeling white paint, brown carpet, and circle of dilapidated folding chairs. He doesn't get paid for this work. Just like he doesn't get paid for being a part of his Wednesday-night recovery group or going to the Budget Inn to talk with people who are struggling or helping young men fresh out of jail find work. He does this because he believes in it, and because, I'm starting to learn, his hopefulness is unbounded.

But it's a hope rooted in reality and in work—it's central to any lecture he gives to a person struggling with addiction. It's also central to what he does. Eric gave his own one-year Narcotics Anonymous coin to C.J., rather than giving him a shiny new one. He had had the coin for a long time, and it carried more value, more weight. When he worked nights stripping, waxing, and buffing grocery store floors, Eric used it to scrape out particularly hard spots. He would get down on his hands and knees and go at the spots. Eric gave C.J. a coin that was weathered but strong.

The group is sanctioned by Licking County's adult probation office, and its members gather to help one another overcome obstacles, "to get real," Eric says. If people complete the eighteen-month program, come to the meetings, and do the right things, they can get time off of their probation. This is no easy task, because most participants have substance use disorders. It's not an addiction recovery meeting, Eric says, but he admits that the ethos of recovery shapes the group.

There's a small crowd tonight, so Eric can take some time with each person who has shown up, check in with them, dispense advice—both practical and spiritual. Speaking with a calm toughness that is all him, he counsels them to be patient.

"We all work real hard to clear the system—to just go back and get high again?" Eric asks.

One woman talks about how she contacted an old friend on social media and then he just showed up at her workplace with dope. She quickly sent him packing.

She didn't need that right now, she says.

"You've got your role models, your people. Be patient."

His bifocals slip down his nose as he talks.

Eric listens, he connects people to resources, he shares. There's not much to it. Except, there is. He's here and he's supportive. He's providing another check-in, another layer of support. All this while he's dealing with his own struggles, serving as the crisis manager in his own family.

After about an hour Eric dismisses the group. He stands up and walks through the door, Kortni following. I shut off the light, and we trudge down the stairs. He grabs a hidden key and locks the door for the night. It's colder—a breeze has picked up and sends small flecks of snow into our faces.

Eric needs a ride home, so I offer and we cross the street to my truck. Kortni is lagging behind and he turns, reaching out his hand. "Come on."

Kortni hops up into my truck, and Eric winces as he sits down.

We drive up past the courthouse and down West Main Street to his apartment. He's quiet, tired. He has no business being out on this cold January night. But he is here. Weathered. Strong.

None of Us
Are Bad People

Trish's son Billy McCall got out of jail about a week ago, and right now he's on Vivitrol (the brand name for naltrexone), which blocks the effects of opiates, and he is hoping that this time sobriety sticks.[1] At the kitchen table in his modest trailer in Newark, he stares through a mostly curtained window to the street. His long, dark hair is pulled back in a ponytail and smooshed down by a beanie. He has a handsome, round face and well-trimmed beard. He admits he's not used to how sober he is feeling right now—it makes him anxious. "The best I can describe it is like, for most people, sex is probably the best feeling they've ever had in their life or whatever and then, say, taking that away for the rest of your life. The thing you like the most, the best, most pleasurable thing you've ever had. Now, all the bullshit that comes with it and the consequences that come with it aren't good, but physically it's just euphoria. To take that away and say you can never have it again is overwhelming."

Billy has struggled with substance use disorder for years now. His use is intertwined with his short list of crimes, mostly theft that leads to probation violations and more complications. He's been to prison twice and jail often enough. Inevitably, it's just more traumatic experiences that don't address the underlying problems. And now he's overwhelmed by probation—the fear that if he slips, he'll go back to jail again. He has to call every day to see if he is going to be tested. He checks outside the window again. "I'm paranoid looking out my window thinking they're just going to show up here."

When they don't call him, he gets nervous that he's doing something wrong. When they do call him, he gets nervous that he's doing something wrong. His main worry? "That at any moment they're just going to come snatch me out of my life again." Because that's what happens, he says, when you go to jail.

"Right now I just want to be a father to my son, I want to be respected by my peers, I want to help people. I got to get myself together first, but ultimately I'd like to take this experience and be able to help some people, man."

He has a lot on his plate, just dealing with life, with the people he has lost, and he doesn't think being wrapped up in the criminal justice system is helping very much.

But Billy is not alone. One of the central narratives of the current overdose crisis is that there has been a softer touch than during the crack epidemic of the 1980s and '90s. There is some truth to that. It's hard to imagine, now, how many lives racist drug policies have destroyed—all the families disrupted, all the men and women killed, all the human beings imprisoned. On the one hand, there is a growing push for criminal justice reform in Ohio. Senate Bill 3, for example, reclassifies some drug possession charges—if possession is for personal use—to misdemeanors.[2] On the other hand, the old drug-war playbook is still in use and some prosecutors have adopted a decidedly "tough on crime" approach—through the usual charges around possession and trafficking.

Also, and increasingly, this has meant treating overdose deaths, one of the key features of the current crisis, as murders and seeking to level harsh penalties against dealers, even small-time drug users, who have supplied people with the drugs that killed them. The federal government and twenty-four states have, as of this writing, what are known as "drug-induced homicide" laws on their books, under which anyone involved in the illegal manufacture, sale, distribution, or delivery of a controlled substance that causes death can be charged with murder or manslaughter.[3] Penalties for charges under the state laws range from two years in prison to capital punishment, which is the case in Florida and Oklahoma. (To date, however, no one has been sentenced to death in a drug-induced homicide case.) Midwestern states, including Ohio, Wisconsin, Illinois, and Minnesota, have been among the most aggressive in prosecuting drug-induced homicides.[4] According to a *New York Times* investigation, there have been more than a thousand prosecutions or arrests in connection with accidental overdose deaths since 2015 in fifteen states where data was available.[5]

While this trend began prior to Donald Trump's election, it has accelerated since he assumed office. According to the U.S. Sentencing Commission, a federal agency, there was a 10 percent increase in 2017 in the number of people who received federal prison sentences for distributing drugs resulting in death or serious injury, and a nearly 200 percent increase since 2013.[6] Trump has made it clear that he favors an aggressive approach to the opioid crisis. "My take is you have to get really, really tough—really mean—with the drug pushers and the drug dealers," Trump said in February 2018 during a speech in Blue Ash, Ohio.[7]

Trump has pushed this rhetoric to its logical conclusion, suggesting that drug dealers should face the death penalty, an idea he said he got from Chinese president Xi Jinping.[8] He has also expressed admiration for President Rodrigo Duterte of the Philippines for his violent approach to curbing drug trafficking.[9] In March 2018, then attorney general Jeff Sessions issued a memo to the ninety-three U.S. attorneys reminding them that they have the power to pursue capital punishment in certain drug-related cases.[10]

This aggressive approach has filtered down to the local level. During the summer of 2017 in Middletown, Ohio, a city of fifty thousand near Cincinnati, city council member Dan Picard proposed a "three strikes and you're out" policy for overdose rescues.[11] Overdose victims would be required to perform community service to make up for the cost of treatment—and if a 911 dispatcher determined that someone who is overdosing has not performed community service, they would not dispatch emergency services. "We've got to do what we've got to do to maintain our financial security, and this is just costing us too much money," Picard told a local news station. First responders balked at this dehumanizing proposal, but the frustration that bred it persists and can foster other misguided "get tough" responses. And according to Health in Justice—an "action lab" out of the Northeastern University School of Law—Ohio is one of the most active states, second only to Pennsylvania, with 385 media mentions of drug-induced homicide charges since 2000.[12] And in Licking County, at least five people were charged for supplying drugs that led others to overdose between 2016 and 2019.[13] One of those cases involved Billy's friend Chad Baker.

The evening before Chad Baker died, his fiancée, Katie Offenburger, came home from her job as an account manager at a credit card company, let the dog out, and smoked a cigarette on the back porch of their three-bedroom house in Newark.[14] The couple had bought the house a few years earlier, after meeting while in recovery.

The next morning, Katie woke up and walked to the bathroom. The door was closed, but the shower was running. She called Chad's name. No answer. She pushed on the door, but it barely moved. Through the narrow opening she could see Chad's feet. She pushed hard and made her way in. "I saw Chad lying on the floor. There was a needle between his legs," she later testified.

The paramedics who arrived on the scene shortly before 8:00 a.m. found Chad Baker unresponsive. His skin was pale, he had no pulse, and his pupils had shrunk to pinpoints. The paramedics performed CPR and attempted to revive him with epinephrine (adrenaline) and Narcan, and then rushed him to the hospital, but he never recovered. Chad Baker was pronounced dead at 8:29 a.m. on May 29, 2015, just three days before his birthday. A toxicology report revealed heroin and cocaine in his system.

Two years later, a man named Tommy Kosto sat in the Licking County Courthouse awaiting a jury's verdict after a three-day trial. Chad and Tommy had met while serving time for drug offenses in a community-based correctional facility for nonviolent offenders about eight years earlier. Tommy struggled, however, and by the spring of 2015, he was using heroin again, sending desperate daily text messages to his dealer, hoping to buy more.

But the county prosecutor alleged that Tommy wasn't just a struggling user—he was a dealer and had sold Chad Baker the drugs that killed him. Tommy admitted to using heroin with Chad days before he died but denied that he sold the drugs that killed him. The jury sided with the prosecutor, finding Tommy guilty of involuntary manslaughter, corrupting another with drugs, possession of heroin, and tampering with evidence—for deleting text messages between him and Chad.[15] Together, these offenses could result in at least fifteen years in prison. As the jury announced its verdict, Tommy wore a look of disbelief, and his attorney just shook his head.

After Tommy was convicted, Licking County prosecutor Bill Hayes—who was present at the reading of the verdict but was not the prosecutor for the case itself—told *The Newark Advocate* that drug-induced homicide laws would help stem the opioid crisis in Ohio.[16] "The jury sent a strong message that cavalier use of drugs in our community isn't going to be tolerated," he said.

The concept of prosecuting individuals in connection with drug-related deaths goes back more than a century. In 1885, a doctor in New York was charged with manslaughter after a patient died from a morphine overdose.[17] The doctor was accused of administering the drug "with wicked, wanton, willful, and reckless disregard of the life of the patient." In 1916, less than two years after Congress passed the Harrison Narcotics Tax Act, which regulated the sale of opiates and coca products, three people were arrested in connection with the death of a fifteen-year-old boy who died of a heroin overdose.[18] And in 1970, a Bronx grand jury indicted two men for second-degree manslaughter and criminally negligent homicide for giving heroin to a seventeen-year-old Barnard freshman.[19] Many drug-induced homicide laws date to the 1980s, however, when states and the federal government used them as part of the war-on-drugs approach to the crack cocaine epidemic. After University of Maryland basketball star Len Bias died of a cocaine overdose in June 1986, Congress passed the Anti-Drug Abuse Act, which mandates a sentence of twenty years to life in prison for dispensing a controlled substance that results in "death or serious bodily injury."[20] Despite their creation as a knee-jerk response to a social crisis, these laws were rarely used for decades. That is changing. Recently, North Carolina passed the "Death by Distribution" law, which reads that someone is guilty even if there is no malice. There are even stiffer penalties when prosecutors can prove malice.[21]

Passing these laws and prosecuting individuals under them might help lawmakers burnish their tough-on-crime bona fides. But there's almost no evidence that stiffer penalties have reduced drug overdoses. Northeastern School of Law professor Leo Beletsky told me that, in many ways, drug-induced homicide prosecutions are a form of political theater: "It's an episode out of a multiseries sort of American story."

A 2018 report by the Pew Charitable Trusts points out that there's no relationship between drug imprisonment rates and a state's drug problem. "The theory of deterrence would suggest, for instance, that states with higher rates of drug imprisonment would experience lower rates of drug use among their residents," the report notes. But according to the study, incarceration is one of the least effective methods for reducing drug use and crime.[22] "With addicted people, it doesn't deter behavior or deter people who have multiple felonies and can't do anything else to make a living," said

Kathie Kane-Willis, director of policy and advocacy with the Chicago Urban League, who has been tracking the outcomes of Illinois's drug-induced homicide law since the early 2000s.

And yet incarceration is still a common policy for addressing America's addiction crisis. One in five of the almost 2.3 million people currently in prison in the United States is there because of a drug-related offense.[23] Most of these people are not violent drug kingpins; mandatory minimum sentencing laws have filled jail cells with low-level drug offenders, primarily minorities.

Tommy Kosto and Chad Baker are both white, and the prevailing narrative around the opioid crisis presents it as a white problem. This isn't factually the case, of course—and the prosecution of drug-induced homicides is likely to affect minorities disproportionately as well. African Americans are dying from opioid overdoses at a rate higher than the general population in a number of states, including Illinois, Wisconsin, Missouri, Minnesota, and West Virginia.[24] In Illinois, deaths from opioids among African Americans increased by 123 percent from 2013 to 2016, faster than those in any other racial group. And Kane-Willis told me that, as the opioid crisis spreads and drug-induced homicide prosecutions become more common, even more people of color are likely to go to prison.

Moreover, while many states, including Ohio, have Good Samaritan laws that are meant to encourage people to call 911 if someone appears to be overdosing, the fact that you could be charged with manslaughter discourages some people who use drugs from seeking help. Besides, Ohio's Good Samaritan law has some serious limitations: it excludes people on parole and probation; you're only allowed to receive immunity twice; and the person who overdosed must seek help from a "community addiction services provider or a properly credentialed addiction treatment professional" within thirty days.[25] Restrictions (and the misunderstandings they create) can have a chilling effect. In a 2017 study, Johns Hopkins public health researchers Amanda Latimore and Rachel Bergstein found that some people who use drugs said that if they knew someone was overdosing they would hesitate to call 911 or not call at all, because they feared being charged with the person's death.[26] Illinois's Good Samaritan law specifically includes language that says it will not protect individuals from drug-induced homicide charges.[27]

Drug-induced homicide laws are ostensibly meant to fight serious drug traffickers. For example, New Jersey's 1987 statute targets "upper echelon members of organized narcotics trafficking networks."[28] In 2003, Vermont used similar language, claiming its law targets "entrepreneurial drug dealers who traffic in large amounts of illegal drugs for profit," rather than people who sell drugs to support their own habit.[29]

In practice, however, the laws often lead to prosecutions against friends and family members. Twenty-five of thirty-two drug-induced homicide prosecutions identified by the *New Jersey Law Journal* in the early 2000s involved friends of the person who overdosed rather than "upper echelon" traffickers.[30] In 2013, Jarret McCasland of Baton Rouge, Louisiana, was sentenced to life in prison because his girlfriend died of an overdose after the couple shot heroin together.[31] In 2016, Lindsay Newkirk injected heroin into her arm and then into her father's arm in a motel on the outskirts of Columbus, Ohio. When she woke up hours later, her father was dead. Facing up to eleven years in prison for involuntary manslaughter and corrupting another with drugs, she pled guilty and was given a three-year sentence.[32] Later that year, Samantha Molkenthen, a young woman in Jefferson County, Wisconsin, was sentenced to fifteen years in prison for delivering the drugs that led to the overdose death of her friend Dale Bjorklund.[33]

A 2017 investigation by a Fox News affiliate in Wisconsin into one hundred drug-induced homicide prosecutions in the state found that in nearly 90 percent of the cases the people charged were friends or relatives of the person who overdosed.[34] According to Lindsay LaSalle, director of public health law and policy at the Drug Policy Alliance, an advocacy organization focused on ending the war on drugs, one reason the last person who touched the drugs is typically charged is because it's easier to get a conviction. "The further you get up the supply chain and the further removed you get from the actual hand-to-hand sale or exchange, the more difficult they become [to prosecute]," she said.

At Tommy Kosto's sentencing hearing in July 2017, Clifford Murphy, the assistant prosecutor, pointed out that Tommy had been in the court before and had been given multiple chances to turn his life around. This time, he asked the judge to "impose a prison sentence that will deter other people from similar type conduct"—a sentence "consistent with the expectation that the community should be aware that people that are going to participate in these endeavors, especially when someone dies, are going to be held accountable."

"We're asking that this court send a strong message through a serious prison term for Mr. Kosto," Murphy told the judge.

Judge David Branstool addressed the court before the sentencing and pointed out that he knew both Chad and Tommy—that Chad had graduated from his drug court, weeks before he died, and that Tommy was also someone with substance use disorder who had been in his courtroom before.

Branstool sentenced Tommy to a mandatory four-year prison term, plus one additional year, a fairly lenient sentence. In May 2018, however, the Fifth District Court of Appeals found there was not enough evidence to convict Tommy of the charges of involuntary manslaughter and corrupting another with drugs.[35] Chad Baker had died from a combination of heroin and cocaine, but Tommy had been charged with supplying only the heroin. The other two convictions still stood, and Tommy would serve another year while the prosecutor appealed the appellate court decision to the state supreme court.[36] At his resentencing, a visibly tired Tommy told the court, "I just want this nightmare to be over."

From 2016 to 2019, at least 131 people died from an accidental drug overdose in Licking County, Ohio. If drug-induced homicide prosecutions are intended to send a message to dealers, there is no discernible evidence that they have been deterred. In a speech at the White House on August 4, 1986, as lawmakers in Washington wrestled with how best to address the drug crisis in the wake of Len Bias's fatal overdose, President Ronald Reagan acknowledged that it would take more than criminal prosecutions to win the war on drugs. "We've waged a good fight," Reagan said. "Drug use continues, and its consequences escalate. All the confiscation and law enforcement in the world will not cure this plague."[37]

That is as true today as it was three decades ago. And yet when Reagan signed the Anti-Drug Abuse Act into law that October, political theater won out over more rational thinking. Out of the law's total $1.7 billion budget, $1.1 billion was allocated for law enforcement: more boats, planes, and weapons with which to fight drug traffickers on land, sea, and air; more federal agents, boots on the ground in the ever-expanding drug war; and, most telling, more prosecutors and more jail cells.[38]

According to Leo Beletsky, handing down harsh prison sentences will do little to address the current addiction crisis. Doing so is simply an emotional response, he said, by people who are looking at a crisis and seeking a quick solution. If the goal is to reduce overdoses, Beletsky told me, then the state has to approach the problem differently. "We've had these laws, and we have more people on drug-related charges behind bars, per capita, than any other nation on earth currently, and yet heroin is more widely available and cheaper than it's ever been," he said. It would be much more effective to focus instead on harm reduction—measures that seek to change user behavior and save lives.

If people are overdosing around loved ones, that's a sign that a community could use better access to naloxone so that people can be quickly revived and have access to treatment, a policy U.S. surgeon general Jerome Adams and others have called for.[39] But programs like these require funding, as well as a dramatic transformation in the country's approach to addressing addiction—and that hasn't happened. Every dollar that goes to a drug-induced homicide prosecution is a dollar not going to support harm reduction, treatment, or prevention of overdoses. These laws underscore the reality that the war on drugs has been a resounding and dangerous policy failure, and that primary policy failure telegraphs other failures that cripple communities and lead to more deaths.[40] To underscore this reality, in 2019, *The Philadelphia Enquirer*'s ever-on-point opinion writer Abraham Gutman coined the slogan "Every Overdose Is a Policy Failure" and made it his Twitter name for a time.[41]

Louise Vincent, executive director of North Carolina's Urban Survivors Union, a group of people who use drugs and who advocate for policy change, says that these laws are about "manipulating people's grief." Her daughter overdosed while in a treatment center. Afterward, she says, she was angry and wanted someone to pay for what had happened. At the same time, she knows what it is like to be in withdrawal, to have dope sent to you in treatment. "And so I'm battling with this emotion," Vincent says. "And it becomes very clear to me that it's grief. Those stages of grief, nobody made that shit up. The anger, blame, all of that stuff. And so we've got a society that's manipulating these feelings, knowing that parents and people that love us typically have a lot of guilt, because we don't have good hard-and-fast answers. Anger feels good and powerful. Anger feels like you're doing something. Sadness and grief feels like you're powerless. And feeling powerless is pretty horrific, especially for somebody who's lost a child."

She wanted to change the narrative, though, to step back and acknowledge that a prosecution wouldn't solve the problem. So Vincent, along with Jess Tilley, founder of the New England Users Union, launched a project in 2018 called Reframe the Blame that allows people who use drugs to sign a "Do Not Prosecute" document, asking that if they overdose no one be held criminally responsible for their death.[42] This is a way, though not legally binding, for people to announce their own desires, to speak, and hopefully to be heard. In an essay she wrote, Vincent noted, "The war on drugs is a war on people and their human rights." Now, it seems, she is fighting back.

When Billy thinks about Chad's death and Tommy's imprisonment, he thinks only of loss. Like Chad, like Tommy, Billy has been through it all.

He started using "one thing or another," he says, when he was twelve. By the time he was twenty-four, he was using a needle. He met Chad and Tommy in a community-based correctional facility, a transition space from prison. They were all trying to recover together.

Billy remembers Tommy as an introvert—almost the opposite of gregarious Chad. "He was just a nice, quiet guy. He was content to get his drugs and sit at home." He certainly wasn't the dealer he was made out to be in the courtroom, Billy says. He was just a user engaging in user behavior. In Licking County, he said, that can mean pooling money and driving to Columbus to buy cheaper heroin and picking up a little extra for four or five other people. Today you help them out; tomorrow they help you out. He recalls a time when he and Chad were working together assembling grills and bicycles for Walmart in western Pennsylvania. They were both sober at first, but months into the work they began using again. "If we were sick and we couldn't get nothing there," Billy says, "we would drive all the way back to Columbus, a five-and-a-half-hour drive, grab our stuff, and then go all the way back."

Billy says that one of the main reasons users feel compelled to buy and share is that they know what it means to go through withdrawal. "If you're compassionate, if you're a human," he says, "you wouldn't want to see anybody go through that, you know?"[43]

According to the prosecutor, Tommy purchased $450 of heroin.

"Is that Trump's death-penalty dealer?" Billy asks. Tommy wasn't living the high life, Billy says.

Billy remembers that one year at the county fair, Chad was playing in a cornhole tournament with a friend. A random guy walked up to him and said, "Man, that's a really nice shirt." Chad replied, "You know what, you can have it."

"He just gave him the shirt off his back," Billy says. "He was like, 'Yeah, you can have it.' But not in a sarcastic way." That trip to the fair stands out in Billy's memory because he was not using then. "When you get clean and you actually do social stuff like that, it's like, 'Wow, maybe we can make it.' When you're getting high you're thinking, 'There's no other life but this. Life isn't going to be fun.' You can't have any good times without using." But then he pauses and adds, "You don't really have any good times while you're using."

He continues, "None of us are bad people. At times we just decide this is our life and we're going to accept it. Eventually you want change, you know what I mean? You get tired of disappointing everybody in your life, you get tired of disappointing yourself, you want more for yourself, you know what I mean? I'm sure he had more of a life planned out than living in his parents' house at almost forty or thirty-five."

As Billy slips from first person plural to second to third, he nervously glances out the window. It's not clear, at times, if he's talking about Tommy or Chad or himself. He sees it from so many sides because that's how he has lived it and, he says, he thinks about it all the time.

Several years ago, Billy and his girlfriend Michelle bought some heroin together and shot up in her car, in the parking lot of a Columbus-area Nordstrom.

"I hope we can feel this," she told him.

"Yeah, me too," Billy said. "There's only fifteen dollars' worth apiece."

She shot up and said, "It's really good."

"Don't overdose before I get mine," Billy responded, joking.

"I'm gonna step out and walk around the car."

Billy hit his and then joined her to take in the beautiful July day.

"I gave her a big hug," he remembers, "and said, 'Let's go to Newark.'"

Suddenly she collapsed on the ground.

"I remember saying, 'Michelle, I'm gonna have to call the squad if you don't start breathing,'" Billy says. Then he, too, lost consciousness. "Then I came to, and I'm spread out, and there's all kinds of paramedics around me."

At the hospital he learned that Michelle was in a coma. He wanted to see her, but he wasn't allowed in her room. Seventy-two hours later, she passed away, and Billy was alone in the hospital at eleven at night with his car impounded, no phone—he didn't even have his shoes anymore. A hospital social worker paid for a cab ride back to his mother's house in Newark. She was shocked to see him.

"What the hell's going on?" his mother, Trish Perry, asked when he knocked on her door.

Trish got Billy back into treatment down south in Pike County, but this time it was even more difficult—now he was dealing with the fact of Michelle's death. Three weeks in, he bought some black tar (a crudely processed form of heroin that is tar-like) off someone inside, locked himself in the bathroom, and shot up. He tied a belt tight around his left arm, found a vein, and pushed the needle in, pulling back dark blood. It felt, he remembered, like the first shot he'd ever taken.

A guy working in the kitchen noticed that he had been in the bathroom for some time. He put his ear to the door and heard Billy gasping. He kicked the door in and found Billy face-first on the floor. He started CPR, stuck him in a cold shower, and called 911. He was rushed to the hospital. According to the ER report, after he became alert again, Billy told the doctor that he wasn't attempting suicide, that it had been "three weeks since he had last used."[44] The last time he used, he said, was when his girlfriend Michelle had "died in his arms."

And then a sheriff's deputy came in and began asking him questions. He told Billy he was being charged with "abuse of harmful intoxicants," a first-degree misdemeanor under Ohio law. Billy responded to the officer, "I've been charged with felonies and sent to prison, and you're going to charge me with a misdemeanor?" He didn't say anything else. The treatment center packed up his belongings and left them in his room there in Pike County. Once again, discharged from a hospital, a long way from home.

"This has been a whole trip for my mom, too," Billy says. "She's evolved a lot through it. At first, she would just get angry about stuff; she would just shut me out, tough love. I'd see anger in her eyes, and she wouldn't want anything to do with me. Now, when I look at her, when I'm using and stuff, I can tell that she's just scared she's not going to see me again. She ain't angry. She ain't mad about the shit. She's more sad than scared. Does that make any sense?"

It does make sense. One of the first times that I met her, Trish told me that she had already put money away for Billy's funeral.

8

The Churn

It's late April 2018, and Your Voice Ohio, a nonprofit helping journalists to collaborate with and learn from their communities, hosts an event at Thirty One West, a trendy music venue in downtown Newark.[1] The event, billed as a community discussion about the addiction crisis, was really an opportunity for journalists from around central Ohio (myself included) to listen to their community and hopefully produce stories that push the narrative away from problems and toward solutions. In a report of the event, the conveners write that "productive and community-oriented coverage of the crisis can be difficult to find." This was meant to be a step forward. The ballroom at Thirty One West was packed. One hundred and twenty people showed. I had never seen so many people gathered in this community to talk about what was happening on the ground. A facilitator offered three questions for discussion. Your Voice Ohio compiled responses into a report. These are some of them:

1. *What does addiction look like in our community?*
   Broken families. Crime and violence. Unmet needs.

Non-stop overdoses—first responders barely catch their breath between calls.

I have no idea. That's why I'm here.

It has taken over.

My neighbor.

Child abuse, homelessness, unable to hold a job, hopeless.

Jail isn't a solution.

Under the surface for those not yet affected. Desperation, poverty, despair.

Loss.

2. *What do you see as causes of the addiction crisis here?*

Lack of moral values, no spirituality or faith in anyone.

Overprescribing pain meds. Trauma.

No singular cause, but the isolation of drug users together . . . creates self-reinforcing culture.

Self-medication to treat undiagnosed mental illness and to cope with trauma.

Trauma.

Greed.

Poor health care.

Loss of community.

Spiritual poverty.

3. *What steps might we take to combat the addiction crisis?*

Addiction is a larger issue, eating disorders, cutting, depression, anxiety.

Reduce stigma.

Treat the soul.

Make addiction less profitable.

Decrease stigma: drug use, mental health, poverty, addiction.

The "Just Say No" mentality does not work.

Listening, collaboration, cooperation, open-mindedness, education.

Harsher punishments for criminals dealing drugs. Put up border wall.

"Attendees agreed," Your Voice Ohio wrote, "that addiction affects every demographic in society, and nobody is exempt."[2]

The attendees at this meeting had reason to be alarmed—the numbers are grim. In 2016, there had been seventeen overdose deaths in Licking County. In 2017, there were thirty-five. The responses—the fear, the anger—all of this is in keeping with the reality. When I spoke with people about the event afterward, many people saw it as a catalyst—a way to get things moving.

As part of their campaign, the Newark Think Tank on Poverty was planning a town hall meeting at the high school in partnership with Newark City Schools, inviting people to "learn about the local resources we have, what more we need to help those who desire recovery, and what steps we need to take to end this epidemic."[3] Trish Perry was one of the slated speakers, along with Scott Fulton and Kay Spergel, the executive director of Mental Health and Recovery for Licking and Knox Counties. They were also beginning to collect signatures to get an initiative on the November ballot that would reduce the number of people in state prisons for low-level drug charges.[4] The measure—which appeared on the ballot as "Issue 1" that year—would make drug possession and use no more than misdemeanors, prohibit courts from ordering people on felony probation to be sent to prison for noncriminal probation violations, create a sentence credits program for inmates' participation in rehabilitative work or educational programs, and require the state to spend savings that result from these changes on treatment, rehabilitation programs, and crime victim programs. If passed, the measure would lead to changes to the Ohio Constitution.

On the corner of Buena Vista and East Main Street, down the street from the Licking County jail, Trish and her friend Jen Kanagy had just started the homeless outreach. Homelessness, they had noticed, seemed like a growing issue in Newark—especially downtown. Minutes from a meeting of a downtown business association reveal concerns over people who may be homeless seeming to congregate in front of a restaurant with free Wi-Fi.[5] Notes from a later meeting record a discussion about how social services bring people to Newark.[6] According to a guest speaker at the meeting, the minutes assert, "The fact that Licking County provides better services to help the homeless than most other counties, encourages more homeless people to the area." It did seem that more people were sleeping on park benches and on the streets, especially in the winter. One popular spot: under the eaves of the county government building, next to the Wendy's on the Courthouse Square.

There has been a concerted and tireless effort by social service agencies and faith communities to address homelessness, both chronic and temporary. In the spring of 2016, Deb Dingus, the executive director of Licking County United Way, hiked for fifty days around the county, sleeping outdoors, in part to raise awareness about homelessness. In this moment, and despite all these efforts, there seemed to be so much more work to do. Frustrated by the slow pace of change and the efforts of public officials, in February Trish and Jen set up in a parking lot directly across from the jail and were soon offered the corner lot a few blocks away.

"People were talking about doing stuff and then we just did it," Trish says.

They are serving between forty and seventy-five people every Saturday, like on this sunny June day in 2018. Trish guesses most of those they serve are people who use drugs, and she sees the offer of food as an opening to work with them. "We're able to give them resources. I give them my phone number, and if they call, I try to find them a place to go to."

But mostly, she says, it's about building relationships, about talking. "You know how it is, Jack. They'll talk. You have to let 'em know they're not forgotten."

I'm following her back and forth from her car to a table set up under a tent. Jen is cooking hot dogs. Other volunteers are folding and displaying donated clothing for folks to take. Trish wants to do more—like offer naloxone training, drug testing strips, and harm-reduction kits. "We've talked to a lot of people down here, and a needle exchange is very much needed. Harm reduction as a whole. A lot of people are homeless because they can't get into no shelters. If you're using, you can't get into any shelter. Where are you gonna go? By the river? Under the bridge?"

When Billy was homeless, he lived in an abandoned house. He drew up a fake lease so that if the police knocked he'd have a response. Billy's why she's here, Trish says. "I can help somebody, but I can't help him. There might be someone that can interject into his life." She says it took a few years for her to realize that she couldn't save him. "I said a lot of bad things to him ... but in the beginning, when you called people, no one knew anything about opiates." And neither did she, really. So what is she doing here on this corner on a day off from work? She calls this outreach. But what is this? Service, amends, penance, atonement?

Right now it's being as close as she can to Billy. He was not out of jail for long before he violated probation, shortly after I spoke with him about Chad and Tommy. This time it's not clear how long he will be there—he's trying to get into a treatment program, trying to end this cycle of going in and out of jail. I go to visit him one day at the Licking County Justice Center. When I tell the officer signing in guests who I'm visiting, a tall man behind me responds, "You're going to see Billy, too! That's awesome. Billy's my boy."

"Oh, well, if you want to go first, that's fine," I say. "I won't be too long."

"No, we can go together. I just want to tell him I'm putting some money on his account. He put money on my commissary when I was inside."

Marcus, I'll call him, told me he wanted to surprise Billy, so we try to get into the waiting room early to let him hide off camera before Billy can see who has come to visit him. The room contains about fifteen booths with monitors and old payphone-style telephone handsets. It takes a while for Billy to appear on the screen, and so we wait. It's busy today, which is no surprise—jails are busy in Ohio and throughout the United States. According to the Prison Policy Initiative (PPI), people go to jail 10.6 million times each year in the United States (some of this number, of course, reflects individuals going to jail more than once in a year).[7] Some will make bail quickly, while those who can't afford to pay will wait days, sometimes years, until their trials—as many as 76 percent of people in jails have not been convicted of a crime, according to the PPI. "It's enough," the PPI notes, "to fill a line of prison buses bumper to bumper from New York City to San Francisco." The initiative refers to this revolving process as an "enormous churn," people in and out of the criminal justice system—not just the accused or convicted but also the family members and friends who also get caught up in it. Those people are left figuring out how to support themselves and their families; who is going to watch the house, the dog, the children; or who is going to speak to the boss or the landlord.

In the visiting room, some of those complications are being worked out. Some people lean in close and speak quietly; others couldn't care less about being overheard and talk as if they're at their kitchen table chatting over coffee. I catch snippets of conversations, intimate moments of connection and confrontation.

"I'm gonna keep my teeth until they fall out my mouth."

"I blacked out—forgot to take my meds."

"Well, you're not wasting any money when you're in there."

"Stop going to jail, bro, and when you're out you need to listen."

"I'm just stressed out."

And then Billy appears on the screen—he's in jail-issued khaki scrubs. He's smiling and looks good. He says hello, and I ask him how he's doing. And then Marcus jumps into view. Billy's head goes down and he cracks up. He's so happy to see him—even though Marcus just got out a few days ago. He tells him he's going to put some money on his account, and Billy thanks him. Billy is on his pod in the rec room, so there are others milling about in the background. It's an odd feeling to be on the outside, free, while seeing others in jail. As people walk by, they can see that Marcus is outside and chatting with Billy, and folks start crowding the camera. I can't hear what they're saying because Marcus has the handset up to his ear, but there's a lot of laughter and joy. Marcus turns to me and says he needs to go. We shake hands and he leaves.

Billy's still smiling when I turn back to him. "He's a good dude," he says, and explains that Marcus didn't have any money, so he loaned him twenty bucks. Billy says he's bored and has been reading a lot. There aren't many options, but he did find a copy of *Eat, Pray, Love*. He says he knows it's cheesy, but he likes that the author is on a journey to better understand herself. He can appreciate that. That's what he's trying to do—walk that path.

To help, Billy goes to a group meeting that's held once a week in jail. This is the highlight of each week he's in jail. The group is run by Pastor Dave Pennington, a man who has earned a lot of respect from people in jail and out. Pastor Dave struggled with methamphetamine use for years and ended up in jail—he has been where they are. He has buried over fourteen people who have died of accidental drug overdoses.

In Licking County there's a lot of meth use. In popular culture there's a lot of talk about opioid overdose. But for him, Pastor Dave says, the problem is addiction.

"It's not really about drugs," he explains. "That's the thing that's most newsworthy because of the deaths. Addiction runs rampant in our society. The need to escape from the reality. The reality of some people that live in Newark is that they live below the poverty level. They are in or have been in abusive relationships. They come from a generation of people who were prosperous at one time and then when Newark fell into disrepair—I'm sure there are thousands of cities across the U.S. that would be the same—you know they're looking for some escape. It does give you an escape for the moment, but it doesn't take away the things that you're trying to escape from. They just get worse."

He talks about a young man who recently died from an overdose and says that he never wants to get used to burying people who die that way, never wants to be jaded or cynical. He still encounters people who will blame and judge the victim. "My compassionate heart says, How are we gonna take care of his family? How are we gonna take care of everyone that's left? And why couldn't we have done something while he was alive?"

Pastor Dave made his fortune with his company, American Kidney Stone Management, which pioneered the idea of mobile kidney stone lithotripsy machines. Today he lives in a gorgeous home at the top of a hill reached by a long driveway, horses in a pasture below. The man who, for the past ten years, has spent much of his time counseling people who are addicted to drugs lives in a pastoral paradise. He's not disconnected, though. The system is stacked against so many people, he says. They can't afford the two-hundred-dollar bond, so they sit in there and lose everything and when they get out and there are few high-paying jobs available, what are their options?

The same goes for the men in the group he runs in the jail. He tells them that most people in the room aren't going to have access to a gold-star treatment program, and besides, he says, treatment programs don't guarantee anything. This can be overwhelming to some—they think they are stuck in one path. He blames this thinking, in part, on the idea that "once an addict always an addict." He insists that God made everyone perfect and sometimes people stray from the path. That's okay. It's possible to get back on it.

"You need to be accountable to something that's omniscient," Pastor Dave says. "You can't get away from it. You can't hide. And then you need to change your community. If you become accountable and change your community, your odds of making it are huge. But you can't play; this is a life-or-death thing."

He doesn't knock counseling, the psychology and pharmacology, but

Pastor Dave says his approach is different. His message must be direct and simple because he might not see these men again and he wants to give them something they can hold on to. A mantra. A way to be in this world. "Don't pick up," he tells them. Many times it will happen. He'll be walking through Walmart and someone will come up to him and say, "I didn't pick up." Dramatic. Quick.

But he says that, long term, you have to adjust your priorities, find some other source of accountability. "I'm talking about a higher form of oversight that stays with you. And you don't have to turn into a Jesus freak or carry your Bible around, but just in your head if you're accountable to something that's loving and greater than you, you will change your behaviors. You just will."

He tries to empower people in his class, which he jokes is truly a "captive audience," but he tries to get people to open up to talk about their lives and goals, their families, and their paths to jail.

"I'll ask a question. I'll go, like, 'Who are you?'" Then he says to me, "Who are you? Answer me. Who are you?"

I gather that he's not being rhetorical and struggle a bit. "I'm a father," I reply.

"That's a good answer. Most people go, 'I'm Jack.' No, that's your name."

"I'm a writer."

"No, that's what you do. What are you? I like to say, you're a precious child of God. So when I go in there and ask my class, every man will say 'I'm a precious child of God.' They know to say that. You're not some piece of shit. You may have been marginalized and your parents won't let you come in their house 'cause you've stolen stuff and people have told you you're a piece of crap your whole life. You've got this big emblem on that says 'loser.' I want you to take that off. Throw that sucker away. We're starting with 'God made you in the image of his son.' That's the floor. 'Cause otherwise, if you believe you're a piece of shit, you're a piece of shit. I want to raise them out of where they've been and let them know that they are cared about and people love them."

Outside the county jail where Pastor Dave runs his group every week, maybe fifty yards from the building, there's a path for biking and walking that runs alongside the north fork of the Licking River, extending north to Everett Field Park and south to a neighborhood called Little Texas. Sometimes people will chalk notes of support on the sidewalk, messages of hope and encouragement scratched in pastel letters so that people looking out can see: "Hope to see ur face!" "Keep ur head up, babe!" "You have someone that will be here."

9

Any Positive Change

On a warm Friday morning in early June 2018, several public health professionals sit in a bland white-walled boardroom. The dozen people gathered here constitute the core members of Licking County's prescription drug overdose task force. The group is discussing new grant funding when one health worker says that what they really need is access to people who use drugs to better collect real-time information and, perhaps, educate them.

Someone suggests a syringe exchange.

"Remember how people responded to naloxone distribution?" someone murmurs.

And then a gentleman speaks up. He's in his late fifties, has a full head of rumpled gray hair, and wears flat-front Levi's, a cotton flannel shirt, and white New Balance walking shoes.

"I'm Dennis Cauchon from Harm Reduction Ohio. The time is now. The time for a needle exchange is here. It can get done."

Dennis explains that from a public health perspective, a syringe services program (SSP) is a no-brainer. SSPs help reduce needlestick injuries (accidental punctures) and the spread of infectious diseases (hep C and HIV).[1] They save taxpayers money. SSPs are also a place to build relationships with people who use drugs, to offer health care, to distribute naloxone, and, maybe, to open a door to treatment.[2]

Dennis, a former *USA Today* reporter and editor who took a buyout after twenty-seven years of reporting, has joined this meeting for the first time, and he's prepared. He notes that SSPs, once frowned upon in many parts of the country, are becoming commonplace. He points out that currently Ohio has fourteen that he knows of and will have, he hopes, twenty by the end of the year (as of March 2020, there were programs in twenty-one counties). Recognizing their cost-effectiveness (needles are cheaper than HIV or hep C treatment), the Republican-controlled Ohio legislature approved syringe exchange programs in 2015 as part of the state budget.[3] This is important in Licking County, where the number of hepatitis C cases has tripled in the last decade and where HIV cases involving IV drug use are on the rise.[4] From 2014 to 2018, there was a 25 percent increase in new HIV cases and a 38.8 percent increase in hep C; from 2015 to 2018, there was also a 20 percent increase in hep B cases.[5]

"You're in the sweet spot—not a leader or a follower. You guys would have to be creative, and it would take someone like me sitting down in my suit and tie." He chuckles.

There's visible support in the room; there's also visible concern. When the Licking County Health Department began distributing naloxone as part of a statewide program, the social media backlash was immediate. People accused the health department of enabling drug use.

Dennis agrees that it will be a challenge—to face down the stigma, the moralizing, the suggestions that people who use drugs should just stop. He's not daunted. It's not in his nature to be. Dennis is scrappy, persistent, and at times an admittedly annoying bulldog who sinks his teeth into a problem and won't quit until it's resolved.

At *USA Today*, Dennis earned a reputation as a bit of a muckraker. After stints at the *Sun Herald* (the paper of Biloxi, Mississippi) and the *Clarion-Ledger* (Jackson, Mississippi), he became a financial reporter for *USA Today* in Arlington, Virginia. Over time, he went on to cover national affairs, eventually trying his hand at editing.

In the aftermath of the September 11, 2001, terrorist attacks, Dennis's editor told him to find a story about first responders—to talk with police, firefighters, and EMTs and find out how they were coping. When he arrived in New York City after the four-hour train ride from D.C., every other reporter was looking for the same story. So he did the thing that still gets him into trouble: he found a problem and began poking at it. He was curious about the number of people who died and felt that it was a knowable number. He started calling landlords and found out who the tenants were and how many checked in to their offices on the morning of 9/11. He discovered that the count was around 2,800 (the total was eventually determined to be 2,606).[6] The story, which included his count, explored why the numbers weren't higher, noting that building design and evacuation drills, as well as fate, played a role. It was a story that fit with his beat, which he describes as "interesting stuff you haven't read elsewhere." Stories about prisons in Alabama, about hurricanes, about Ted Turner, about elections, about African American church burnings. For almost thirty years. Story after story.

After the buyout, Dennis became an independent local journalist in the tiny college town of Granville, Ohio, just west of Newark. Given his affinity for numbers and slicing through bureaucratic red tape—as well as his investigative chops—he became a bit of a lightning rod in the community. He blogged about making the community safer for walkers, about the need to scrap a proposed plan to drug-test high school students, and about the village fire department moving its headquarters.

"I was doing nothing different," Dennis says. "They were getting the full monty. Little town gets this investigative reporter."

One of the hallmarks of a good investigative reporter is that they can sometimes irritate people and court controversy. But Dennis never seems to let it get to him.

His office, in a narrow hallway above a local coffee shop, even looks like a journalist's. He works at a desk shoved in the corner of a room with half-opened file cabinet drawers, empty coffee cups, and a view of the highway through a window that hasn't been cleaned in years—there's an old wasp's nest stuck between the window glass and the storm window. Old Wi-Fi passwords are tacked to the walls above piles of books and files.

For several years, Dennis sat in this room writing stories for his own blogs and doing freelance work to pay the bills. But as the overdose numbers began to rise in Ohio, Dennis could not help himself.

"To me the greatest social injustice of our generation is the drug war. Half a million drug offenders in prison. The destruction to black neighborhoods. The damage to families is largely due to the drug war."

He says that, as he heard prosecutors announce that they knew they couldn't arrest their way out of the overdose crisis in one breath and then try to do just that in the next, he couldn't keep quiet. He had found a new problem to poke.

Dennis started a blog called *Harm Reduction Ohio*, which became a nonprofit with the same name advocating for policies that reduce the negative consequences connected to drug use. He also began blogging about the need to actually treat the spike in overdoses as a health crisis rather than a criminal one, and began sharing his stories through social media. He wrote op-eds. He spoke in legislative hearings. He began pestering state crime labs for access to drug seizure data. He discovered that the Ohio Department of Health had failed to submit a form to the U.S. Centers for Disease Control and Prevention that would give the state access to $7.6 million that could be used to support needle exchanges. (The state eventually did submit the form after he wrote a blog post about it.)[7] He began applying his reporting skills to his work as an activist, to promoting harm-reduction policies around the state.

For people who use drugs, harm reduction encourages making positive changes: using sterile equipment, encouraging safer use by testing drugs for fentanyl, creating calm spaces for people who are "overamping" from stimulant use.[8] It can also simply mean providing housing or a place to hang out during the day for people who are homeless. Harm reduction can also mean evidence-based but controversial things, like safe injection sites, places where people who use drugs can do so in the company of others and mitigate the chances of dying from an accidental overdose. Harm reduction also involves SSPs and community-based distribution of naloxone, an idea pioneered by Dan Bigg and the Chicago Recovery Alliance in the 1990s.[9] Bigg thought then that if it was a helpful medicine that was used in hospitals, giving it to people who know the most about drug use and making them the first responders was an even better approach, one that could save even more lives. Research shows he was right—community-based naloxone distribution is one of the most effective tools we have to address the overdose crisis.[10]

As a way to address substance use disorder, a harm-reduction approach counters the widely accepted wisdom of an abstinence-only approach, noting that addiction is complicated and sometimes it's best to start where people are.[11] Maia Szalavitz writes, "To help people overcome learning problems, they must be treated with compassion and respect. All types of students do better in schools where they feel welcomed and safe . . . People learn best in environments where they feel connected to others—not places dominated by a sense of threat and fear."[12] Harm reduction, she continues, "allows people to learn new skills and then move away from drugs, rather than attempting to force them to do the reverse."[13] Harm reduction isn't in opposition to treatment; it could be viewed as a low-level part of a continuum of care that includes outpatient and inpatient treatment. To that end, medication-assisted treatment for addiction is an important part of a good harm-reduction program.

It's important to keep in mind the broader context of harm reduction. Applied medical anthropologist Lesly-Marie Buer reminds us that harm reduction is political, that it "is a social justice movement that supports the dignity and rights of people who use drugs." She explains further: "Many harm reduction programs have roots in 1980s activism around HIV, and most of the organizations I have worked with exist thanks to the unrelenting labor of queer activists."[14] (And, I would add, poor people and people of color.) Harm reduction counters neoliberal attitudes toward drug use, she says, as "exemplified by the War on Drugs focus on punishment. Instead of trying to enforce abstinence—viewing individuals as the site of punitive state intervention—these initiatives try to reduce the harms, both medical and social, associated with drug use." In other words, central to this public health approach is that addiction is a public health issue, not a criminal one.

Dennis decided to see if the county where he lived could support a syringe exchange program—and perhaps provide space for one. Harm Reduction Ohio was started as an advocacy group, but now they're becoming a service organization as well because in some places they are advocating for something that no other organization is prepared to take on. So in Licking County, the first step was to find a space and resources to start one, and the second was to get the approval of the county board of health (which oversees the department of health). For that, he would need community support.[15]

In late August, Dennis walks up to a microphone at an Overdose Awareness Day rally in downtown Newark that Trish organizes.[16] There's a good-sized crowd for a hot, humid afternoon. The summer has passed, and there's still no syringe exchange in Licking County. People are still overdosing.

He begins awkwardly. His hands are shoved into his pockets. And his voice is not coming through the speakers. Someone walks forward to adjust the microphone, moving it closer to his mouth. He's wearing a long-sleeve light pink Oxford shirt and his walking shoes. He looks uncomfortable, nervous.

"We hear a lot from people about the crisis, but not enough from the addicts themselves," Dennis says. He explains that if anything is going to change, we need to start listening to people who use drugs. He talks about the disability rights movement and the slogan "nothing about us without us."

There's some feedback from the mic.

Dennis picks up speed, saying that users are also people. They are people with families. People with homes and lives and jobs. They are people who also happen to be users. Drug use does not and should not define them. And, he says, we need to support them. We need to promote harm reduction. We need a syringe exchange.

"Go to a needle exchange and meet real users; they are humans, too," Dennis says.

This is a new role for him—the activist, the public face of a growing movement that is bringing people together from around the community and the state, a movement that doesn't judge, that is accepting.

Billy McCall has been in treatment since June at a place called The Landing, just east of Newark in Muskingum County. In journals he kept from that time, it's clear that Billy was in need of nonjudgmental love and acceptance, if not from others, then from himself. He marked off each day, to measure either his sobriety or his stay in treatment. And he describes his choices in black-and-white terms: sobriety or using, life or death. He's severe at times, criticizing himself, remembering Michelle especially, and feeling guilty that he lived and she did not.

"No amount of guilt," Billy writes, "can solve the past." He fills the pages of three wide-ruled composition books, the ones with the stiff black-and-white cardboard covers. On one of them he tapes a photo of his granddaughter. In another, at the back of the book, he writes "I Love U" in permanent marker.

He sketches a timeline of life events—when his house caught fire as a kid, when his mom went to prison, when he first smoked pot, when he was first arrested (for skateboarding), when he dropped out of school, when he first tried heroin. "I would take back the first time I used heroin," he writes. "I see this as a turning point in my drug use."

He also writes a letter to "dope," saying that it loved him when he was "unlovable" and that it brought him joy when he was low. He writes about his love of the ocean, of being by the sea with a girlfriend in San Luis Obispo; with his grandfather in Hyannis Port, where he went to deliver a boat; Destin Beach, where he worked on a painting job for ten days. He thinks of the ocean, imagines the ocean, imagines swimming, and then remembers where he is and what he's doing.

On the day that Billy gets out of treatment, he attends a public information session and forum about SSPs that Dennis organized at the county library. Billy's hair is cut short (he donated the ponytail to Locks of Love). He looks like a new man. He tells me he's ready to help push for a syringe exchange. It's needed, he says. In a letter Dennis wrote to *The Newark Advocate* alerting the community of the event, he pointed out that on the ground things seem to be shifting, that a 2017 poll indicated that 50 percent of Ohioans support SSPs and 38 percent oppose them.[17] This, he says, is because more and more people are connected to this overdose crisis. "When we know people who've died, we don't see one-dimensional stereotypes," he explains. "We see fathers and mothers, sons and daughters, friends and co-workers—people who are more than a struggle with drugs." While SSPs may be cost-effective, he continues, "We [as an organization] care about drug users as people and want to keep them healthy and alive."

At the event, Dennis is wearing a tie, the first time I have ever seen him wear one. He is hoping the community will support a syringe exchange program—and perhaps provide space for one. He has traveled around the state visiting exchanges. He also knows the rules: that the county board of health must approve the exchange, but that there must be a committed location for the exchange before they can approve it. To do that, he knows he must also have popular support.

Experts, including a professor from The Ohio State University, are given space to present the evidence, but there is also space for people with lived experience. They are front and center. They are also experts. Dylan Stanley has been sober for ninety days. Months ago, she was an active heroin user, and she remembers one morning with intense clarity. She was waiting to buy dope—tired and getting sick as she sat in her car in a parking lot. She saw someone jogging by in the early-morning light. They were healthy, living a "normal life," she says. And she hated them for it. "When your money is 'dope tokens,'" she told me later, "life is exhausting." Tonight, though, Dylan speaks up with confidence and empathy for her present and past selves. Here, in a windowless meeting room at the Licking County Library, decked out in a purple "Overdose Awareness Month" T-shirt, she chokes up. It frustrates her that "the things you do become your identity," but she says she was and is more than her addiction. She talks about keeping the same needles for months, but then she got access to a needle exchange and it changed her life. "These are people that matter. Just because someone is addicted to drugs does not mean that they don't matter." Dylan says she's here tonight because the harm-reduction community takes her seriously and has empowered her to speak up. It's a new feeling.

Dylan says that she got where she is today because she had access to an SSP in Columbus, Ohio, called Safe Point. She looks over to Rick Barclay, a program manager from Safe Point, a dark-haired man with a big grin and a can of Jolt Cola. Rick smiles at her in agreement.

Rick is also in recovery and dismisses outright any suggestion that harm reduction is enabling. "We have to meet people where they are," he says. Some people in the room nod in agreement.

The library kicks everyone out after multiple calls over the intercom asking people to leave. Folks reluctantly exit and stand around outside in the cool of the evening, a hint of the setting sun over West Main Street. Billy is there, and Trish is grinning as she circulates through the crowd. I meet folks from OhioCAN, and Gordon Casey and Oona Krieg, two people from Vancouver, Canada, working on an app to help prevent overdoses. An hour after the event is over people are still talking. Dennis is chatting, engaged. He has found his legs.

The Foot of the Mountain

I pick Billy up from Trish's apartment at 6:30 a.m. Billy has to be at the Pike County Courthouse, in Waverly, by 8:30. It's less than two hours south of Newark, so we should make it. He's going there to deal with the "abuse of harmful intoxicants" charge from when he overdosed while in treatment in August 2014, just weeks after his girlfriend died. He's been trying to resolve this for over a year, and he's already been down there twice, only to have his appearance rescheduled each time. He's growing weary of this legal dance.

But today he's hopeful. It's November 5, 2018, the day before the midterm elections. The day before Ohio is set to vote on Issue 1, which groups like the Newark Think Tank on Poverty and the Ohio Organizing Collaborative helped get on the ballot, and which some believe will help address the ways the justice system handles drug offenses.

The sun is shining as we travel south through the stately town of Lancaster, where Civil War general William Tecumseh Sherman was born. Lancaster is also home of glassware manufacturer Anchor Hocking, a company that once employed some five thousand people but now employs only about nine hundred.[1] In the past couple of decades, the company has been bought and sold by private equity firms three times, a story told by Brian Alexander in his fiercely prescient book *Glass House*.[2] Some Rust Belt cities were victims not just of new technology or companies moving overseas but also of people in boardrooms putting profit ahead of people and communities. In a 2017 article for *The Atlantic*, Alexander writes that the factory's workers and the people of Lancaster don't necessarily know this story: "They only know that the old social contract has disintegrated and that nothing has come to take its place."[3] The hospital is now the biggest employer in Lancaster. The town is also home to a state prison housing over 1,500 people (as of this writing). There are many prisons scattered about the postindustrial landscape of southeastern Ohio, some more or less along our route today—in Ross County there are two, and in Hocking County there is one. In Portsmouth's Scioto County there is another.

The leaves are bright reds and yellows, outlining fields of corn cut to stalk that we pass as we drive south. Despite his legal and health struggles, Billy has started a lucrative house-painting business, with contracts around central Ohio and two employees. Billy is on the phone talking to the guys who work with him. One person hasn't shown up to the work site yet, and Billy's playing triage. A disrupted day like today is another obstacle, another inconvenience.

On Highway 23, we enter Pike County and pass billboards advertising treatment centers and addiction recovery support. A large one offers a reward for help finding the people who killed eight members of the Rhoden family execution-style in rural Pike County in April 2016.[4] As we enter Waverly, we turn left into a large strip-mall parking lot anchored by a Kroger's and a Burger King. In the far right corner, out of place it would seem, is the Pike County Courthouse. We're early, so we get coffee and biscuits at the Burger King. After we eat, we go outside and Billy leans on my truck and smokes a cigarette, and then we go wait in a long line outside the courthouse entrance.

At 8:30, folks file through metal detectors and into the courthouse lobby, where there are rows of folding chairs for those waiting to hear their names called. At first there are no seats. The demographics of the room lean white and working class, with people who seem to be on their way to work—lots of Carhartt clothing, muddy boots, and sneakers with paint stains, just like Billy's. Lots of people who look like they have been living hard.

As if on cue, Billy scans the room and remarks, "Lots of people in here are dealing with the same things."

For an hour we sit. Waiting. Staring at our phones. Staring ahead. Staring out the windows. A man in a red polo walks out into the lobby. Takes down the clock on the wall and sets it an hour back—it is the Monday after daylight saving time ended. He reaches up, puts the clock back in place, and retreats. The only thing that signals we are in a courthouse is the stack of docket books and a woman behind the counter who answers the phone by saying "Pike County Courthouse."

"This place looks like an old Walmart," I say to Billy.

A woman chatting with a man wearing a cowboy hat pipes in: "Used to be a Kmart!"

"I stand corrected," I say, and we all laugh.

"But they still have the blue-light special," Billy jokes.

As of 2017 (the latest year for which official numbers are available), there were roughly 2.3 million people incarcerated in the United States—almost half a million of them for drug offenses, as noted above.[5] According to the Drug Policy Alliance, about 198,000 are being held in state prisons for drug charges; in jails there are 118,000 not convicted and 35,000 convicted; and in federal prisons there are 81,000 convicted and 16,000 with marshals. These numbers do not include those who committed crimes to support drug use or other drug-related crimes.

Police, prosecutors, and judges spend a lot of time and resources punishing people for drug possession—over a million people arrested every year. These kinds of arrests disrupt low-income communities and communities of color especially, making lives more complicated, causing people to miss work, and causing families to lose mothers, fathers, and siblings. Felony convictions create even more complications. Surprisingly, or maybe not, Issue 1 has little support from law enforcement. Licking County sheriff Randy Thorp told *The Newark Advocate* that the measure was "decriminalization, plain and simple."[6] He argued, "Law enforcement requires the weight of proportional criminal consequences not just to curb abuse and trafficking but also to rebuild and save lives." In other words, sometimes it takes a stick to help someone get sober.

Sitting in the lobby of the Pike County Courthouse, a.k.a. the stick, I ask Billy what he thinks of Issue 1.

"Well, it's time to stop criminalizing the disease of addiction," he answers. "The way we're doing things now is cultivating addiction, not addressing it." He looks anxiously at his phone. "Not too many nice days left before snow comes." He looks around the room and says, "All this hurts the community."

Billy's life since I first met him underscores this—he rolls a rock uphill, only to have it roll back down again. After treatment, as part of his probation, Billy had to go to "day reporting," a program for adults on probation that requires attending a Monday–Friday, nine-to-five program rather than having weekly check-ins with probation officers. Like drug courts, day reporting is a holistic approach, an alternative to traditional probation that offers a packed schedule of GED, parenting, mental health, trauma awareness, art, writing, and recovery classes. Licking County's day reporting program began in November 2017. The research findings on these programs are mixed. A study of day reporting in Allegheny County, Pennsylvania, found that the program saved the county money and that participants had lower recidivism rates than those in traditional programs.[7] The study also found that the program was most effective for high- to medium-risk participants.

A study in New Jersey, however, found that participants in a day reporting program there were more likely to be arrested and convicted than the control group.[8]

Billy saw the program as just another step toward moving on with his life—it was also an opportunity to talk to people about harm reduction, about Issue 1, and about the need for an SSP. When he graduated from the program—always a festive event to which those graduating invite friends and family—that's just what he talked about: the work he has been doing with Harm Reduction Ohio and how that gives him meaning. He also talked about learning to appreciate the daily rituals of life. How his son let him get up with his granddaughter recently, how he fed her and enjoyed being with her. He has, he said, been practicing patience.

And yet day reporting is still a criminal justice response to what amounts to a health crisis, just like this day is for Billy in the Pike County Courthouse.[9] Rather than seeking counseling or group therapy to help him deal with the trauma he experienced, rather than doing a job that gives him hope and helps him build a future, he is sitting in this dinky waiting room. His experience is the norm rather than the exception; it is the consequence of policy on the daily rituals of mostly poor and working-class people. Billy is waiting here to find out what will become of charges that could result in jail time, maybe more probation, and certainly a fine.

In Greek mythology, as a result of his many attempts to trick the gods, King Sisyphus was condemned to carry a boulder up a hill, only to have that boulder roll back down again. Endlessly. Forever. Carrying the boulder up the hill.

At 11:00 a.m., Billy becomes justifiably frustrated. He still hasn't been called to appear. He walks up to the desk to ask if the public defender is around. The man with the red polo shirt says he will check. Billy sits back down and tells me about a guy he met while in treatment here in Waverly.

He looks him up on Facebook and discovers that he has since overdosed and died.

Billy says this wait is nothing. One time he came here for a drug test that came out positive and was arrested on the spot. They transported him to a holding cell where he waited for about nine hours before being loaded onto a van. The van drove all over the state—to Circleville just up the road in Pickaway County, then farther west to Montgomery County, ending up in Butler County—all because there wasn't enough room in the Pike County jail. The whole while, he had no idea where they were taking him. He was hungry, tired, and wanted to get well. When he got off the van in Butler, he was finally given something to eat. It was six in the morning.

The waiting room thins out. Some people give up. "I gotta get to work," the man in the cowboy hat says as he limps out.

It's 11:30 a.m.

"How do you plan a life around this stuff?" Billy asks out loud. He goes outside to smoke a cigarette and make a contingency plan with his co-workers. An hour later, Billy is rescheduled. He never entered a courtroom. He never saw a judge.

On our drive back from Pike County, Billy and I talk about the future and he says that at this point in life, he just wants to run his painting business and be proud of it. He says there was a time when he strived for other things, but now he wants to appreciate where he is and what he's doing.

The next day, Issue 1 is defeated by a wide margin. Advocates are surprised; folks involved in the justice system are relieved. They can, for the time being, keep their stick.

Weeks later, Billy attends a meeting of the Licking County Board of Health as a representative of Harm Reduction Ohio. According to state law, each county's board of health must approve the location of any SSP.[10] Billy speaks during public comment in order to share with the board that Harm Reduction Ohio is currently looking for a suitable place to host a program. They were trying to partner with one organization, but the landlord of the building the organization occupied would not permit it. Once they have a location, he tells them, he hopes that the board will approve of it and they can create a program. When he speaks he is casual—it's a small group, and there are no other members of the public in the room. Matter-of-factly, he asks if anyone on the board has any suggestions or contacts and then invites them all to a harm-reduction conference taking place in Columbus next month.

"I know the needle exchange isn't only about getting people into recovery and everything; we're looking to cut hepatitis C and HIV and promote safe use," he explains. "But it's my passion to put together a resource sheet with treatment centers that I have relationships with." He says he has a few places that are already committed to helping—he knows it can be hard for people if they don't have cash or private health insurance. "Anyway, if you guys could help get something going by next month, in any way, because it's real urgent." He asks the board members if they have any questions. They don't have any, but they smile and nod and thank him.

As we leave he says to me, "Having people like me on the front lines that have been there getting high, and when people see that I'm doing good, they're like, for real, 'It's possible if he can do it!' I'm not bragging or anything, and by no means proud of it, but I'm about as far down the scale as you can go without being dead. You know what I'm saying? If I can come back from it, anybody can."

Billy is moving against the currents of his community—standing in public and going on record as a person who is in recovery from drug use, as a person who can talk about the need for sterile needles.

In his essay "The Myth of Sisyphus," French philosopher Albert Camus writes that we must look to King Sisyphus as a model for confronting the absurdities of our lives. Sisyphus incessantly pushes that rock up the hill and watches it fall down again. This is decidedly absurd. But Camus is more interested in how Sisyphus approaches the journey back down the hill, back to the rock. A translation of the essay reads, "I see that man going back down with a heavy yet measured step toward the torment of which he will never know the end."[11] It is in that moment that he is free and, as Camus writes, "He is stronger than his rock." He accepts the absurdity of his life, that struggle will always be a part of it, but he also masters it. "The struggle itself toward the heights is enough to fill a man's heart. One must imagine Sisyphus happy."[12] He does not despair. If you are melancholic, Camus writes, the rock wins. If you are joyful, you master the rock.

A few months later, Billy was able to settle the matter in Pike County, paying a fine of $250.

The Person Next to You

I t's late fall 2018 when I meet Gordon Casey in downtown Columbus. He is a long way from home, if only he could pinpoint where that is exactly. He was born in Zambia, raised in Qatar, went to primary school in Ireland and then high school in Canada, studied law in South Africa, worked for a service provider for a hedge fund in Curaçao, and then moved to Vancouver, Canada, where he runs a tech start-up called Brave Technology Coop. I first met Gordon at the needle exchange open forum at the Licking County Library. I was astonished he was there—with his all-black attire and long hair—but given his peripatetic lifestyle, I'm not now. He's back in central Ohio, working to get his company off the ground.

Brave makes technology that can help prevent overdoses and promote safer consumption.[1] They developed an app called Be Safe that makes it possible for people not to use alone. A person about to use would alert a network they've created. If they don't check back in after a certain amount of time, the network is alerted and can call for help. A long-term goal is to create a wearable that will be able to check respiration and set off an alarm remotely. They've also created a system that uses buttons to activate a care network—

similar to what is used in elder care, but super simple to install if a wireless network is available. Buttons are pushed before use and then pushed again to signal all is well. In a shelter, if the button isn't pushed again, a neighbor or building staff member could check. In the first pilot of the button, three people overdosed and were all revived. There were also two cases in which a person felt threatened and pushed the button as a call for help—it was an unintended but positive outcome, recognition that there are many vulnerable populations that could benefit from the awareness of a community in their midst. Because that's really what this is—using technology to affirm and enhance a community.

In Vancouver, Gordon was watching the overdose death toll climb, even though the city had a progressive health-care system and a vocal harm-reduction community. He had been thinking about the ideas behind Brave for a few years.

"I had this concept in my mind from this TED Talk that I heard in, like, 2013," he says, "about how a crowd could respond to emergencies and mitigate the harm that's done between something happening and professional help getting there."[2] Like, for example, giving chest compressions to a heart attack victim. "I was like, This has to exist, right? We have Uber, and we have pizza delivery apps, and surely for something urgent like this there's something out there. And it turned out there wasn't."

There were crowdsourcing apps that had been created at hack-a-thons, but mostly they languished in purgatory and didn't have a lot of buy-in from people who use drugs. Gordon suspected there were reasons why such technology hadn't taken off; he just needed to find out what those reasons were. So he made a sharp turn, from living in the world of hedge funds to devoting his whole self to this start-up. He puzzled over the question of how to give access to this technology to the people who could benefit from it the most.

Outsourcing health care to a community would require real-world organizing, not just a trip to the app store. It so happens that Gordon's office is in a co-working space called 312 Main, in the old police station in Vancouver's Downtown Eastside, a neighborhood known for its single-room occupancy (SRO) units and its social service agencies. The neighborhood was the cradle for the movement to organize people who use drugs in North America. The building at 312 Main is just blocks away from several overdose prevention sites and from the headquarters of the Vancouver Area Network of Drug Users (VANDU), the first drug users' union in North America. From the people in this neighborhood, Gordon learned that to prevent overdose deaths, it's important for somebody, somewhere, to know that a person is using. Believing that people who use drugs can and do care for each other, that they are capable of helping each other out, is a radical approach that is contrary to the dominant narrative.

"We are a drug-user-first organization and we're an action-based organization and if that requires talking to some other folks in a different way than we're used to, then we'll do that," Gordon says of Brave. "And probably that means hiring people here to do that talking for us. Right?"

"What does that mean?" I ask.

"I mean, speak to them first, find out what their needs are first. Build it from there."

Brave is now part of Ohio's Opioid Technology Challenge, and its members are also preparing for a pilot project working with people just out of prison, a particularly vulnerable population.[3] People who use drugs and who have been in prison may start using again when they are released, and they may use at the same level they did before incarceration—with often deadly outcomes. A 2018 study published in the *American Journal of Public Health* revealed that, compared with the general population, formerly incarcerated people in North Carolina are forty times more likely to die of an overdose from an opioid (including heroin) in the first two weeks after release from prison.[4]

Gordon says he remembers worrying a lot as a child about why people didn't help each other out more. "It sounds cheesy, but I remember thinking that if everybody just looked out for the person immediately next to them, then that was the answer to everything. Because then everybody would be fine, by definition. And thinking through it, as I got a bit older, like, 'Oh, but then there'd be people who are alone who didn't have anybody next to them. But then you'd find them too. Because you'd see the one person who didn't have somebody. So I think in a lot of ways Brave is me feeling that I found a way to do that, that's actually real . . . and that's what I felt when I first read an article about Insite [North America's first safe injection site] in Vancouver. I thought, 'Wow! This thing is radically kind.' And that's what it is. Just being really, really kind to people."

"Isn't that what harm reduction is?" I say.

"Yes. I just don't understand why more people aren't trying to come up with things to keep people alive. Just fucking keep them alive. It's weird. But it's also disheartening."

It is disheartening, but the reasons are in my face all the time. Scratched on a wall in Sharpie in a hallway in downtown Newark: "Fuck Tweeker Ville of Shit County, Ohio." A bumper sticker on the back of a truck in the YMCA parking lot: "Shoot your local heroin dealer." (Dealer and user are, as I've noted above, very often the same person.)[5]

There's a young man who comes to the corner often. When we first met, he was tired, had red splotches on his face, and was wearing a gray sweatshirt that hung on his frame like a choir robe. He had lost everything at that point and was sleeping in his car. He had started with pills and then moved on to heroin or meth; he would go back and forth. He was using meth then—mostly because he didn't have anywhere to sleep safely. I asked him if he saw a way out. "Yeah, I could die," he told me. He has tried treatment, but nothing seemed to work. He was nervous about fentanyl in the drug supply and was getting some testing strips from Trish Perry, who had a small supply. But he was more worried about what people would think of him. He had run into a family member at the grocery store, and the way they looked at him hurt. "The stigma is real," he said. "You get treated like a piece of shit."

The anger and hate in that graffiti and that bumper sticker, and the pain in the eyes of the young man—they are all connected. The revulsion, the disdain with which our culture treats these people must be addressed and interrogated because it permeates so much of how we have come to understand the overdose crisis, the narrative we want to believe, the stories we share. It's much easier to blame Purdue Pharma for the downfall of working-class white men than to swallow the deeper truth that the overdose crisis is affecting more than just those people.[6] It's easier to blame something rather than recognizing the deeper issues, like economic and social inequality, like racism, that help perpetuate stigma, addiction, and the war on drugs. Besides, as Bruce Alexander notes, we live in a culture that lauds certain addictions, like the addiction to power, and derides others, like the addiction to meth.

Two weeks after I first talked with that young man at the corner, I saw him there again. He looked much better—not tired, well fed—because someone had taken him in and given him a place to sleep. Now he was able to think more clearly, he was showing up to work on time, and he was able to imagine a future, albeit tenuously. He was still using but not as much. This is a good example of harm reduction—meeting this man where he was led to a kind of transformation, if only for the time being.

Katherine McLean, the sociologist from Pennsylvania State University, acknowledges that a lack of harm-reduction services exacerbates already-present risks for poor people especially.[7] She writes, "While drug policymakers can hardly be tasked with reversing the economic and social ruin of deindustrialization, such phenomena must inform the creation of overdose interventions accessible to low/no-income users who are wary of law enforcement and isolated from other institutional sources of help."[8] But harm reduction must be part of a broader social movement to change the conditions that foster substance use disorder and exacerbate it. The stigma that people who use drugs face is fundamentally a human rights problem— part of a larger human rights crisis confronted by people who use drugs. It is characterized not only by the ways in which the criminal justice system is being used as a tool—in some cases, weaponized—to treat a health crisis but also by all the daily indignities faced by people who use drugs. It is at once a crisis of institutional and personal relationships that degrade people's humanity so much that they are afraid to go to the grocery store, to step into the light, to speak in a public space, to take up space, to be—in a word—human.

Human rights are those rights or privileges one has simply by virtue of being human. These rights come above and beyond what we are entitled to as citizens of a nation-state—they are moral claims for the dignity of every individual. Historian Lynn Hunt writes, "Human rights require three interlocking qualities: rights must be *natural* (inherent in all human beings), *equal* (the same for everyone), and *universal* (applicable everywhere). For rights to be human rights, all humans everywhere in the world must possess them equally and only because of their status as human beings."[9] The popular narrative is that the concept dates back to the eighteenth century, when a coterie of white men in Paris and London opined about the rights of man. I would argue that if we want to look at the eighteenth century, the concept is rooted in the freedom movements of enslaved peoples around the world.[10] Calls for human rights echo in movements to end slavery, to abolish the death penalty, and to ensure women's and civil rights. Calls for fundamental human rights are heard when people are not being treated as citizens or as humans; they come from those most marginalized and degraded. In this moment it would be hard to argue that people who use drugs are not particularly marginalized and degraded, to the extent that we hardly give them a space to speak in the public sphere.

The overdose crisis is a human rights problem because the human rights agenda is predicated on the fact that all humans want to be treated with dignity and live with dignity. We're not doing that; we've never done that. There is still too much stigma, despite all that we know about drug addiction, despite all that we know about our criminal justice system and the ways in which criminalization is driven by racism and the ways in which stigma is reinforced by criminalization. Despite all of this, Hunt writes, "The history of human rights shows that rights are best defended in the end by the feelings, convictions, and actions of multitudes of individuals, who demand responses that accord with their inner sense of outrage."[11] Doing so opens doors and puts one in conversation not only with neighbors but also with those around the world. The person who uses drugs and is brutalized by Rodrigo Duterte's regime in the Philippines is allied with the person who uses drugs and sits for a month in jail because she can't pay the two-hundred-dollar bond for a possession charge in Ohio. And the person protesting to end drug-induced homicide laws is in partnership with the mother handing out naloxone on a corner.

In Licking County, Dennis Cauchon continues apace, advocating for a syringe exchange and educating people in the community about harm reduction. He hosts a gathering in Granville, about ten minutes east of Newark. The purpose is to build a group of allies prepared not only to address their neighbors' concerns but also to begin the work of connecting those doing this work already. Billy speaks, as do others with experience. Billy seems comfortable in this new role, but also inspired and wanting to do more.

At a meeting of an ad hoc harm-reduction committee, Dennis asks the group why there are no members of the task force who actively use drugs, speaking from their lived experience. In the room there are certainly a few people who have experience—Trish is there, as well as folks with many, many years of sobriety. But I think Dennis was asking about people with recent experience—people who can help the social workers, counselors, and providers gathered around the table understand what was actually happening on the street. Maybe someone like Billy?

Waiting in the lobby at city hall, Billy is fidgeting and reading through notes he's written on the back of an invoice from work.

"You should have seen the first draft with coffee stains all over it," he says.

"That ain't what you said yesterday," Trish says. "Said you were gonna wing it."

"Yeah, I said I was gonna shoot from the hip."

"Yeah," she says, "but then I seen you sittin' in your truck taking notes!"

Trish and Billy laugh.

Billy is with his girlfriend, Samantha, and his friend Jayson. He says aloud that he's nervous. This is an open meeting. People will be scrutinizing him. People will wonder what he has to say to the city council.

"Yeah, but you got a PhD in drug use!" Jayson says.

When the meeting starts, Billy sits alone in the front row, wearing a blue hoodie and jeans.[12] Dennis is on the agenda, so he goes up during the first public comment period after his name is called by a council member. He speaks quickly and nervously. "I'm Dennis Cauchon, president of Harm Reduction Ohio. We're a statewide organization based in Granville. However—"

A council member interrupts, "Hold on a second, hold on a second, let me finish. So we all have a presentation by Dennis Cauchon, who is president of Human Reduction Ohio."

"Not *human* reduction. We're trying to maximize the humans," Dennis says, waving his arms up and down in a lifting motion.

Some laughter from the audience.

"*Harm* Reduction Ohio, thank you," the council member says, "regarding starting a syringe exchange in Newark."

Dennis hands the podium over to Billy, introduced as the organization's director of syringe advocacy, a big title that I hadn't heard used yet, but it makes sense. Billy steps up nervously to the podium. It's standing room only. He puts his notes down on the podium, holds them in place with a shaking hand, and speaks. He's too far from the mic at first, and then, when asked to do so, he leans in.

"Okay," Billy says slowly, "what we're trying to do here is gain community support in starting and operating a syringe access program in town. We're trying to get a location." He explains that they would like to have a place settled on by January before they go back to the Licking County Board of Health. They don't need the city council's permission, but they want to work with them and have their support. "We're trying to build a culture of safe use among people who are using. A lot of people ask, 'Why Newark?' Newark is the heart of Licking County, metaphorically and geographically. We have a strong community. Strong core values. Somewhat progressive I think. And we have really motivated leaders. As a community we need to face this issue with addiction head-on. There's no one answer to the problem. A syringe exchange is just one element to it. Some people say it's enabling drug use. I can answer that many different ways. We think of it as prevention, not permission." He cites CDC research that shows that exchanges do not promote drug use.[13] As a ten-year IV drug user, he says, the syringe exchange is not why he used—but it did keep him healthy. There are many different paths to recovery, but when somebody gets there, they shouldn't have to suffer from HIV or hepatitis C or other infections. Billy tells them that by meeting people where they are, we can build relationships that can keep people who use drugs healthier and, he hopes, get them into treatment.

"As a community," he says, "we've used drug addiction as an excuse for poor public health for too long." He says that he didn't care about any of the other services when he was using Safe Point in Columbus, but now he is seven months sober and he's lobbying for people who use drugs. "People do change. People should have given up on me a long time ago, but they didn't." Billy tells them that people think that the majority of people to use these services will be homeless, but that others could be people in this room. People who work. People who have jobs and just don't have access to syringes.

The council members ask a few follow-up questions: The syringes are used for what? How does an exchange reduce needlesticks? And then Jonathan Lang, a Republican from the Fifth Ward, congratulates Billy for his seven months of sobriety. "You're really doing some good work in the community," Lang says.

Billy continues. "A lot of people ask me, 'You're clean now, why would you care about getting clean needles into people who use's hands?' And I say, 'Maybe if someone would have helped get some clean needles to me, I wouldn't have hepatitis today.' Now that I'm clean and living my life, I wouldn't have to clean up so many messes that I made for myself, and if that's one that we can prevent for somebody, I'm all for it."

The reality on the ground, though, is that Trish has already started distributing needles, buying them with her own money or getting them donated. Because her work has not been sanctioned by the board of health, she's risking arrest. Now, on Saturdays at the corner, people are learning through the grapevine that there is a lady handing out "clean works": brown paper bags filled with condoms, Band-Aids, Neosporin, vitamin C packs, tie-offs, fentanyl test strips, cottons, heroin cookers, and sterile needles.

12

Punk Rock Harm Reduction

n February 2019, at about the same moment that Donald Trump declared a "national emergency" to secure funds to build a wall, I was waiting to meet Sheila Humphrey-Craig, an activist affiliated with Harm Reduction Ohio, at a McDonald's in Dayton.[1] A lanky, twenty-something white man with pockmarks on his face put a blue backpack over his red coat, walked out one door, ambled down the sidewalk, and then entered through another door of the restaurant. He took off his backpack. Sat down. Stood up again. Walked out. Repeat. Two booths away, an African American woman wearing a bandanna began nodding off, clipped moaning noises coming from somewhere inside her.

The big news, the reason I am here, is that Verily Life Sciences (whose parent company is Alphabet, which also owns Google) is building an opioid use disorder treatment and recovery center in Dayton, a city once referred to as the overdose capital of America. The center, called OneFifteen, is slated to open in a few months, with transitional housing opening in 2020.[2] Verily will apply data analytics in an effort to tailor treatment and track the progress of patients in and out of health care and criminal justice systems.

Community and business leaders are excited. They cite Dayton's impressive turnaround as the main reason for Verily's interest. In November 2018, *The New York Times* ran a story about how Dayton has managed to significantly decrease the scourge of opioid overdoses as citizens banded together to address the problem.[3] The Center for American Progress has called Dayton's community coalition a model for other communities to follow.[4] They note the city's all-hands-on-deck approach, which includes better data collection, a disease model for treating addiction, and widespread access to naloxone.

Sheila Humphrey-Craig doesn't seem impressed by all this talk of Dayton's turnaround or of "Google" coming to town. An ex–punk rocker, the fifty-something Sheila wears a black hoodie that reads "I love people who use drugs." When she can, she drives around town in her pickup, handing out naloxone and fentanyl testing strips. As soon as I see her walk into the McDonald's, she turns around and walks out with a man she recognized, knowing he needed some naloxone. Like Trish, Sheila does this because she has seen too many young people overdose, too many young people die. Handing out fentanyl testing strips and naloxone is a quick way to prevent more. And like Trish, she has a son who has struggled with heroin. Sheila's son has been sober for a while now. "He exercises," she says. "That's his trip, and he practices mindfulness." But if he ever goes back to that lifestyle, she wants him to be safe.

"And I'm doing it for all these other friends that he's lost and are gone."

"How many friends has he lost?" I ask.

"Oh God, too many," she replies. "Too many. I'd say over twenty. Really. 'Cause all of his friends are gone. That man I was talking to before I came in, all of *his* friends are gone. It's sad, that everybody you know is gone. They're so young. I've had all my life peppered with death here and there, but I'm an old woman and I absorb it . . . How can a young person, twenty-one years old, how do they deal with twenty of their friends dead?"

"Yeah."

"That right there does a number on their brain. They don't realize it, but they are in shock, and they don't know to deal with it, except to just ignore it. They can't dwell on it—if they sit and dwell, they just become so depressed. Then they go back."

That's why she does it, she says, because none of those people deserved to die. And when the overdoses were highest around here, when a lot of people were dying, her son was using. At that time, between mid-2016 and mid-2017, things were especially dire as Ohio was hit by a surge in overdose deaths.[5] The drug supply was tainted with potent opioids, and many people who use drugs were dying. In May 2017, *People* magazine ran the story of the tragic drug overdose death of a handsome airline pilot and his beautiful wife.[6] The couple was found in their home by their son—their Centerville, Ohio, community was shocked to learn that the coroner found cocaine as well as illicitly manufactured carfentanil—a fentanyl analog that's a hundred times more potent and is used primarily to tranquilize elephants and other large mammals—in their bodies.[7] Of course, theirs was just another story about an overdose death amid a national frenzy over opioid overdose deaths.

A 2018 CDC study revealed that from July 1, 2016, to June 30, 2017, there were 1,106 carfentanil-related deaths in Ohio versus 130 in nine other states.[8] The death rate was 9.52 per 100,000 residents versus 0.45 per 100,000 in the other states. Something was definitely happening in the Buckeye State—something that wasn't happening elsewhere. Numbers were high in Dayton, but they were also high in Cincinnati and Akron, which had to use refrigerated trucks because the city morgue was full.[9] Search-and-seizure data from the Ohio Bureau of Criminal Investigation during this period makes it clear that, of the thousands of seizures, very few were of pure carfentanil, an indication that this super-potent drug didn't need to spread throughout the drug supply to wreak havoc.[10]

Dennis Cauchon wrote several stories for his Harm Reduction Ohio website arguing that the spike in deaths was directly attributable to the increase of carfentanil found in the drug supply:

In the illegal drug marketplace, the speck-sized potency of carfentanil kills at a magnitude that is multiples beyond fentanyl. The increase is not incremental, it is exponential—just as fentanyl kills at a magnitude beyond heroin, and heroin kills at a magnitude beyond morphine, and morphine at a magnitude beyond opium. The drug war's relentless pressure on smugglers, sellers, and users to switch from bulky drugs (heroin, morphine, opium) to tiny, compact ones is why carfentanil is used in drug markets. Small drugs are a rational choice for smugglers and dealers.[11]

He pointed out that the high from fentanyl and carfentanil is not as long-lasting at that from heroin, and therefore its control of the market can't be because of consumer demand. "Although it may seem counterintuitive, easing up on heroin—by reducing sentences and cutting back on eradication of poppy fields—is the smart 'supply side' way to get rid of carfentanil and reduce overdose death," he writes.[12] This is, essentially, "the iron law of prohibition," a concept attributed to cannabis activist Richard Cowan, which asserts that the more we ramp up law enforcement, the more potent illicit substances will become.[13] In his book *Chasing the Scream*, Johann Hari explains the idea this way: "If no mild intoxicants are available, plenty of people will use a more extreme intoxicant, because it's better than nothing. Prohibition always narrows the market to the most potent possible substance."[14] The war on drugs has pushed people who use opioids toward more dangerous substances.

Dennis Cauchon writes:

Ask the wrong questions and you get the wrong answers. The objective questions to ask are hinted at in drug seizure data:

1. What exactly is causing sudden overdose deaths? and
2. Why do so many drugs contain deadly contaminants and adulter-

ants? May I suggest a hypothesis: Prohibition kills. Always has, always will. Is doing so right now.[15]

Using data from the state, Dennis showed how quickly overdoses went down as carfentanil disappeared. State officials attributed the reduction in deaths, in large part, to their public policy reactions.[16] Dayton's mayor asserted that the drop had a lot to do with Governor John Kasich's expanded Medicaid.[17] And Senator Rob Portman helped push for the STOP Act, intended to keep carfentanil out of the U.S. mail—but that came almost a year after the spike in overdoses leveled out.[18] The *Dayton Daily News* suggested there was no one reason for the decline, noting that efforts by law enforcement, work to expand access to treatment, programs that have "increased the availability of naloxone," and even people who use drugs switching to other drugs have helped.[19] The overdose spike certainly wasn't the result of a spike in drug use, which seems to have held steady over time. Data from the Institute for Health Metrics and Evaluation out of the University of Washington suggests that in 1990, 5.33 percent of Americans had some alcohol or drug dependence. In 2016, the number was 5.47 percent.[20] That's only a slight increase over twenty-six years, and the figure itself is not as high as some people might imagine. So what happened to cause so many overdoses?

Sheila Humphrey-Craig is less polite than Dennis Cauchon and others in her assessment. "They didn't do shit," she says. "The drug supply got tainted, and then it wasn't. That's it." Activists like Sheila might say that as long as we criminalize use, the drug supply will remain subject to becoming tainted. A spike like this will happen again—and as long as there's a black market, we won't see it coming. Ever.

Sheila and I finally leave the McDonald's, and she takes me on a tour of Dayton. She shows me the West Side and where she used to live, where the treatment centers are, where the exchanges are. As we drive she points out landmarks, neighborhoods, and places where people have died from a drug overdose. Dayton is a beautiful city, but many parts are still recovering from its heavy industrial heyday. At one time NCR and GM employed tens of thousands; today the economy is dependent on health care, education, and the Wright-Patterson Air Force Base.[21]

"We used to have great tool and die shops all over Dayton. If you wanted anything fabricated . . . people had stuff set up in their garages. You could find somebody to make a prototype of whatever here in Dayton, Ohio."

"Yeah."

"We had a lot of innovations, a lot of inventors, but they're all gone, they're all gone. This is where they invented the pop top. You know, cans?"

In some ways, Sheila's an innovator, an inventor, trying to figure out ways to meet community needs, to meet people where they're at. Today, though, she's frustrated by those she feels are slow to join her, to advance harm-reduction policies in her community. She looks at new construction and new businesses and sees panhandlers being run off. As we go through one neighborhood, she says, "See, this is all gentrification here. This is all crap. And then they put in these hipster doofus things."

We drive through a warehouse district. Sheila points to one building that used to host punk shows back in the day when she was a punk rocker with a shaved head.

"Well, they're all cleaned up now, but that used to be a big punk warehouse. We'd have shows there, and . . . you could rent a space for fifty bucks a month. We used to put on all kinds of shows. We brought in the U.K. Subs and Broken Bones, all those. NOFX. Dead Kennedys. They all played Dayton. Dayton was a fucking cool town at one time."

Today Sheila is a full-on harm-reduction activist. She tells me that during the time when carfentanil first came through, her son was using. His girlfriend overdosed, but he had naloxone; then he overdosed, but someone near him had naloxone. "That's why I always have it," she says, but adds, "You don't really know, you can't, if it's carfentanil unless you can test some way. Otherwise, it's just a guess. And that's the rub. Given the ways opioids are being sold these days, it's a real crapshoot. It's like the Wild Wild West. You know there is nothing uniform about it. Where one goes down, another one pops up and takes their place."

But then, she says, it disappeared. "It disappeared just as mysteriously as it came to town. It's gone. Okay. Who had control over that? Nobody. No public official had control over that."

There had to be another way to deal with a tainted drug supply. When she learned about testing strips, she was sold. And now she has learned about safe injection sites (also called safe consumption sites)—it's now her mission to educate others about them. This summer, she plans on driving around the state with a mock safe injection site to demonstrate to a skeptical public how they work. Sheila is not interested in waiting, or in joining committees, or in taking part in trials and feasibility studies.

"I'm not going to sit here and waste my time and try to convince people that don't want to see. How can you reason with the unreasonable? You can't. So you have to take matters into your own hands, and go around them. That's what I do, I go around them. Yeah. I don't give a damn anymore."

Rainbows and Unicorns

O n a frigid Saturday in February 2019, a group of protestors lined the
spiraling central gallery of the Guggenheim Museum in New York
City.[1] They dropped flyers and dumped fake prescriptions down to
the museum's lobby below in protest of the Sacklers, the family who owns
Purdue Pharma and who made donations to the Guggenheim as well as
the Smithsonian and the Metropolitan Museum of Art. The protest was
dutifully covered by *The New Yorker*. It's important, though it does reinforce
the trope that Purdue Pharma and the Sackler family are solely responsible
for the opioid crisis, that the problem is only the drug and their greed. It's
a good story (but not the complete story) and certainly money from the
lawsuits people have brought against Purdue could be useful to those addressing the overdose crisis. But what happened in that art museum made
only a slight blip here in central Ohio, a momentary story passing through
my social media feeds.

At the same time, Dennis Cauchon and Billy were busy trying to
find a site for an aboveground syringe services program, meeting with local agencies, networking with politicians. Billy was attending every health

department board meeting he could—he even sent Christmas cards to all the board members. On February 19, Billy stood up at another meeting and talked about what he was now referring to as syringe services programs (SSPs), using the best terminology available. An SSP differs from a one-for-one syringe exchange program (SEP) in that it's not always based on how many needles you bring in—though participants are encouraged to bring as many as they can. An SSP is, more specifically, a distribution site for sterile needles as well as a point of contact between people who use drugs and health professionals.[2] In some cases, it's the only contact they have. At an SSP, a person who uses drugs can get help with injuries they might have as a result of injecting drugs—abscesses, needles in their arms. They can also learn how to safely inject, how to use alcohol to prevent infections, how to use a fentanyl test strip, or how to administer naloxone. If they wish to go into treatment, someone is around to help. They can also get new syringes. An SSP, Billy would say, is really about building relationships.

It seemed inevitable that Licking County would get one. The commissioner of the health department, a quiet but self-assured man with years of experience named Joe Ebel, was on board—as were other folks working at the health department.[3] They understood what was at stake and could see the rising number of hep C cases, not just in Licking County but also around the state. And everyone knew about what happened in rural Scott County, Indiana, one state away, in 2015—an outbreak of HIV resulting in 215 new cases, due in no small part to Governor Mike Pence's opposition to SSPs.[4] Writing in *The Lancet*, Gregg S. Gonsalves and Forrest W. Crawford explain that "the HIV epidemic in Scott County might have been prevented or mitigated with an earlier response," including the establishment of SSPs.[5] Ellsworth M. Campbell and his colleagues, writing in *The Journal of Infectious Diseases*, suggest, "Had an SSP been in place prior to recognition of the outbreak, the explosive phase of the outbreak may have been blunted."[6] That incident transformed many in the public health community and certainly influenced U.S. surgeon general Jerome Adams, an outspoken advocate for SSPs. It seemed inevitable that the Licking County Board of Health would concur with Billy, with research, with evidence.

After Billy left the meeting, he texted to tell me that it went well. And then the board of health went into an executive session and afterward voted 8–0 (with two members not in attendance) to oppose any syringe program in Licking County.[7] A vote was not on the agenda, there was no public discussion of the proposal, and Billy wasn't notified they were going to vote, even though he was at the meeting.[8] At the time, twenty-two of Ohio's eighty-eight counties had SSPs in place already, and Licking County's board of health may have become the first in the state to vote against an exchange in recent years.[9] Billy was devastated. Only one board member, Jim Glover, offered a comment to the local newspaper, *The Newark Advocate*: "I don't see a reason for us to do something like that. I feel we're giving them all the chances they need now. When a person decides they want help, they'll come and get it. Giving them needles just furthers their problems."

The Saturday after the vote, it's partly sunny and unseasonably warm. The corner is busy. Across the street, two sheriff's vehicles are parked side by side near the jail. Trish Perry thinks they're watching the corner, but they could just be idling, waiting on calls. Trish is running back and forth, handing out harm-reduction kits, pulling more supplies for the tables from her trunk. She's not too surprised by the vote—she says she has come to expect it from this place. She will keep doing what she's doing. There will be another meeting of the board of health in a few weeks. Some folks from around the state will likely come—allies from Canton, Dayton, and Columbus. But she is worried that nothing will change, that there will never be an SSP in Licking County. Can she keep doing this on her own? Can she sustain? Right now *she* is the county's SSP—serving forty to fifty people every week. She's in good company, though. There are others around the country risking much to distribute syringes to people who need them. There's a group called Shot in the Dark out in Phoenix distributing "clean works" out of the back of their cars.[10] In Iowa, a group distributes sterile needles around Cedar Rapids.[11]

The number of people—almost all women—working to distribute food and clothing with Trish Perry and Jen Kanagy is growing. Some of them are in recovery; others are former teachers and social workers, people who have learned about the work Trish and Jen are doing and just want to be engaged. Every once in a while, a nice car will pull up and some middle-class person will step out and hand them boxes of food or clothing to distribute. And sometimes, like on this day, a white-haired woman in a coffee-stained overcoat will slip Trish a couple of dollars. Trish thanks her profusely, knowing how much that gift means.

The woman, like a lot of people who come here for the hot dogs or the harm-reduction kits, looks like she has lived hard. Many of them have—either they are homeless or close to it. One man tells me that he used the naloxone Trish gave him on someone this week. A woman with blond hair tells me her boyfriend just went to prison, and she's been sleeping under a bridge—she's hurting and desperately wants to get high. A man with a crew cut says he's having a hard time finding work that pays well and is close enough to this side of town. They tell me how many times they've nearly died, how many times they've overdosed. They know these things. They also know how many people they have saved, how many overdoses they've reversed.

Jen would love to get some of these people to the next board of health meeting—many are already planning to attend. People who use drugs or who are homeless are not usually given space in public settings—nor do they often seek it—especially in a small community like this. People who use drugs are being talked about but not with, Jen Kanagy says. She wants to try to see if she can get them to this meeting. She was distributing handbills to everyone at the corner. "I can seat ten people in my van," she tells me, but then wonders aloud if it is even possible to organize people who use drugs.

Billy drives up in his truck. He's helping move a woman into a shelter today. Jen says, "Billy is like a camel—his back is sagging from all that we put on him." As if on cue, he walks over and talks about the meeting, saying he wishes he could organize a harm-reduction group at the center in Newark with people who use drugs.

On the day of the board of health meeting, I meet Trish at the corner. It's a blue-sky evening; the trees are still bare, but spring feels imminent. We wait around for fifteen minutes, but no one shows up. It was a long shot, she says, to get people from the corner to come. She says she knows that people who use drugs are nervous because they're afraid of being seen in public or because they have warrants. But she just hoped. To stand up in that room and talk about themselves, their drug use, and their desire to be treated with dignity—it would be unprecedented. I can see she's a little disappointed.

"Well, Jen's going to come by in a little bit," Trish says, still hopeful. "See you over there."

I drive across town to the health department. It's located in an old tuberculosis sanatorium on the far north of town, miles away from the corner. In the parking lot in front of the building, about a dozen or so people are hanging out—there's a positive buzz in the setting March sun. Reporters from local papers, along with a couple of TV crews from Columbus, are already getting a story.[12] As more people show up—including a contingent from Canton, Trish's friends from OhioCAN (Change Addiction Now)—one of the crews asks all those present to assemble on the steps, an orchestrated photo op. There are some new faces among the handful of people on the steps, but also some familiar ones, people coming together to support one another: Allen, C.J., Billy, Dennis, Trish. They hold signs that read "Science over Stigma," "Reduce Infectious Disease Rates Now," "No Body Benefits from Disease," and "Meet People Where They're At."

A reporter from Spectrum News 1 asks Billy if he'll go on camera. Billy tells him how he had attended board of health meetings for months asking for support for an SSP, how the board voted in executive session without public discussion and without listing it on their agenda, how they have yet to explain their decision, and how he is here today to seek answers, and hopefully change some minds.[13] "If they'd paid attention to the research and science and all the counties that have done this," Billy says, "it's a no-brainer . . . It's easier for them to say 'no comment' than to say, 'We've made a decision based on scientific fact and we've decided to go against it.'"

Billy is clearly fired up and the reporter asks him why.

"I'm a ten-year IV drug user," Billy answers. "Been in recovery for over a year now. During the ten years of using, I contracted hepatitis C. I've had abscesses that almost took my life. I've been hospitalized for endocarditis. A small thing like a twelve-cent syringe could have prevented a lot of that. What we've been doing for so long with the war on drugs is not working. In fact, it's cultivating addiction. We gotta start looking at other pieces to the puzzle. There's no one fix to the opioid crisis in America." He's on message. On point. And he seems more comfortable with this camera in his face than he did standing in front of city council.

Then the reporter asks him what advice he would give to people who, like him, are no longer using drugs, trying to be abstinent?

"As cliché as it sounds, take it one day at a time. Once we stop using drugs doesn't mean our life turns into rainbows and unicorns. Life is difficult at best, but taking life one day at a time, one obstacle at a time, what I've been able to accomplish in this last year has blown me away."

About ten minutes before the meeting starts, everyone files into the building and up to the already packed boardroom—standing room only when I walk in. Dennis speaks first, and he's visibly angry, saying that for months now they have been "midwestern nice"—attending meetings, joining task forces. "Billy was at your meeting last month," Dennis continues. "It wasn't on the agenda. You revised the agenda. You went into a secret meeting and outlawed exchanges, not just our exchange, all of them. It's not courteous. It's not how government is supposed to function. If we had been Park National Bank, would you have done this to us? I think there's no way you would have backstabbed us like this. Who did you backstab? Billy. Who has been coming to every meeting. And what do you call that? It's called stigma. And that's why we're here . . . We are in the mainstream. You are out of the mainstream in how you have behaved. Polls show that most Ohio residents support needle exchanges . . . We're here to promote science over stigma. You are the board of health, not the board of moralism. These people, you are increasing their chance of dying. It's a serious issue. You need to take it seriously and look at the evidence. These are real people." He says that what they did in February was an open meetings violation and that they will be challenged on that. All the while, he is holding a sign that reads "Every Human Is a Human."

Billy follows. "Hello, everyone," he begins. "Good to see you again. Appreciate you letting us come in. I'm curious, if it was an evidence-based decision, if it was based on public health, I think it would been a no-brainer for the board of health to agree to this. So I'm wondering if there's some sort of pressure, political, or what exactly it is. Because I think we've proven that the community overall supports this . . . Would it be possible to come out and let us know how you guys came to this decision to all vote no?" He says they should go visit one of the state's exchanges, get out of their comfort zone.

And then Trish speaks. And then a retired nurse, two working nurses, a mother from Canton named Cindy Koumoutzis with OhioCAN, a man with hep C, several mothers, a chemist, a woman who used drugs, and another who says, "I used needles from people who had hep C because I couldn't find a clean one. It didn't matter. I've seen needles break off in people's arms. I've had abscesses. I've had MRSA . . . I can't speak enough for it—I've lived it." Throughout the testimony, Billy stands focused, back against the wall, nodding in agreement. At times he squats and listens intently. After each speaker finishes, he claps and offers a generous smile as he tells each person thank you.

The last person to speak is Dr. Robert J. Masone, chief medical officer at Life Spring Recovery, a local outpatient substance use disorder treatment facility. He says that there's no one way to help people with substance use disorder. There are several approaches, just like with any problem, and offering "clean needles" is one way. It's practical, cost-effective. "But," he says, "I heard some talk here about love. To provide a clean needle to someone is a sign of love. They don't get it, but they need it." Not having love, he says, is probably one of the causes of addiction. "And that love can cause them to open up, and we can approach them and get them to another level of treatment. I look at needle programs as intake—harm reduction, cost reduction—but also an intake to give hope to the people."

The World Health Organization and the U.S. Centers for Disease Control have supported syringe programs for many years. The Ohio Department of Health supports them. In Licking County, the United Way and the Licking Memorial Health Systems support having one.[14]

The members of the board of health are silent. They listen but offer no explanation for their decision. No comments. No questions.

Board of health president Neisha Grubaugh issues a statement that doesn't respond to questions but just says the board appreciates the comments and that the health department is committed to disease prevention, offers hep A vaccines, gives out free naloxone, and educates "the public about the dangers of opioid abuse."[15]

After public comments are closed, we file slowly out of the building, chatting excitedly along the way, energized, galvanized. As a big full moon begins to rise, the crew from Canton and Billy and his girlfriend, Samantha, are gathered by Billy's truck, which is loaded down with ladders and painting supplies.

Years before, in the late 1980s, activists, especially in New York City and San Francisco, advocated for needle exchanges as a way to prevent the spread of HIV. They attended forums with health officials, they demonstrated, and in some cases they broke the law. Needle exchanges had already started in Europe (even in Margaret Thatcher's England) and been proven effective. Indeed, research from Amsterdam, Sydney, and elsewhere showed that people who used new syringes had lower rates of HIV infection. Acceptance for syringe exchange programs moved more slowly in the United States; indeed, there was significant pushback from law enforcement, community leaders, and politicians. Dianne Feinstein, as mayor of San Francisco, opposed her health commissioner's proposal for one. In 1988, Senator Jesse Helms pushed for a law banning federal funding for needle exchanges.[16]

But the mood was shifting. In late-1980s New York City, ground zero in the United States for the AIDS crisis, around half of the city's 200,000 IV drug users were infected. The situation was dire between 1988 and 1992: according to CDC numbers, 202,520 Americans had AIDS. In 1987 alone, 13,329 people died from the disease; by 1990, that number jumped to 21,628. There was a growing awareness that while the spread had been slowed among gay men, AIDS was spreading quickly among IV drug users, especially in poor communities of color, and this was why, as William A. Schwartz reported in *The Nation* in 1987, the street price for "clean works" seemed to have doubled in Boston since the beginning of the AIDS epidemic. Given the stigma around drug use, needle exchange was a hard sell. Noting that the common refrain from naysayers is that exchange promotes drug use, Schwartz writes:

> But even if it were true, there is no comparison between the dangers of cleanly administered i.v. drugs—which, while real, are limited, can be escaped through treatment and are uncontagious—and those from AIDS, which is always fatal and can be spread to other users, sex partners and babies. Where drugs are available, needles generally are; the question for public policy is whether they are to be clean or dirty. Few would openly

support making intravenous use of heroin and cocaine capital offenses, but this is what withholding sterile injection equipment effectively does.

He cites a "profound contempt for addicts in our society" that is reinforced by racism.

The only pragmatic way forward is to highlight the risks to everyone—not just people who use drugs. "It is clear that compassion for the dying is insufficient to produce serious action. Fear may prove a more powerful motive."[17]

In a 2011 study of the movement for access to syringe exchange in New York City, researchers Daliah Heller and Denise Paone note, "Even today, 'winning' arguments for the expansion of syringe access have been rooted in the crisis of HIV/AIDS rather than the need for a continuum of care and treatment services addressing problems of drug use."[18] It's the fear of the spread of disease that seems to matter—not the individual who uses drugs.

In a short 1988 documentary by the Gay Men's Health Crisis, a gray-haired nurse from St. Luke's Hospital named Cynthia Corcoran says that people need to stand up, that many people are dying from AIDS and the hospital can't handle all the deaths. "I won't handle them," she declares, adding that health professionals need to give out needles. Her father went to jail to fight prohibition, she says, suggesting a new round of civil disobedience: "I think all of us should be willing to do the same to literally save them."[19] People must be willing, she asserts, to call out the immorality of laws and policies. They must be open to discomfort and have the courage to break unjust laws—indeed, at the time eleven states, including New York, New Jersey, and Massachusetts, had criminalized possession of syringes: no one except medical professionals or people with prescriptions could have a needle. The law, of course, led to a lot of sharing—and even renting—of needles. Today, all but five states have laws prohibiting possession of syringes without a prescription. In Ohio, possession of a syringe is a second-degree misdemeanor punishable with up to 90 days in jail and a $750 fine; if a person already has another drug-related conviction on his or her record, the punishment goes up to a first-degree misdemeanor with the possibility of 180 days in jail and a $1,000 fine.[20]

Many early exchanges were low-budget and illegal. The people involved were aware of the law but didn't care. They had done their research and viewed providing sterile syringes as an effective method for reducing the transmission of AIDS, first and foremost, but also for treating people who use drugs like human beings. The apparent first exchange in the United States, started in 1988 in Tacoma, Washington, by a biker named Dave Purchase, was little more than a TV tray on a corner from which he exchanged new works for used ones.[21] In San Francisco, also in 1988, an underground program called Prevention Point offered syringes, bleach, alcohol wipes, cottons, and condoms to affected communities, transporting supplies in a baby carriage to avoid suspicion. In New York City, groups like the AIDS Coalition to Unleash Power (ACT UP), Jon Parker's National AIDS Brigade, and the Association for Drug Abuse Prevention and Treatment (ADAPT) were behind the work to establish a needle exchange, at a time when "60 percent of I.V. drug users were HIV positive."[22] They set up shop on street corners and in single-room occupancy units around the city. Indeed, Parker had already set up exchanges in New Haven and Boston, and ADAPT had started giving out needles on its own around the city. ADAPT's president, Yolanda Serrano, told *The New York Times*, "We know whoever does this is going to get arrested, but somebody has to take the first step. This virus is spreading like wildfire in minority neighborhoods. It's getting out of hand, and no one is really addressing the issue."[23]

When New York City's health commissioner, Dr. Stephen Joseph, proposed a small experimental program, it was supported by then mayor Ed Koch and the state board of health. In late 1988, New York City finally had a legal syringe exchange, but not for long. That program ended in January 1990, when Mayor David N. Dinkins made good on a campaign promise and stopped it. Most activists felt it was too small to have any real effect.

On March 6, 1990, ten activists set up a table at the corner of Delancy and Essex on the Lower East Side of Manhattan.[24] At the time, this was a working-class neighborhood, a place where they had done this work before. Tipped off by a story in *Newsday* the day prior, the press knew they'd be there, and so did the police. Activists from ACT UP were on one corner, and members of Curtis Sliwa's vigilante anticrime organization Guardian Angels were on another, shouting, "No drugs! No needles!" And then, after a brief meeting at Katz's Deli (according to *The New York Times*), a needle exchange was set up on a third corner around noon. Those at the exchange tried handing out "AIDS-prevention kits," which included condoms, bleach, and new needles. But police rushed in shortly after they set up a black card table, and with the police presence and a mess of reporters and cameras, nothing was distributed. The people at the table, including Jon Parker and Richard Elovich, were arrested. Mayor Dinkins remarked about the incident, "I do not wish to see people assisted in becoming addicted."

In court, the activists relied primarily on the justification or necessity defense—the idea that public policy is supposed to address public problems and that, if it doesn't, citizens can intervene.[25] For example, breaking into a cabin in the midst of a blizzard or trespassing in your neighbor's yard to put out a fire can be excused as a necessary action. The lawyer for the defense called the activists modern-day John Snows, a reference to the British doctor who sabotaged a town pump to prevent the spread of cholera in 1854. Obviously, people were angry when Snow took the handle off the pump. But he was right. This was a situation, the lawyer argued, when the body count was increasing and the problem had to be addressed.

In the end, the New York City activists were acquitted.[26]

Syringe exchange became an official part of the public health response to AIDS in New York City in the late 1980s, and today the U.S. surgeon general and the CDC support SSPs, though federal dollars cannot be used to purchase syringes.

On a Friday in April 2019, I spend the afternoon at an SSP in Canton, a guest of Trish Perry's friends from OhioCAN, Cindy Koumoutzis and Ron Stromsky. The program is called the Stark Wide Approach to Prevention (SWAP), and there are 430 people enrolled. During my visit, there are forty-five visitors and the program gives out likely thousands of needles. Some of the people who come in look like they've been struggling for a while, but others do not; some are coming from work, and there's a mom talking about getting her kids from school. Ron offers peer support to those who request it, and anyone can get Narcan training and hep A shots.

Public health worker Amanda Archer sits at a desk when people walk in and show their ID card, which gives them safe space within up to a thousand feet of the place, though the police tend to stay away, they tell me. Amanda asks them which services, in addition to new syringes, they are interested in. She worked at the coroner's office until 2014 and remembers when she first started seeing prescription opioids (Percocet and OxyContin, in particular) and when she did her first autopsy on someone who died of an overdose from heroin. She remembers thinking, just before she left the coroner's office, that things were peaking. She was wrong.

Amanda is sporting straight black hair, black-framed glasses, and a navy-blue Canton Health Department hoodie. She has a good laugh, too. Despite the seriousness of the work, she erupts every once in a while as if decompressing. The space is reminiscent of a doctor's office, but then there's Amanda laughing and Cindy in the corner making grilled cheeses on a sandwich press. Today, Cindy chats it up with folks about travel, dieting, and Greek Easter. Amanda launches a debate about the relative merits of morning glories versus petunias, with a sidebar about the latest season of *The*

Great British Baking Show. And they all seem to know everyone who comes in and can ask them personal questions, can check in with them, can show them a little love.

A few days after the board of health protest, Trish went with her grandson Ethan, his wife, and Billy down to Myrtle Beach, South Carolina. She takes this trip every year, but this is the first time she has ever taken Billy. So many times in the past he couldn't do it, wouldn't do it, or simply made their vacations next to impossible. One time they were driving to Kentucky's Newport Aquarium, on the other side of the river from Cincinnati. They made it to I-70 before Trish had to turn around and bring him back. She and the others continued the trip, but Billy messaged them the whole time that he was going to kill himself.

But now, throughout this week in Myrtle Beach, Trish posts photo after photo on social media of Billy and his son, Ethan. Billy in the ocean, blue sky. Billy in the pool with Ethan. Smiling.

Part 3

NOTHING ABOUT US WITHOUT US

Spring–Summer 2019

Sometimes we have to do the work even though
we don't yet see a glimmer on the horizon that it's
actually going to be possible.

—ANGELA Y. DAVIS

14

Beyond Rat Park

I call Bruce Alexander on a Friday morning. On my computer screen I can see he's sitting comfortably in his living room somewhere on an island near Vancouver. Evergreen trees outside the windows, light coming in, but we talk about Ohio. He went to Miami University in Oxford, just a couple of hours southwest of here. He remembers it fondly, remembers, too, how he connected with the ethos of the liberal arts while he was there. That tradition of holistic and free inquiry, he says, followed him throughout his life. Although his "Rat Park" experiments are well-known (see chapter 2), he eventually reached the limit with that kind of study and was looking for something else. When his funding ran out, there was only one place he could go do research for free—the campus library. To Alexander, that felt comfortable, appropriate, and in keeping with what he had been doing before: "I read Plato. I read Saint Augustine. That's the source. Our wisdom is cultural, I think."[1]

To understand the genesis of Alexander's more recent work, we must recognize his methodology, rooted in the tradition of the liberal arts, one that speaks to the many ways in which we must address the problem of addiction, overdose, and the war on drugs. We can't address these problems only through data or historical analysis, through psychology, and through clinical trials. These problems, he seems to say, require a holistic approach. Scholars, policymakers, and activists must push on the horizon.

"The last few days," he tells me, "I've been reading psychology papers on gambling addiction because I have to give a speech on gambling addiction." But he's frustrated with the work he's encountering. "It's too narrow. You can't get anywhere doing what they're doing, even though I know them, they're good people, and they want to help. But it's just too narrow."

And yet where he began his own career was quite narrow—an experiment that could fit indoors, focused on rats and substance use. Rat Park, he says, "starts by saying, well, the 'demon drug' myth is wrong. It's just wrong. Let's forget it. But the fact that rats are less inclined to take opioids when they have decent housing, community housing, doesn't really tell you anything about people. It's just a metaphor. And then you say, well, let's try this out on people. Well, we can't do it with people experimentally, but we can do it with people anthropologically. We can look at where people have been taken from their natural cultural setting and put into horrible restricted housing or lives. And it has happened thousands of times. So we have thousands of natural experiments to look at with people."

If you look at the natural experiences of human beings, he says, rather than just the experiences of rodents, the idea begins to evolve. It's not a cage per se that harms people; it's the larger economic, social, cultural, and historical context. "So it all follows from Rat Park," he continues. "[That] was just a moment of clarity which said, wait a minute, these rat studies look like bullshit. Let's change your conditions a little bit. And sure enough."

Alexander thinks that some psychologists use the word *environment* in too limited a way. "Really, what's around you is surrounded, is concentric circles, right?" he says. "There's what's around your house, and then there's what's around your community, and there's what's around your nation. And maybe there's something around that and we call that God or religion." If we want to understand who a person is and why they are the way they are, then we need to explore those circles.

Bruce Alexander is reaching for bigger ideas now, and that is why, it seems, he does not agree with much of contemporary thinking about the overdose crisis. "We're screwing the Big Pharma companies. They deserve to be screwed; I don't mind that at all. But it's the exclusive narrative. We crush those guys and the problem is solved. Well, no. And that's why I love to talk about the history, because we had the same problem in 1970. All of the same panic and all that stuff here. But of course we didn't have fentanyl. We didn't have Big Pharma being part of it. It's a different problem. And yet I think the deindustrialization now is an extension of a long period of whatever you want to call it."

I tell him about how Lisa Roberts reads the history of Appalachia as one of extraction—outsiders coming in, taking things, and leaving. And with each subsequent leaving, the people remaining in the area were just devastated. Penalizing the pharmaceutical companies will provide some temporary relief for overburdened social service, health care, and law enforcement systems, but it will not solve the larger problems facing Appalachia. As Alexander says, addiction is a political problem, wrapped up in structures that need to be transformed.

One way to begin to address this crisis is to rebuild communities, and that is apparent throughout the places hardest hit; it is apparent in the relationships described in this book. But Alexander would argue that it's still not enough. As an example, he points me to the addiction recovery movement. It's an important movement, he says, but the addiction recovery communities are operating within a larger, more damaged framework. You might build a thriving community in, say, Columbus with a recovery house where people can connect and find fellowship, but you're in the state of Ohio, with mounting overdose deaths and people sleeping in the streets outside the house. The house is just an island in a rough sea.

"And as soon as you talk to somebody, you realize there's all this hate in the air," he says. "And you can't just erase that stuff by building a nice house, or by funding a nice house. We've got to live within that world." And to live in our world, he says, requires a kind of fortitude that can exacerbate addiction. Our modern world, with our myriad screens and devices, with the catastrophe of global warming, with the threat of mass shootings. Our world. In the United States, where life expectancy has declined for three years in a row—in part because of drug overdoses, suicides, and organ system diseases (such as heart disease and diabetes).[2] And in Ohio, where five people died of suicide every day in 2018, where suicide is the leading cause of death for people ages ten to fourteen.[3]

"We're not all that strong," says Alexander. "We try to take care of our kids, and we try to do our job properly, and we try to be good citizens and recycle and all that stuff. But it's hard to have the strength to do that when you get up and read the news, and see all the misery that falls on people who don't deserve it for any reason. We don't have that kind of strength. We need environmental support, and it isn't just our house or our community. It's these concentric circles. They're with us all the time."

Alexander says that things will have to change at a national level, really, a global one. "That's where it's going to be resolved," he says, "*if* it's going to be resolved." He does not proffer cheap hope.

In the smallest of places, in the city of Newark, Ohio, people are trying their level best to rebuild those circles, but it is a slog. When the syringe exchange is voted down, when the board of health meeting leads to nothing, the collective energy seems drained, the movement stuttering. But Trish Perry keeps on. She's starting to collect shoes for an event she's organizing in May—a rally at the courthouse at which she will display a pair of shoes to represent all of the people who have overdosed in the last year as well as the nearly five hundred homeless adults and children. Her apartment is slowly filling up with shoes. When I suggest that it's a lot to be reminded of all the time, she politely suggests that at least she has not had to deal with death like some mothers have had to. It's a check on me, a reminder of the empathy present in Trish's work. It is also a reminder of how much trauma all of these overdoses have inflicted, how they have broken those circles, and how much repair work we must do.

I want to believe that there are many strong people out there, strong enough to face the powerful systems that seek to dislocate and to disorient us. On the radio I hear stories of protests in Hong Kong, Bolivia, Chile, Lebanon, Ecuador, Colombia. I hear that people are putting their lives on the line for human rights, for autonomy, and for economic justice. Some of us are that strong.

After filling up plates from a taco-salad bar, about twenty people sit around a large square of folding tables. Around the tables are little signs filled with Bible scriptures. The one in front of me reads 1 Peter 5:7, which in the New International Version reads, "Cast all your anxiety on him because he cares for you." The drop-ceilinged room is dominated by a large cross at the front, and the walls are covered with faux-hand-painted signs that read: "His mercies are new every morning" and "Grateful-Thankful-Blessed."

It's a Wednesday night at Vertical 196, a recently opened and much-needed drop-in day center for people who are homeless in Newark. Vertical 196 gives people a place to rest during the day, a place to wash clothes, to take showers. Tonight, the Licking County Champions Network is hosting a Bible study and discussion connected to The Refuge, the free Christian-based treatment program where Johnathon stayed briefly. Chris Gargus, a fifty-something organizer with a full head of curly white hair, welcomes everyone to "this awesome gathering of saints." There are some announcements about free meals and some rumblings about watching out for the police, to which Chris adds, "I'm a little annoyed with the popo right now, running off our homeless people." Heads nod around the table. Chris reads a passage from the New Testament (King James Version), John 1:17—"For the law was given by Moses, but grace and truth came by Jesus Christ." God loves you, Chris says, no matter what, and you are deserving of that love. It's because of God's grace, he adds. Grace is central. "Grace is unmerited favor all the time."

A young man sitting next to me wearing a ball cap and jeans responds to that: "If you don't believe that, look at the people Jesus hung out with. He didn't hang out with the rich and the people in fancy houses." Jesus, he says, hung out with those who were struggling, those who were ostracized, those who were othered. The implication in this space being—he hung out with people like you. A man across from me responds, "That's true!" Others just nod in agreement. But a young woman sitting to the left of Chris rolls her eyes, straightens her shirt and hair in fun as if to say, "You talking about me?! You can't be talking about me?!"

Beth Bline, who helps Chris run these meetings, stands up and starts talking. She is full of light and energy and speaks with a twinge of an Appalachian accent. She is in a zone, infused with some spiritual energy, her faith, I think, taking hold. Her eyes are closed, she's so moved by the message that has quickly lit up this room. Beth talks about grace, how we all need it but don't believe we deserve it. We may need to use our spiritual imaginations, she says, to see and understand this grace. We're all transfixed by her energy, by her joy—and for me, a guy who grew up in a rather staid Presbyterian church, there is almost too much feeling in this room. "It is no accident you all are here tonight," she says. "You are meant to be here." God sees something in all the people who are here, she says, and she calls people out by name, forecasting their futures. Mary, who will one day be a counselor. Steve, a preacher who will write important books.

It goes on like this for over an hour, a Bible study that zeroes in on just a few passages, close-reading them within an inch of their lives, a freewheeling, free-associating discussion. The central message is that even if you do wrong, Jesus still loves you. It's simple. It's nourishing. Chris says, "You wanna put your eyes on God, put your eyes on Jesus . . . The walk with Jesus isn't complicated. We make it complicated." The message must mean something to the people in this space, because no one is forced to stay—indeed, some get up and leave after they eat—but mostly, everyone stays, even the woman rolling her eyes.

One man wearing a black T-shirt waxes eloquent on his experience of twelve-step programs, how he feels alienated when he goes to meetings. It's not for everyone, folks around the table seem to agree. Everyone needs something different. Chris brings up his own struggles and says, "God sees you the whole time. When I got ready to drink I had a decision to make, but I didn't have Jesus in my life. I can empathize with drug use . . . I knew they were bad decisions, but I made them." It's simple, he says: "Jesus loves you. That's what you need to know and that's where we start. We're trying to bring the Word to life here."

The woman next to him giggles and rolls her eyes again. She chats with a young man sitting next to her. Chris is unfazed. He was in the military for almost two decades. When he was training as a paratrooper, he remembers standing on the edge of the payload door, wind whipping around him. He was thinking in those moments that he didn't need God, didn't need anything but the courage to leap. Years later, his teenage son Tyler was at the house of his best friend, Zach, who was playing with a gun, pointed it at Tyler, and pulled the trigger—the bullet hit Tyler; he was gone within minutes. Chris says in that moment he needed God. When his world was turning upside down. When the wind was whipping around him again. His son. His family. His future. That was the moment, he says, that he figured it all out. That was the moment he did something unusual. He forgave Zach. He let it go. He did the unthinkable, crossed into a place most can't or won't. No judgment, only hope. For him, he says, that was the moment when he knew God was really with him. Chris told me later that he knew staying angry wasn't going to help him and it wasn't going to help Zach; if he held on to hate, it would hold them all down forever.

After Zach's sentencing to "indefinite probation," a bevy of TV reporters surrounded Chris. "They were all over it, because they knew that it was a light sentence, and Channel 6 came out, and they go, 'So, what do you think about the sentencing?' It was right before Christmas, and you know what I told her, I said, 'I'm not really concerned about that.' I said, 'This is the season of forgiveness and I'm just going to stay there.' "[4]

Watching Chris in action tonight, it makes sense. Chris continues his lesson despite the responses, despite the incredulity of the woman sitting next to him. He's not here to judge anyone but to love.

It's this lack of judgment—from a man who talks about his own struggles with addiction and the experience of losing his son—and also a persistent desire to keep people alive. Chris admits that the latter has a lot to do with his son.

The Bible study started as a way to reach out to the homeless in a way that wasn't aggressive. Chris likes being able to minister, but it's also about having a meal together. He thinks of this as a kind of harm reduction—meeting people where they are—and even uses the term. And it's one of the reasons he supports syringe exchange. "At first, I was just skeptical," he admits. "Kind of thought, 'Well, isn't that kind of enabling?' But as I studied it, and looked into it and realized how fast people die from fentanyl, I'm like, 'No. No. This is good.' "

Chris says that it's normal for people who are actively using to come to their meetings. "I've had them come out of the street live. It's pretty open for them." But to put up barriers, that doesn't work, he says. "I don't care if they relapsed or not. I want them to stay. I want them to come back. Come back, man. Don't be ashamed. A lot of guys have shame and guilt. I'm like, 'Man, don't be afraid. Don't be ashamed of that.' See, that's what happens. The church sometimes will beat them up, and once they get beat up by the church, they're done." Chris adds, "Jesus always was moved by compassion. He felt empathy for people. He felt that, and I try to do the same thing, and it's not always easy for me to do."

In *Down and Out in Paris and London*, published in 1933, George Orwell immerses himself in the lives of unhoused people in and outside of London between the world wars. He writes about "tramps," men who are not allowed to stay in a shelter more than one night, so they wander and wander on a seemingly endless circuit of despair through the English countryside. He pays close attention to the ways these people are treated and cared for or not. He describes the slumming parties of the early twentieth century; the preachers who went to poor communities, Bible and crucifix in hand, singing in the kitchens of flophouses; and the many churches that would open their doors wide to the poor and slam them shut once they were inside, preach at them, and only then let them go.[5] In one instance the tramps are shut in a church that has offered the requisite tea and two slices of bread. The church leaders make them sit in the balcony. The church service is down below, all the middle-class people in the church pews, and the poor people above. The preacher launches into a sermon, and the tramps jeer and laugh and chatter away. The preacher calls the men "unsaved sinners" and directs the final moments of his sermon at them. "Even while the minister was threatening hell fire, we were rolling cigarettes, and at the last amen we clattered down the stairs with a yell, many agreeing to come back for another free tea next week."[6] Orwell found the whole scene fascinating, noting that this was charity with expectations, charity directed at a people deemed morally inferior. The men were exhausted and dumbed down from poor nutrition, their ceaseless wandering, and the complexities of poverty. But here they were, yelling and screaming, and part of it has to do with how they were being treated. Orwell's attuned to the effect of that, to the damage such expectations can do to a person. And so the people who ordinarily are spoken to but not listened to, they scream, they curse, they claim the space they are in.

In another instance Orwell describes a clergyman who would meet homeless men under Charing Cross Bridge and distribute meal tickets.[7] He said little to the men, had no expectations. Orwell concludes, "The consequence was that, for once, there was genuine gratitude."

This Bible study here in Newark in 2019 is the latter. The table is set. They have opened a door—people get up and leave if they are bored or not interested. They comment and push back. But the effect of this lack of judgment is another kind of harm reduction.

At the end of the evening, Chris and Beth ask everyone what is on their minds, what they want them to pray for. I think it's almost over—I'm getting a little antsy. But then the praying begins. People rise and pray. Sit and pray. Individually, collectively, everyone prays over everyone, putting their hands on them or above them, and with an energetic and empathetic voice, they pray for recovery, they pray that someone can find a home despite a felony charge, they pray for families, for safe childbirth, for rebirth, for life. Then we all stand up and hold hands in a circle and pray that the whole community will be protected and loved. And I'm humbled and ashamed that I had been so antsy, that I had wanted to leave.

Author and psychotherapist Francis Weller notes, "The work of the mature person is to carry grief in one hand and gratitude in the other and to be stretched large by them . . . If I carry only grief, I'll bend toward cynicism and despair. If I have only gratitude, I'll become saccharine and won't develop much compassion for other people's suffering. Grief keeps the heart fluid and soft, which helps make compassion possible."[8] Weller says that when we think of grief, we often think of it as a complete state of despair and "deadness." But, he says, "Grief is wild; it's a feral energy." Grief can fuel a movement for transformation and change. That wild energy can lead people to do things in this world that they did not imagine were possible. Eric's resilience. Trish's resilience. Billy's. Chris's. It must be acknowledged that behind some of it is grief, but that somehow they each have managed to transform that grief into bold and transformative action.

15

Moments of Recognition

During a cold stretch of winter in 1986 when New York City officials moved homeless people off the streets and into Bellevue Hospital, author Barbara Lazear Ascher wrote that such efforts are really about not having to address complicity. "Raw humanity offends our sensibilities," she notes. "We want to protect ourselves from an awareness of rags with voices that make no sense and scream forth in inarticulate rage. We do not wish to be reminded of the tentative state of our own well-being and sanity. And so, the troublesome presence is removed from the awareness of the electorate."[1]

We protect ourselves from humanity, and yet in recent years homelessness in places like Newark, Ohio, has become more apparent: more people are sleeping on park benches, more people standing on corners. The most recent Point-in-Time homeless count—a count of both sheltered and unsheltered homeless people on a given day, as specified by the U.S. Department of Housing and Urban Development (HUD)—claimed about two hundred homeless people in Licking County. Deb Tegtmeyer, executive director of Licking County Coalition for Housing, who has been working hard on this issue here for years, told *The Newark Advocate* that the actual number, according to HUD, was likely 2.5 to 3 times greater than that.[2] And at the end of 2017–18, Newark City Schools counted 300 homeless students in a district of 6,427 students. Many of the homeless are women and children—couch-surfing one night, sleeping in a car the next, staying in a shelter or at a motel the next.

But when we see people who are unhoused, when they are not hidden in the woods, as some people are in rural and Rust Belt Ohio, Ascher writes, "it may be that these are the conditions that finally give birth to empathy, the mother of compassion." Compassion, she believes, must be learned, and it is learned by seeing adversity and learning to empathize with it. Referring to Aristotle's treatise *The Poetics*, she notes, "The object of Greek tragedy was to inspire empathy in the audience so that the common response to the hero's fall was: 'There, but for the grace of God, go I.' " She adds, "Of course, there is a difference. The play doesn't end—and the players can't go home." Indeed, the tragic hero's downfall, due to some fatal flaw like hubris, evokes in the audience not only pity but also fear that the same thing could happen to them but for a change in circumstance. It is a recognition of common humanity. It is what the Greek philosopher called a "moment of recognition."

In late January 2019, local photojournalist Jessica Phelps played cards for hours, late into the night with the men and women at the warming shelter at Jeff Gill's Central Christian Church. A polar vortex had sent temperatures to as low as –7 degrees, with wind chills clocked at –26 degrees. Churches, community-based organizations, and grassroots activists had scrambled to organize low-barrier warming shelters—that is, shelters open to all, regardless of criminal record, mental illness, or substance use. Through Facebook posts and phone calls, two shelters had been established, one at Central and another at Faith United Methodist on East Main Street, just down the street from Trish's corner, the latter organized by the pastor there and the Crossroads Crusaders.

Jessica saw an opportunity to tell a story—the crisis pulled people together but also put a spotlight on a growing concern. So she went, settled in, and played cards. She spoke with people, got to know them, learned their stories, and then she asked if she could take their photos. She had started working on the story early in the fall. One morning she drove around Newark with Jeff Gill, looking for people sleeping outdoors who might want to speak with her. She went to the corner one Saturday and hung out for several hours talking with people—and then the cold came and, with it, the emergency shelters.

Jessica asked people if they wanted to share their stories. If they did, she listened. "I just wanted to be there and let them know I was a person first," she says. She was interested in knowing how big the problem of homelessness was, not to point fingers at people who were homeless or to frame them as a problem. She asked: Where have you been living? How long have you been unhoused? She wanted to humanize these people, these neighbors. "I wanted them to be able to have their story told in their own words, and I told them that's what I was going to do," she explains. "I wasn't going to take their interview and then rehash it and write something else." She wanted them to be able to speak for themselves in the public sphere.

On Sunday, February 17, 2019, *The Newark Advocate* ran a story about homelessness in Licking County alongside Jessica's striking photos, many from that night at the warming shelter but also others based on relationships she established and from visits to homeless camps in the community.[3] Online, the paper published even more photographs.[4] One is of "Cowboy," a man in a wheelchair known affectionately by that moniker because of the hat he often wears. He's at a snowy street corner, gray Ohio sky surrounding him, holding up a cardboard sign that reads, "Homeless vet. Hungry. Happy Holidays. Please help. God bless all." His eyes look away from the camera, thoughtful. There's Larry, smiling on a cot at the shelter, almost as if in mid-joke. There's Seth, formerly homeless and in recovery, volunteering at the warming shelter. There are people in tents, in their homes. We don't see drug use. We don't see stereotypes. Instead, Jessica captures men and women who are struggling but who are willing to tell their stories—men and women who are human and part of this community. She had hoped to dispel rumors that people come to Newark from other places—she has heard folks say Columbus and Mt. Vernon—in order to access services. Her photos helped to document stories from people who have always lived in Newark and Licking County.

The initial response to the article was overwhelmingly positive, especially from the activist circles, Jessica says, from people who had long wanted a spotlight on the problem. But about a week later, rumors spread that police visited and later cleared out camps belonging to some of those photographed, including that of Cowboy. The result of Jessica's work, this labor of love by a thoughtful photojournalist, became the center of a controversy.

Days later, a visibly upset Jen Kanagy, Trish Perry's partner at the homeless outreach, went to the city council.[5] At that point, it was all hearsay, but she confronted the city nonetheless. "It was supposedly our Newark police department," she alleged during the open-comment session. "I'm just saying that was what was reported to us, that threw them out of their camp and bulldozed their camp down." She explained that after learning this, she and Trish spoke with people who confirmed the story and reported that two other sites had been destroyed—she also proposed creating a tent city with adequate facilities.

The public safety director denied the allegations and said that Jen was seeking "fifteen minutes of fame" (she was running for city council at the time).[6] He later corrected his story after reportedly "learning more information from the police department," noting that police had visited the location because of a "reported assault and while there arrested a man on an unrelated warrant."[7] The camp was on private property owned by the Columbus and Ohio River Rail Road Company at the end of Bolen Court, a street just off East Main not too far from the corner. The investigating police officer writes in his report, "I explained to them the issue at hand, that they could not erect tents within the city, especially on property that was not theirs, and live in them."[8] The officer describes piles of trash and a few tents. He gives the people at the camp some time to clean up and leave before a crew from the parks department would arrive. "The first crew members to arrive came in a small dump truck, pulling a trailer with a Bobcat equipped with a small bucket that allowed them to grab items," the report says. They cleared the space and disposed of the tents. The officer writes, "It was discussed with these persons where they could go to access camp sites, whether it be Dillon State Park or the campgrounds along Dry Creek Road." Dillon is twenty miles away, and Dry Creek is about ten.

According to sociologist Alex S. Vitale, breaking up encampments pushes unhoused people toward danger, "into more remote and isolated conditions that leave them more vulnerable to robberies, assaults, and the elements."[9] It's also something that seems to be happening more often in the United States. The National Law Center on Homelessness and Poverty has noticed an uptick in laws around the country that seek to "criminalize behavior associated with homelessness."[10] From 2011 to 2014, for example, bans on camping increased by 60 percent.[11] A survey by the National Law Center on Homelessness and Poverty found that 50 percent of cities surveyed have one or more laws restricting living in vehicles and that, since 2006, there has been a 103 percent increase in laws prohibiting "loitering, loafing, and/or vagrancy."[12]

The timing was, perhaps, a coincidence. Maybe it wasn't the photographs, the story. Maybe. But Jessica Phelps says it hurt. She says she felt like it was her fault: "So you had the activist circles who were really excited about it and okay, now we can come together and figure out how to solve this problem. But then you have the other side of things, where people say, 'Oh, we have this problem, let's just get rid of it. We don't want it. It's ugly, it's unsightly, it's dangerous.' And they complain loudly enough, and that happens. And so if the article hadn't happened, maybe those people wouldn't have known, and they wouldn't have complained."

Now, Jessica says, she's gun-shy even though she knows that she needs to keep documenting the problem. But she's not sure the homeless community would trust her after what happened, and she says she understands that: "I was afraid there would be negative consequences, and I tried to do it as responsibly as possible and it just feels like I failed. These camps got bulldozed in the middle of winter when it was freezing cold outside. My heart broke. I just can't imagine how terrible that must have been."

About a month after the last polar vortex and just days after Cowboy's camp was razed, the temperatures dip again. Another overnight shelter has been set up at Faith United Methodist, and others have gathered to help: a woman named Peggy Ruton who works regularly at the corner, Jeff Gill, Chris Gargus, and Tresa Jewell, the former nurse who delivers food to people living in homeless camps around the area. Outside, I talk to a guy smoking a cigarette who tells me that he ended up homeless because when he returned to Newark after prison, his family was gone. He has a locker at The Main Place and is getting help from counselors there, but he's still spending many nights underneath a bridge. The night before, he says, a fire burned up much of his belongings.

Inside, people are gathered to pray before dinner in the dimly lit tiled basement fellowship hall of the church. In one room, there are about thirty green foldout cots set up, and a table with coffee and hot cocoa. In the next room are Tresa's chicken and noodles, pizza, a platter of veggies, cake for dessert, and, it seemed, more volunteers than guests. I sit down at a booth with Peggy and Jeff and Chris. Jeff tells us that the day before there was somewhere between fifteen and twenty. Tonight he expects the same. The barriers for entry are low, and they aren't taking names.

The talk turns to the camps, to the rumors, and to the confrontation at the city council meeting the other night. We had all read the police report, but as for other incidents, there is no way to know for sure what happened. What is real is that there are some scared people and that there are a growing number of grassroots groups interested in helping. These groups also are skating around the edges of the overdose crisis or are deep in it and approach it from many angles. For example, there's Jeff, the Scout leader and pastor. There's Chris, who says he supports harm reduction because, in his words, "Can't teach them about Christ if they're dead. That's what I tell the churches!" Then there's someone like Peggy, whose sentiments might not align with anyone else's. And yet here they all are, groups that cut across political and ideological lines—doing the work that needs to be done. And here we all are, talking with one another over Styrofoam cups of weak church-brewed coffee, finding common cause.

The truth in this community right now is that there are people sleeping in tents, in cars, in abandoned houses, and they are scared and isolated and some of them use drugs. The next Saturday at the corner, Jen and Trish start handing out flyers that read "Rise up! You matter" spreading word about the next city council meeting—they want to get unsheltered people there to testify. Their efforts are part of a growing movement—Chris's group, Tresa, the Crossroads Crusaders, and the Think Tank. The word spreads that people need to speak up.

At the next city council meeting, the lobby is packed: Allen Schwartz, Trish Perry, Jen Kanagy in her blue nursing scrubs, and C. J. Wills, who is waiting on surgery for a hernia and in pain but still present. As of late, C.J. has had some great news: his advocacy for more support for treatment for meth users has helped encourage the Mental Health and Recovery Board to use a new grant to support people who use and wish to stop. And he's gotten news that he will be getting a new home through Habitat for Humanity—he has so much, he says, and he wants to speak up for those who don't. During public comment, he explains how he became homeless. He is confident and strong. He says he comes from homelessness and then gets to the point: "It's time for Newark to care about its people . . . Stop caring about bridges and streets and buildings and care about people."[13]

It's a learning experience for the council, for everyone in the room.[14] People talk about homelessness in an intimate and personal way. The second speaker, a young man named Daniel Crawford, who also happens to be running for city council, testifies that he was homeless once and that he has never before spoken publicly about it. When he was younger, his family went to a campground; he thought they were on a trip, but they stayed for a long time. Then, he says, his family lived in the Budget Inn. "I know what it's like to live in desperation," he says. "Unconditional compassion—that's the kind of society I want to live in ... It should not be illegal to exist without a home."

Carrying a pile of large photos, Trish walks up to the podium and says confidently that she's just here to confirm what Jen said at the last meeting. People are afraid right now, she says. People from the corner didn't show up for this meeting, but who can blame them? At this point there had been three reported incidents of camps being destroyed or shut down. She asks the council, "Who took the initiative? Who made the complaint?" One man had a child support warrant, she claims. But that's not something to bulldoze a camp over. She then shows the audience the pictures, which she's had blown up, and her voice begins to shake. "We've got to stop talking and start doing," she says, which is essentially her motto.

Bill Hammond, who helped to transform the local St. Vincent de Paul into a significant service organization, says he's getting old and he thinks a lot about judgment. "We'll be judged by how we treat each other," he concludes. Local organizer David Greene then suggests the city issue a proclamation to honor Jen Kanagy and Trish Perry.

And then, after all that, Allen Schwartz speaks. He's fired up. He says people talk about gentrification in Columbus but not here in Newark. "This is a situation where we're creating more homeless. That's the plan, and it looks good in the fancy magazines that we're putting out to try and get people to move to Newark so we can justify the rents on the second floor around the square. And it looks good. It's good business. But it creates homelessness. And only you have the power to deal with that situation. With rent control and any of the number of well-known strategies that they're using in Columbus. But we can't do this unless we're brave enough to have a discussion about gentrification, which is the other side of the moon from development."

He names some of the people most involved in development in Newark, then says, "Y'all are not brave enough to create a community discussion about this. We'll create a community discussion in a second about how beautiful the downtown looks, and thank you for doing that, but it's much more complex than that." There are examples all over the country, he says, but we're not brave enough to look. In some places they create homeless camps and provide services for them. It's not a solution, but it's better than bulldozing tents. "Nothing will work if the development is going to create more homeless people . . . Can y'all say that word? Gentrification," he says slowly, leaning in. "I'm challenging you to have a real conversation about the development that's going on in our city."

Weeks later, over a dozen Newark Think Tank on Poverty members, decked out in their blue T-shirts, show up at the council again and speak openly about their own experiences of being unsheltered, demanding an encampment, a city-sanctioned tent city immediately.[15] Some of the council members thank folks for speaking up.

City council member Jeremy Blake urges quick action, responding to requests for a tent city. "But we need to bring some urgency to it," he says. Newark mayor Jeff Hall does not speak in the meeting, so when it's over, Lesha Farias confronts him, asking why grassroots organizations like the Think Tank had not been invited to meetings on this issue.[16] When Hall says he wasn't in charge, she presses, "You could ask for representatives from each of these grassroots groups. All you have to do is make a phone call. That's the power you have. We don't have that power. We want a voice."

In the wake of the polar vortices and the recognition that the community lacks enough space to shelter people—especially people who use drugs or who, for whatever reason, can't get into a shelter—a warming shelter task force was created to prepare for the future. Deb Dingus, a longtime advocate for the unhoused, organized a meeting to discuss the warming shelter problem and to create a countywide plan.[17] Eventually, this became a task force that has been meeting regularly and includes people with ties to the grassroots community, like Linda Mossholder, a retired teacher and social worker who sometimes wears a shirt that reads: "Your First Mistake Was Thinking I Was a Nice Little Old Lady." Some of these grassroots people have also been invited into a larger discussion about chronic homelessness and about funding a low-barrier shelter. And after those city council meetings, a local grassroots activist named Nancy Welu from the Freedom School in Licking County stepped in and helped organize the people who spoke up, people like Chris Gargus and Trish Perry.

In her 2004 essay "Reclaiming the Commons," author and activist Naomi Klein writes, "We need to be able to show that globalization . . . has been built on the back of local human welfare. Too often, these connections between global and local are not made."[18] She asserts that community-based activists and those with an eye on global questions need to be in conversation with each other: "What is now the anti-globalization movement must turn into thousands of local movements, fighting the way neoliberal politics are playing out on the ground: homelessness, wage stagnation, rent escalation, police violence, prison explosion, criminalization of migrant workers, and on and on."[19] These local movements, she says, need to think about how they fit into the whole. "The goal should not be better far-away rules and rulers, it should be close-up democracy on the ground." She adds, "We need to show some humility where now there is so much arrogance and paternalism. To believe in human diversity and local democracy is anything but wishy-washy."[20]

I'm walking deep into the woods near the Licking River in Newark on a sticky early-summer morning. There's something of a path, but due to weeks of constant spring rain, it's either mud or puddle. I'm wearing waterproof muck boots, but my guide, I'll call him Jeremiah, has only discount-store hiking boots. I keep falling into the puddles like an idiot, splashing mud on my jeans. Jeremiah's movements are much smoother, like he's done this many times. He's patient with me, the novice. We're both carrying bags full of still-warm Styrofoam food containers to a few campsites hidden in these woods, part of a network of campsites back here, a group of people, some of whom I've met at the corner, others at the Champions Network meetings. It's not a place you want to go to alone or without a guide or a connection, but this is where people live. My connection is Tresa Jewell, the army veteran turned rogue social worker, who drives around Licking, Perry, and Fairfield Counties delivering food and supplies to people who live in tents and camps. She's been covering this circuit twice a week for about four years now.

Jeremiah is short, bearded, and in his forties. He got out of prison eight months ago after serving time for a drug-manufacturing charge, a charge that has put up all kinds of roadblocks. At this point, he says, he can only get work off the books. He hasn't been able to find a place to live through local service providers, though he could get a place in a men's shelter. He refuses to be split up from his wife, who was recently diagnosed with lupus. She's his best friend, he says; he can't imagine leaving her. He's been in these woods for two months now and says there are maybe ten other campsites that he knows of.

After about ten minutes of walking, we turn off the main path and go deeper into the woods to a space dominated by a large oak and several cottonwoods. There are a few piles of garbage here and there, and then his tent comes into view, covered by a large tarp.

"You can see my tent's just falling apart at the doors," he says. "Raccoons did that last night, trying to get in. And they got in there, got in the food, and destroyed all kinds of stuff. But you can see how." Despite that, he thinks that they have a decent setup, considering—they have two air mattresses. It's also hidden, a bit of a secret alcove in these woods.

So far, Jeremiah says, no one has been run off of this land. But who knows, it could happen at any moment and he would have to move on. It's a precarious and perilous existence. They hear the coyotes coming through at night. They can't leave any food that raccoons might smell inside the tent. He worries about his wife's safety because the darkness is so real. It can be scary. So, he says, they often gather around a fire at a neighbor's "house"— he uses that noun—and they talk through the night.

"What I notice here, with this group of people that's back there. We all go to these programs. We all go to get help. We're trying to get help. We're not just going down there to eat. We show up for the programming. We do everything we're supposed to do." And then, he says, they get put on a waiting list. "That's what we get, a waiting list."

We walk out of the woods, back to where Tresa is waiting. He asks her to keep an eye out for a new tent on account of the raccoons.

"I'm going to go over to AMVETS," Tresa says, "to see if they'll help me with getting you a tent."

"Thank you so much."

"And I'll look for some more boots."

"Thank you guys," he says, and he turns to walk back into the woods.

We drive away and Tresa says she wasn't worried about my safety back there with Jeremiah. In some of the camps, if they have been drinking and they don't know you, it can be dangerous. She points to a long gash on her arm as we drive out of a parking lot and back toward town.

"Got in a fight, as you see. Guy pulled a knife on me."

"Out in the woods?"

"Yes, sir. He didn't know who I was. He was new to the camp. But as soon as it happened—I mean, I'm conceal/carry. And I always carry a stun gun when I go back. I just stunned him a couple of times, and then my veterans was right out there."

I had noticed the scar the second she picked me up, but I'd been too nervous to ask her about it.

"But if they know you, and you're going to bring them food, they're going to protect you."

They protect her, not because she brings them food, but because she takes them in—sometimes quite literally. Last winter, she tells me, she took people to her house, a small trailer in nearby Buckeye Lake. There wasn't enough room for everyone in her house, so most of them camped in her yard.

She's driving. I'm riding shotgun. Brandon, a slight young man, sits in the backseat. He rides with her when he can in part because she likes the company but also because he can get in and out of places that she can't with her bad knees. Brandon has been homeless—she met him at one of the warming centers last winter—so his knowledge is useful. And she gets a lot of help, she's quick to point out.

"I have a lot of real good friends that help out. If they didn't help me out, I couldn't do it. I'll tell you right now. Like yesterday, I got a call. 'Hey, I'm cleaning out my freezer. I got two turkeys, some chicken. You interested?' I said, 'I'm right there.'"

"Tresa, you've got your own struggles, and you don't have a limousine and a helipad," I point out jokingly.

"No, I sure don't," she laughs. "I get more help from the less fortunate than I do from the people that have money." She gets help from the service organization American Veterans (AMVETS) in nearby Thornville—they give her money for groceries, tents, phone cards, boots and socks, propane, and whatever else people might need.

"Mainly, this is all being done because it helps me cope with losing my son," Tresa admits. She came to this work after her son was killed in a car accident one Christmas Eve. It devastated her so much, she says, that she just wanted to be with him. So she tried to hang herself from a ceiling fan.

"I jumped off for it to hang me, ceiling fan come off, hit me in the head, and I started laughing. 'Okay, good Lord, I got it. I got it.' So then I got to thinking what I could do instead of sitting around moping, because I am terminal. I have cancer and everything else you can imagine. After he died, I started fixing stuff up for underprivileged families that was on low income at Christmas. And every year I'd do their Christmas. The whole family. I paid their rent, I would fill up their car with gas. I got the Christmas trees, all the toys, paid their gas, electric, and rent for that year. Or that month."

She met some veterans who were homeless in Newark. Was appalled by their situation. And, well, here we are driving around Newark with stacks of Styrofoam containers full of Tresa's chicken and noodles. She has been doing this for ten years now.

"I always knew there was homeless, but it's like it didn't register with me," she says.

"Yeah. Out of sight, and all that."

"That's the way it is with everybody, pretty much."

Since Tresa had served as a nurse in a MASH unit, at first she was focusing on "her veterans," as she refers to them, but now she looks for anyone she can help.

There's not much that can stop her. She lost her grandson last year. About a month ago, a family member died of an overdose. And recently her oncologist told her she should have been dead six months ago.

We turn onto Wilson Street, not far from a bridge underneath which a number of people live, and Tresa spots a man walking along. He's carrying some bags. She slows the car and rolls down her window. "Want a meal?"

"Sure," he says.

Brandon passes a couple of Styrofoam containers up to Tresa, and she hands them over. We drive on. She moves on. She keeps on. Seeing the people and the harms around her and doing something.

16

Corners

It's Good Friday, the day the veil was torn in two. It's drizzling, gray. The sky is so low it feels like it could crush you. The last time I visited Billy McCall's place, he was recently out of jail, on medication-assisted treatment, and nervous as all get-out. At that time he was telling me about his friend Chad Baker's overdose death. Today, the death of his friend Tyler Shue, who overdosed the week before, weighs heavy. The funeral home is across the street from Billy's house, but he says he's not going. We look out the open window, into the space between two houses across the street as the parking lot fills and people walk to the funeral home in suits and dresses to pay their respects.

Billy has seen so many die. It's not that this is "just another one"; it's that he doesn't know if he can take it right now. Things are going well for him, even though he is still technically on probation for two charges—a forged check and possession of a pill press. He is remodeling his trailer—pieces of wood and debris litter the floor, and there's a new coat of paint on the walls.

And Billy feels like he's giving something back to his community, to the people who have supported him. He recently recorded an anti-stigma advertisement for the Licking County Health Department that features the head of the health department, the chief of police, and the executive director of Mental Health and Recovery for Licking and Knox Counties.[1] The ad shares information on getting access to treatment and connecting with resources. In his segment Billy says, "No addict wants to be an addict. I promise you that." He has started rebuilding a relationship with his mom. And he has four guys in recovery working with him. His painting company has contracts lined up for weeks. But today he's not working on account of the rain, and he's in a mood—somber, contemplative.

He's keeping a large white pit bull named Laser that belongs to a woman he knows who's serving a six-month sentence in the county jail. When I came through the front door, the dog was jumpy, but now she has calmed down, panting at his feet as he rubs her head and ears and coos, "Good girl." Then he explains, "Another victim of the drug crisis right here! She just wants to be loved."

Billy went to the last board of health meeting and spoke once again. The board members nodded their heads.

"They have to listen because it's public comment," he says. "I think if they had a choice they wouldn't. I think they're probably tired of us coming. But I'm not gonna stop going until they do something different." He says he's not sure they believe in science. "And if they say they made that decision [against supporting the proposed SSP] based on moral values, I still can't see how they came to that decision." He called them out and said he thinks someone is putting pressure on them. It's going to take some new elected officials, he says. One of the board members gave him a hug and said he was proud of him. "Sometimes I think it's condescending. You know what I mean? And sometimes it motivates me."

A few weeks earlier, Harm Reduction Ohio hosted its first statewide conference in Granville, near where a statewide meeting of the Ohio Anti-Slavery

Society was held in 1836.[2] Back then, abolitionists were considered "fringe" or "radical," and this group was met by a mob throwing eggs and punches.[3] Now, in 2019, it was, perhaps, serendipitous that people with lived experience of the drug war—some who use and some who have in the past—were meeting here to strategize forming a union in Ohio. At one point, on a sunny afternoon when the daffodils were just starting to bloom, Sheila Humphrey-Craig set up a mock safe consumption site outside the conference space. She had also set up a table in honor of people who had died of an overdose, people who would have been saved at a safe consumption site. Trish and Billy were there. Trish had to leave early to do the "Lord's work," handing out naloxone and needles at the corner, but Billy was in his element, working the crowd and making friends with everyone there by the end of the weekend. He sat on a panel about law and drug use with Professor Doug Berman from The Ohio State University's law school.

The conference was uplifting for him in many ways, but it exposed gaps in the work he wants to do. He felt like he was preaching to the choir. He wishes more people would come, people from outside the harm-reduction community who know nothing about the issue. People need to keep an open mind and be willing to learn, he says, and be willing to admit when they are wrong. "And admit that the way you've thought of things and the way things were done and the way everybody's been doing things for the past one hundred years with addiction is completely wrong."

Today, on this Good Friday, he stares out the window again. "The funeral is right over here, but I'm, man, I'm just not going to go. It's in ten minutes. The parking lot's filling up over there. There's nothing good to come out of it. I love Tyler and all, but it's gonna be all emotional and there's gonna be a lot of people in active addiction. Tyler knows I'm thinking about him."

It's silent for a beat. I am not sure what to say. There are many ghosts in this room with Billy. There are many people he has lost, and he knows that it did not have to be that way. The room is crowded, the ghostly people fall over each other, they push on the walls and windows, press on each other and memories. Billy wrote while in treatment that he wished there was some sense that could be made of these deaths, Michelle's in particular. "Why her? Why then? I'm sure I'll never understand the answers to those questions, so I guess I'll just pray for acceptance," he writes. Pages later, a list of overdoses, of people who lived and people who died. Death is always so close.

Today, it seems, overdose death is just too close. He says that he didn't realize the funeral was going to be across the street. He googled the address. Too close. And the people he cares about the most, the people he wants to keep safe, the people who are actively using—they are too close at times as well. He's torn, doesn't know where he belongs. It's too risky for him to hang out with them because if he sees people using and seemingly being okay, he might think that maybe he could do it again. At the same time, he says, he feels isolated when going to twelve-step meetings.

"It's all about self-awareness. I got goals and shit I'm working on. It's not worth throwing it away for a shot today."

"That sounds like the twelve steps," I tell him.

"It does."

Billy says that he got a lot of flak from people working the steps when he posted on Facebook that he had received a medical marijuana card. He got a call from someone who said he didn't want to see Billy get shunned.

But then the other night, after Tyler died, Billy spoke up in a meeting. What he said was this: "I'm probably gonna piss a lot of you off and I really don't care right now. If you or someone you know is out there still actively using, see me after the meeting to get some Narcan. If you need clean syringes, I can help you. If you are using, don't get high alone in a bathroom. Use with somebody. Get on a phone call, on a video chat. Do half. Wait thirty seconds and do the other half. It's unrealistic to say that everyone here is completely abstinent. If you're using, don't be ashamed. Don't let anyone in these rooms shame you."

You're not supposed to do anything that might enable people who use drugs, he says. Heads went down, and when the meeting was over, most people took off quickly rather than hang out and smoke and drink coffee. But a couple of people took him up on his offer, and he gave them naloxone. "For people who think I'm enabling, yeah I am. I'm enabling people to live. I'm enabling them to stay healthy. I'm enabling people to get their lives together. You ain't gonna do that if you're dead."

He realizes that he's radical in his approach for this community. "Alcoholics Anonymous. Narcotics Anonymous. 'Get clean. Get off drugs. Get your shit together and shut the fuck up about it.' That's what it says to me. Obviously, it's more complex than that, but that's what it tells me. It may cost me work in the future. It may cost relationships."

Tyler, he says, had been in treatment and had just left. And now this.

"Let's be real," Billy says. "They're just using drugs. People are just using drugs. They're not out raping and killing people." He shakes his head.

Weeks later at a Think Tank event, Billy spoke publicly about why he shares his story. "It's vital," he said, "that every time someone changes their life and puts down the drugs . . . that they share their story." He had done that—again and again—repeating the mantra of harm reduction, to meet people where they're at but not to leave them there.

And then Billy's story got complicated. Dennis Cauchon later said that he knew Billy was in trouble. That he had been doing a painting job in Columbus and had gone into a convenience store to get a Gatorade; it was the same place where he used to buy drugs, and the smell of the store triggered him. He fled the store and raced back to his job. Dennis said when Billy told him that, his heart raced. Still on probation, Billy was in a risky place.

Trish could see it, too, she says. There was a lot going on in his life all at once. Billy's brother, Joe, came for Billy's son Ethan's high school graduation. Billy hadn't seen Joe in thirty-six years. And then there was all the work—the painting, the activism—on top of all the daily duties he had to take care of in order to manage his life. Trish thinks about all Billy had accomplished over the year and says that the thing that made him most proud was that he was able to pay for regular trash pickup. To him, it meant that he was stable. Had a home. Had resources. Was not putting his extra resources toward dope.

But then one day, Trish says, Billy asked for naloxone, asked that she drop it off at his house. He told her it was for someone else.

"You know," she texts me after the incident, "that's when harm reduction gets real."

She called his probation officer, and Billy went in for a urine test. He could not piss because he was so high.

Billy was upset with Trish. And Trish texted me and asked if I thought she had done the right thing.

On the morning of Billy's bond hearing, a transformer blows in downtown Newark. I walk into the eerie, pitch-black basement of the courthouse with Dennis Cauchon wondering whether or not Billy would be getting out. After a cursory pat down from guards, we go to the magistrate's office and learn that court has indeed been canceled. We start walking away—Dennis tells me that he had planned to post bond for Billy. And then, all of a sudden, the power cuts back on. Billy's hearing will happen as planned, so we wait in the hallway together. Trish shows up—she took the day off from work—wearing a pink-and-teal tie-dyed shirt with "Myrtle Beach, South Carolina" written on the breast pocket. She's just spoken with Billy on the phone and learned that as he was sitting in the recreation room at jail last night, the health department commercial he's in played on cable television.

"Now people are saying to him, 'You're on fricking TV and you can't keep your shit together?'"

He told her he wants the Vivitrol shot—which he's had before to block the effects of opioid use—as soon as he can get it, as well as accountability of some sort, which might mean going back to treatment.

We file into a small courtroom for the hearing—the magistrate is seated behind her bench with Billy up on a monitor in green prison scrubs, standing in an empty room. He tells the magistrate that he has a plan of action if he gets a bond. He explains that he's a small-business owner and that he would like to get back to work. But this is a justice system response. This hearing is all about legal minutiae and not Billy, not really. When he says that he's a small-business man, the judge doesn't ask what kind of business he owns or what his exact plans are or what kind of support he needs or who he is or what he thinks is the source of his substance use disorder or his thoughts about the drug war. The state merely requests a bond of fifty thousand dollars. This gets negotiated down to forty thousand.

On the way out Trish says, "Look up how much a rapist gets." She is shocked that the amount is so high.

"I have to go," Trish says, and pauses.

"Recover from a heart attack?" Dennis interjects jokingly.

Billy was released later that day after Dennis posted bond for him. Trish tried desperately, but unsuccessfully, to get him into a suboxone clinic. A couple of days later, the police found him high at a Red Roof Inn. When they tested him, they found cocaine and fentanyl in his system.

The recently renovated Licking County Courthouse is situated in the middle of a lush square of green grass and hardwoods. The limestone building, completed in 1878, has four statues of Lady Justice standing sentinel on each side of the building. In one corner of the square, facing South Park Place, the Ten Commandments are inscribed on stone; in another is a memorial to the victims of 9/11. At Christmastime the whole courthouse building is decorated in elaborate lights, and at the lighting ceremony, the square and roads around it are packed, standing room only. In the summer it's home to the Kiwanis Strawberry Festival.

But the courthouse square is also contested space: Who owns it? Whose ideas does it represent? Who can even be there? Can the unhoused be there? Can they sleep there? In 2016, an old-fashioned, straight-out-of-*The-Music-Man*, white-painted gazebo was removed almost overnight. This upset many folks who believed it was removed because some of the unhoused were sleeping in it.[4] Months later, the county commissioners announced a new lighting system that would be up year-round. Organizers for Newark's first Pride Festival in 2018 petitioned to have the courthouse lit up in rainbow colors in honor of the LGBTQ+ community in the county. The petition was denied.[5] Supporters responded by packing a county commissioners meeting, speaking out in favor of the rainbow lights. The commissioners were unmoved. Ultimately, my friend Sheilah ReStack, an artist and activist, gathered dozens of people around the courthouse on the first night of the Pride Festival and created their own rainbow with flashlights and colored gels.[6]

Over a century earlier, another sort of confrontation: After Ohio passed a law in 1908 permitting counties to vote on whether or not they would permit alcohol sales, Licking County voted to be dry. At the time, Newark was a major producer of glass, which included beer bottles. Whenever you drank a beer in one of Newark's saloons, it was customary to break the bottle on the ground afterward. Beyond that, many of Newark's residents were recent immigrants from countries where drinking beer was part of the culture. Thus the town was an island, surrounded in part by older farming communities that had voted for the alcohol ban. The tension was real. On the morning of July 8, 1910, the mayor of nearby Granville deputized a group of detectives to shut down Newark's speakeasies. Things did not go as planned, as the community turned on the detectives. Deputy Marshal Carl Etherington, a seventeen-year-old white man from Kentucky, shot a former police captain named William Howard and was then locked up in the jail.

When Howard died from his wounds, a mob used a large piece of train rail to knock down the jailhouse door. Etherington was dragged through the streets to the courthouse lawn, where a decent-sized tree could not be found, so they hanged him from a telegraph pole on the corner of Second Street and South Park—not too far from where the Ten Commandments are today.[7]

In 1914, four years after the lynching of Carl Etherington in Newark, the U.S. Congress passed the Harrison Narcotics Tax Act, chapter 1 of which describes it as "An Act to provide for the registration of, with collectors of internal revenue, and to impose a special tax on all persons who produce, import, manufacture, compound, deal in, dispense, sell, distribute, or give away opium or coca leaves, their salts, derivatives, or preparations, and for other purposes." In some ways, this is where the drug war begins—this ban on opium and cocaine.[8] Economist Fadhel Kaboub told me once, "War on drugs is a war on the wrong thing. When you're facing a public health crisis, you need public health solutions. The root causes of drug abuse are economic, psychological, social . . . If you only deal with the problem from a criminal justice side, you're making it worse because you're allowing the other root causes to ferment even more." This approach has not worked—it has only helped construct our prison-industrial complex. Ten years after the Etherington lynching, nationwide prohibition of alcohol began and led to an increase in organized crime as well as to deaths from poisoned moonshine and bathtub gin—not all bootleggers were experts, and some drinkers ended up with denatured industrial alcohol or wood alcohol.[9]

On a warm July day, I walk into Judge Thomas Marcelain's courtroom, an homage to the neoclassical with a gorgeous rotunda, gilded false Corinthian columns, and heavy light blue window drapes.[10] The judge, wearing a black robe, has a full head of white hair and a closely shaven round face. His demeanor is stern and then some. The "revocation hearing" has already started, and the judge is asking Billy if he has anything to say. Billy says that he made some bad decisions in the last six weeks that led to his probation violation and that he hopes the court will take into consideration all else that he has done over the past year.

When Trish speaks, she notes that Billy has worked especially hard to remodel his house. Judge Marcelain interrupts her, saying, "I think that's the residence where he was arrested for making counterfeit substances"—in other words, the place where a pill press was found.

"That's his—that's his home," Trish says.

"That the house you're talking of that he was maintaining?"

"Yes," she replies, a bit flustered, off her game. She explains that Billy had cleaned up and was able to file his taxes for the first time in years. For Billy, she knows, these were major accomplishments.

When Dennis stands to speak, he begins by joking, "If anyone should be pissed at Billy, it should be me, because his team did a great job painting my house inside and out; however, it's not finished." He adds that he also bonded him out, but that he's not mad about that either, because he knows about opioid use disorder. He points out that it takes many tries for people to be able to have a long period of sobriety. Like Trish, Dennis says we should focus on Billy's upward trajectory: "What he accomplished in the last year is just extraordinary and his kindness is extraordinary. Just like if you're on a diet or trying to commit, it's not a linear line. You're going to have many, many setbacks and, in my view, it's a mistake to give up on him."

"Who's given up?" Marcelain responds.

"Well if—"

"Nobody's given up on him that I can . . . I don't see anybody giving up on Mr. McCall."

"If he goes back to treatment . . . or, I'm sorry, to prison."

"That's not giving up on anybody. That's a consequence of his actions. That doesn't mean anybody's given up on him by any means."

"Right. But you have discretion."

Marcelain says he's never given up on anyone.

Dennis tries to get a word in edgewise and eventually sputters out, "Sending him to prison—"

"We can disagree," Marcelain says.

"—is not giving up on him?" Dennis asks, incredulous.[11]

After all the testimony, Judge Marcelain speaks directly to Billy: "Mr. McCall, you obviously get your skills from your mother, I would say, as far as community outreach and organizing and care and compassion for others." He then riffles through the letters and notes the number of people who wrote. He says the letters all seem very similar, asking for long-term treatment and drug court. He cites one that reads, "I'm not sure he's been given a fair chance."

"Wow, not been given a fair chance," Judge Marcelain says in a condescending tone. "I can't give a pass to a person because of their good works." He points out that he has seen Billy in his courtroom a lot over the last ten years. "It insults me that I'm supposed to treat him differently than I would a homeless guy who's done the exact same things, who's never spoken in front of a public group, or the board of health, or Newark City Council, who doesn't have powerful friends, who doesn't have, you know, relatives who run committees of concerns or organizations."

Judge Marcelain then asks, What is it that has caused Billy to relapse? Was it all the pressure of people depending on him? "I'm not sure what it is," he concedes. And then, seeming to respond to Dennis: "I'm not a credentialed treatment provider. I'm not a nurse or an LSW. I don't lead groups that advocate for homeless people or drug addicts. I'm only responsible for supervising a caseload of one hundred and fifty active criminal cases, [and] overseeing a few hundred other [cases for people] who are on [probation]." He then lists all the addiction recovery services available to someone like Billy in Licking County and points out that the county is better served than most places. His point, it seems, is that Billy wasn't taking advantage of assistance available to him. With that, he sentences Billy to eleven months in prison.

About a half hour later, we gather just down the hall in the courtroom of Judge David Branstool, the judge presiding over Billy's other case. Again, Billy's lawyer speaks on his behalf.[12] This is the same courtroom where Tommy Kosto—the man the court held responsible for the death of Billy's friend Chad Baker—was tried and sentenced two years before.

Judge Branstool asks Billy, "What do you think the problem is here? You are gonna kill yourself. You'll be dead. And if I had to guess, I would venture to say that Judge Marcelain probably decided to send you to prison in part because he's worried you're going to OD and die. So what are we supposed to do? I get the drug epidemic. It's a public health crisis. And the criminal justice system doesn't deal with it very fairly or justly. I get it. But some people are so sick that they're contagious. So what would you expect to have happen to somebody who's done what you've done? Is there any more treatment that's available?"

"Yeah, I was screened and accepted back into The Landing," Billy replies. "It's a twelve-week program. I was hoping to get sentenced back into there and get a chance to get back on Vivitrol and take that ninety days and try to build a foundation and go back through and look and see what I missed over the last year that sent me back out."

"Right. There's no magic treatment program. You gotta want it. Right?"

"Absolutely."

"Going through a program again, what's different about it?"

"Just if I was to go through the program again, I can take that time and utilize all the counseling and the therapy and everything."

"Okay, right. I get it. You can do all that stuff in prison, too, right? Have you been to prison?"

"Yes, Your Honor."

"How many times?"

"Twice."

"Right, right, right. Do other folks want to say something? Does anybody want to say anything?"

Chris Hawkins, an ally of Harm Reduction Ohio with a head of thin, curly white hair and round spectacles, stands up to speak. "Your comment about drug use being contagious struck me. And I think that's true. The other thing that's contagious is people working hard to try to get themselves back to where they need to be." Billy is not just anybody, Chris says, not just somebody who got busted for violating probation or for using. "That's not all of him. That's only a part of him. The other part is all the people that he's dragging with him." He is all the people he hired, the people working with him, the people in recovery he's friends with. The good work that he has done, that is contagious, too."

"I don't disagree with what you're saying," Judge Branstool responds. "I run a drug court . . . And I mean it's a complicated situation. Human behavior is complicated. I get it. I appreciate your remarks."

Trish stands up and pulls out a rumpled piece of paper, a letter from Billy's girlfriend, Samantha, who was caught with Billy and is currently in jail:

> I'm writing on behalf of Billy McCall and his probation violation. I'm not going to make any excuses up for his sick behaviors or choices here, lately for himself and for this society. I'm not here to waste your time or mine. There was a time my hope was completely broken and all I had to hold on to was a program that you've created—the [drug court] and the true inspiration that Billy gave me every day. I know that Billy wants to help. He just needs accountability back in his life. Billy needs and wants to learn and love himself again.
>
> So if you could please take that into consideration and let him get into an inpatient program into your drug court rather than prison sentence. I buried too many of my loved ones and I'm not ready to bury an-

other one. The community loves Billy. He does a lot of love and service for those that are in need. I've watched him hand out meals to the homeless and set up homeless outreach every Saturday. And he speaks for Harm Reduction Ohio. He's a huge motivation to so many. So and as you know, people make mistakes. And it takes a lot to hit rock bottom and become completely bankrupt to all aspects of our lives. I truly do hope that you will take this into consideration. Thank you for your time.

Then Dennis stands up and says that imprisonment increases a person's risk of overdose in the first days they get out.[13] He says that many people will say that jail saved them, but that we don't get to hear from the people for whom it did not. But by then, it all seems decided.

That's not lost on Judge Branstool. He has been running a drug court for ten years and has lost people. He tells Dennis he doesn't disagree. "Does jail or prison save anybody's life? Maybe it might extend it. It might make it more difficult for people to get a fatal dose of a lethal drug. Not impossible. I'm not naive enough to think that there's no drugs in jail or prison. But part of the analysis here is at what point do we say, 'Look man, we've invested so much and so many resources into trying to get you on the right track and keeping you there that it's denying our ability or minimizing our ability to help other people.' Especially when you've been through this program and that program . . . It really is a triage kind of a thing. So we only can, we only have so many resources. We only have so many probation officers that it becomes a situation where we say, 'Okay, where can we help the most people do the most good?' And when you've been an addict for what, twenty years?" He pauses. "I mean, at some point we just have to kind of redivert our resources into people who we think we can help. Or who haven't had the benefit of all those programs and things like that. Right? I mean, you understand that?"

After we walk out of Judge Branstool's courtroom and stand in the hallway, Trish is upset. She wonders why the judge said they needed to redirect their resources. Can't we try to help everyone? she asks. "I don't know why they choose one over the other." And then she cries.

Dennis immediately leaves the courthouse and drives back to his office above the coffee shop. Sits down and writes a story titled "HRO Syringe Program Advocacy Director Billy McCall Sentenced to Prison for Addiction to Heroin" for the Harm Reduction Ohio website.[14] Dennis rarely hides his opinion. In this case, though, his tone is particularly acrid. Dennis reports that Billy was in court for having a "dirty" urine test last month. "Billy, one of the smartest and hardest working men you'll ever meet, had been sober for nearly a year but started using again in June. His 11+ months of sobriety was Billy's longest period of sobriety since he dropped out of high school in 9th grade to work, use drugs and deal them." He points out the hard work he did over the course of the last year. And that, now, "Billy appeared in court in a prison jump suit, shackles and paper slippers. This is the stigmatized life of peaceful people who are addicted to opioids." Dennis writes that what really happened was that "the court sent a drug addict to prison for being a drug addict."

He points out that once Billy is out of prison, he could have three years of court control, which means of course that he can't fail any drug test when the process starts again. In a Facebook post sharing the blog article, Dennis writes, "Harm Reduction Ohio judges people by the content of their character, not the contents of their urine."

Billy's charges—having a pill press, trying to pass a check—are about drug use. They are about not having the money to buy drugs. There is no doubt that these judges must have some compassion fatigue—who would not in this situation? But is it even fair for us to burden the system, to burden them, with the task of helping people with substance use disorder?

"Every Overdose Is a Policy Failure"

ordon Casey meets me at my hotel in downtown Vancouver, Canada, and we walk over to the Downtown Eastside together, along West Pender Street, cutting across Victory Square. Across the square, actually a tiny triangular park that slopes down toward Hastings Street, is the Victory Square Cenotaph, a monument to the 59,544 Canadians who died in World War I. Facing Hastings Street, the granite pillar reads: "Their name liveth for evermore." Facing Hamilton: "Is it nothing to you." Facing Pender: "All ye that pass by."

The park is quiet, still. It's a sunny day. A few people are asleep on benches.

"I wonder if we'll put up memorials to all the overdose victims, if we'll recognize this as the health disaster that it is one day?" Gordon asks aloud. He points out that the number of dead honored by the cenotaph is far fewer than the over seventy thousand Americans who died of a drug overdose in 2017.[1]

"I wonder," I mutter, "for the drug war."

We walk across to West Hastings and after a few blocks, after we pass a mural in honor of the Ohio-raised activist-poet Bud Osborn, Gordon stops by a man leaning over in the middle of the sidewalk. He asks the man if he's okay, gives him a little nudge, and sees that he's still breathing.

"I always like to check to make sure people are okay." But he also says he's careful to give people their space and respect.

This community of about eighteen thousand people is one of the poorest not only in Vancouver but in urban Canada in general.[2] Over the years, the Downtown Eastside has become a nexus for all kinds of harm-reduction interventions, with multiple methadone clinics, a bank for the unhoused and people who use drugs, clinics offering heroin-assisted treatment, a community center for women and indigenous people, and the headquarters for Vancouver Area Network of Drug Users (VANDU), a community center with couches and a chill-out room. With its SRO housing, the neighborhood attracts people who are poor and who use drugs. In some ways, the community is a safe space for them, a place where they can live without judgment and have access to resources.

For my first visit to the Downtown Eastside, Gordon hands me off to Gerald "Spike" Peachey, who'll be my community guide. Today happens to be "cheque day," and as Spike says wryly, "Everyone's a millionaire today!" Combine that with the dry weather, and the sidewalks for several blocks are packed with people using drugs or leaning over, those on stimulants shaking a bit. It is, at first glance, overwhelming. Spike walks quickly, and I struggle to keep up with him and pay attention to the world around me. He takes me from one safe consumption site or overdose prevention site to the next. On one alley he points out an outdoor space for people who smoke their drugs to hang out.

Spike has a mustache and long, straight black hair, topped by a black ball cap. His face is long, animated—he reminds me of Frank Zappa, thin and quirky and brilliant. As he shuffles up the sidewalk, he greets everyone he recognizes admonishing, "Stay safe!" And when there's a lull in our conversation he says, "We don't have an overdose crisis. We have a stigma crisis."

He repeats this phrase several times throughout the day. He's wearing gray slacks and a button-down like he's fighting that stigma as hard as possible.

"Once you're labeled poor or drug seeking, you get treated like shit," he says. "We're not human, we're just drug users." He is more than one thing, he says.

His life has been complicated. Spike was hit by a distracted driver on September 5, 2007, and spent ten months in a hospital suffering from numerous fractures including to his back and skull. The pain was intense and debilitating. He was on oxycodone and methadone for two years and then was cut off and went to the streets and did whatever he could to support his habit. Now he runs an anti-stigma campaign in his community, which includes taking nurses, doctors, and journalists like me around, and he also works at Brave Technology Coop as an outreach specialist. In 2018, he received the Nursing Excellence Award from Nurses and Nurse Practitioners of British Columbia.[3] Spike is more than one thing, more than one life, more than one experience.

The current overdose crisis in Vancouver is really the second one in the city's history. The first was in the 1990s. At the time, a drug users union formed in response to the rising number of deaths, especially in the Downtown Eastside neighborhood. The union members organized and protested publicly, in ways that no one expected drug users to do. They planted a thousand white crosses in Vancouver's Oppenheimer Park, disrupted city council meetings, and started underground safe injection sites. As journalist Travis Lupick describes in his thorough and important chronicle of the VANDU, published in 2017, the people who risked so much to make these things happen are little known outside of certain circles.[4] When Lupick visits Ohio, he has trouble finding anyone who knows who Bud Osborn was—he was an activist, the poet laureate of his Vancouver community, and a key advocate for a safe injection site. Born in Battle Creek, Michigan, but raised in Toledo, Ohio, Osborn wrote of and for his community in his poem "1000 Crosses in Oppenheimer Park":

Our purpose is to live in community
and community is care
care for one another
care for those least able to care for themselves
care for all
care in action
and there is no one to care
if you do not care[5]

Eventually, in 2003, the city's underground safe consumption sites became Insite, North America's first safe, legal injection site, a place where, as of writing, no one has ever died of an overdose.[6] That's saying something, given that in 2018 alone there were 189,837 visits to Insite by 5,436 individuals.[7] People bring their own drugs—the site has an exemption from the government—and inject while being monitored by nurses with naloxone and oxygen at the ready. Insite can also be a gateway to treatment if people are interested: there's a withdrawal management and treatment program above the facility.

But since fentanyl and its analogs arrived in 2016, the overdose rate in Vancouver has shot up over 80 percent and there has been an even more urgent need to figure out ways to keep people alive.[8] Once again, activists responded by setting up their own emergency facilities, calling them overdose prevention sites (OPSs), in places where people who use drugs frequent. Even in a country with universal health care, it took activists to launch this public health response. One person I spoke with referred to them as "death prevention sites" or "lifeguard stations." Now there's a network of at least seven OPSs in the Downtown Eastside and over forty in British Columbia. These low-barrier sites, run mostly by people who use drugs and their allies, offer a quiet, dry space off the streets for drug use with naloxone at the ready. Most sites are for intravenous drug users, but there are also sites for people who smoke. Since December 2016, according to the Portland Hotel Society,

"OPS have facilitated over 130,000 visits and reversed over 1,000 overdose events, without a single fatality."[9]

After Spike takes me to visit the lobby of Insite, which feels a bit like a doctor's office waiting room, we move on to the Molson Overdose Prevention Site (MOPS), run by the Portland Hotel Society, the same nonprofit that runs Insite. Molson is set up in an old corner bank; along the walls are eight metal tables below a gorgeous vaulted ceiling. It's less medicalized than Insite, and with its white walls and wood floors reminds me of a yoga studio. Doug Dees, who works here, says that MOPS relies on the expertise of people who use drugs, who better understand overdose than "any Joe Blow, white middle class, white bread, is gonna have." MOPS's status here is temporary, though, he says. Its three-year exemption ends this year—but the problem of overdose persists. Dees says that will just send people back to the alleys and the back rooms, and more will die. He asserts that OPSs keep the proverbial bathtub from overflowing.

The real problem is that there is no safe supply—it's a refrain I heard time and again in Vancouver. As long as there's prohibition, there will be no control over what enters the drug supply. Nothing is regulated. People who use drugs are at the whims of the market and of drug dealers who are not chemists by trade. Dennis Cauchon's research on carfentanil in Ohio underscores this point about the iron law of prohibition.

As Doug and I talk in the alley outside MOPS, a steady stream goes in and out of the site. Young people. Old people. People who are homeless. People who are housed.

"Does it ever get to you?" I ask.

"Of course it does. My mom passed away in 2016 and my dad passed away in January. And I'm finally able to grieve, but I don't know how to grieve anymore because I've lost so many people over the years."

He says that in the past sixteen years of doing this work, he has lost at least two hundred people, people he knew and loved and respected. The juxtapositions of his life haunt him as well—the people suffering through cold winters standing in doorways waiting for a warm space to open up. Just knowing that people he cared about were suffering. "I would go home and feel guilty 'cause I had my fuzzy blankie with an adult beverage," he says.

Spike jumps in and says we have to keep moving—there are still many places to go. So we move. To VANDU's headquarters, to Brave's headquarters, to another OPS. After a couple of hours he asks, "Are you hungry?"

I am. I'm also tired and need a minute to sit and process all I've seen and heard. So we stop at a diner called Save on Meats and belly up to the counter.

As soon as we sit down, Spike asks, "Have you been trained to use naloxone?"

I have, but not with the intramuscular kit he has—it's all needles and vials and intimidating to an amateur like me. I've been trained with a nasal spray (Narcan) that reminds me of the allergy medicine Flonase I have to take in the spring. Spike walks me through the steps. A few people in a booth behind us stare as he pulls out the needle and one vial. Spike ignores them, rushing through the steps two times, and then asking me if I have any questions. Over the sound system in the background, Dolly Parton's voice croons, "I can see the light of a clear blue morning."

I'm about to ask him to go over the part where you pull the drug up from the vial when Spike says, "I need to go get my medicine. I'll be back in about fifteen minutes."

He dashes out as Dolly sings, "Everything's going to be all right. / It's gonna be okay," and I watch as he heads across the street to Providence Health Care's Crosstown Clinic, which claims to be the only clinic in North America that provides prescription diacetylmorphine, a.k.a. heroin, as part of a heroin-assisted treatment (HAT) program.[10] One of the doctors there, Dr. Scott MacDonald, explained to me later that the Swiss have been doing this since 1994. Now, he says, the United States and Canada are in the midst of a health emergency, and yet, even after multiple randomized control studies have proven that HAT is safe and effective and certainly cost-effective, Crosstown is still the only place offering it. Select patients come in every day for injections under the supervision of medical professionals. In Canada, some clinics are now offering the opioid hydromorphone (Dilaudid) for a similar treatment, but Crosstown is the only clinic offering prescription diacetylmorphine, the real deal. Decades of research from Europe and Canada suggest that it works for people who do not respond to methadone or buprenorphine. Dr. MacDonald says that research also shows that HAT is associated with reduced mortality, property damage, and violent crime, and reduces taxpayer burdens. His patients' lives are stabilized because they are no longer out seeking illicit drugs. There should be widespread support for this treatment, he says. And yet there isn't—even amid a crisis.

There are only two hundred people in the Crosstown HAT program. Spike counts himself among that lucky few and has come to Crosstown up to three times a day for his dose for the past eight years.[11] It's the only treatment that has really worked for him, he says, and he believes it has saved his life by giving him access to a regular and safe supply. He is now able to work part-time and is no longer, in his words, "wheelin', dealin', and stealin'." Research bears this out. In the first study at Crosstown, conducted from 2005 to 2008 and published in *The New England Journal of Medicine* in 2009, researchers from the University of British Columbia found that HAT was superior to methadone.[12] With HAT, Dr. MacDonald explained to me, "you have better attention and care, and it reduced illicit drug use and accessing of the illicit opioids."

That's just it—HAT gets people in the door, people like Spike, who says that he hadn't had regular access to health care for years until he started at Crosstown.[13] Now he does. And, Dr. MacDonald points out, no one in the program has died from an illicit drug overdose. Some people use less and less heroin or transition to oral treatments, or to methadone. And some stop using altogether.[14]

It's difficult to move public opinion on something like this, but

Dr. MacDonald is hopeful and sees HAT as key to the larger project of harm reduction. "It is an incremental step towards safe supply and decriminalization or regulation of opioids and substances," he says. "There's no risk to the public. There's no drug that's being diverted." Besides, it is so much cheaper to provide HAT than to deal with the social costs—from incarceration to emergency services to theft—that can be connected to the use of illicit opioids.

When I talk about HAT with people back home in Ohio, some are shocked and others feel sorry for folks who must go to a clinic to get medicine three times a day. But the alternative? For someone like Spike, it could be a whole lot worse. Spike says this treatment has saved his life and I believe him. In and around the Downtown Eastside there are many IV drug users injecting illicit fentanyl. There are people overdosing and dying. Spike circumvents those hazards by safely injecting a pharmaceutical-grade drug.

When Spike returns to the diner from getting his medicine, our food is ready. I devour a cheeseburger, and he polishes off a plate of fries and a milkshake. We talk about fast food, the weather, about his plans for doing more tours around the community as a way to fight stigma.

Then he says, "You ready to go? There's more to see."

Coco Culbertson, senior manager of programs at the Portland Hotel Society, reminded me that none of the harm-reduction programs established in Downtown Eastside came without a fight. "Activists in this community twenty years ago," she says, "dragged [those in power] kicking and screaming, and publicly shamed people in order to get anything done." It took years of educating voters and citizens and implementing programs without permission. It took activists willing to risk their freedom in order to protect the ones they loved.

I will admit that when I first walked into an OPS, I felt uncomfortable (all those needles and all that blood). But then when I took a deep breath and observed what was actually happening—people working together, wiping seats down with disinfectant, distributing sterile syringes, looking out for one another, helping one another—I realized I was looking at an empowered community.

Few people are more responsible for fostering this empowered community than the folks who helped organize VANDU, like Bud Osborn, Dean Wilson, and Ann Livingston. Ann, in particular, is sort of a grande dame of activism in this neighborhood. After some back and forth, she meets me in the lobby of the swank Parq Hotel and Casino. She's helping check in people from the Canadian Association of People Who Use Drugs (CAPUD) who are attending a conference organized by the British Columbia Centre on Substance Use.[15] The juxtapositions are uncanny—the gorgeous lobby with a waist-high glass table in the center covered in fresh cut flowers and Livingston, sitting in a high-back chair in jeans and a dark blue polo, a large bag of naloxone in front of her, and a pile of papers in her hand.

"Well, we're going to have users here, so I just want to make sure everyone's safe. Do you need some?" she asks.

"No, Spike gave me some already," I tell her.

"Oh, Spike's good!"

And then a group walks in, lots of jeans and leather jackets, one woman in a camo crop top. A knowing smile comes across Ann's face. She shouts, "Here are the drug users!"

They all turn and walk over to her—lots of hugs and hellos. She tells me that these are some of the folks from the drug users union who have come to speak at the conference and, more important, to hold people accountable and to have their seats at the table. In many ways, they do have a seat at the table.

Right now, though, they are struggling with the overdose deaths. CAPUD is arguing for a safe supply—for better access to heroin and not fentanyl.[16] It will be another struggle, but it is a struggle Ann seems ready to support. In a concept document published in February 2019, CAPUD writes, "In the midst of the worst overdose epidemic in Canada's history, 11 people are dying every day. Most of the deaths are related to the rise of fentanyl and its analogues adulterating the illicit drug market."[17] This is a human rights crisis, the writers argue, precipitated by a drug policy that dehumanizes people, and a regulated drug supply would help to address this. In my own "baptized in Just Say No" mind, this document, this idea, seems at first beyond radical. And yet, there is overwhelming evidence to support it, not the least of which is Spike and his vibrant and beautiful life.

Ann Livingston has the social and cultural capital to help the safe supply effort—she has the look of a somewhat-crunchy baby boomer, is kind almost to a fault, and is the smartest person in the room. She's also absolutely funny. When she's checking people in to make sure they have a room in the hotel, she carries on a running conversation with me about her own work as a community organizer, and how to do that work with a stigmatized group like people who use drugs. She says she learned a lot from Chicago-based activist John L. McKnight's idea of asset-based community development, building on a group's available skills and potential.[18] One second she's talking theory, and the next she's cross-checking her own list of attendees with the hotel's list. She's trying to read the names and, exasperated, says, "What the hell happened to twelve-point font!"

Then she catches herself, takes a deep breath, and gazes across the hotel lobby as two tall and pouty blond women in heels—one carrying a toy dog—flounce by. She chuckles, self-aware enough to see the humor in this scene, two worlds colliding.

People who use drugs are rarely given the space to organize and to build fellowship—when they do so, it disrupts so many middle-class assumptions. The challenge that the Newark Think Tank on Poverty faces—to open up a space and to admit anyone into it—is similar. Ann says she learned early to try to do some basic things: Keep out of the way. Have something for everyone who shows up (VANDU offered five dollars and a snack). Meet on Saturdays. Listen to their words and then use them. Be observant and take notes. (Use big paper so people can see what you're doing and can correct you). And always start by asking: What do you think a drug user group could accomplish?[19]

"And then you have to ask, 'What are the issues?' and then it's just a tsunami," she says. She pauses, then says, as if to reiterate, "So you have to listen, and the facilitator should have a strong middle-class sense of 'No one should take that shit!' Then you discuss and figure out a solution, and then you act."

Two days later, in a packed conference room at the same hotel, Judy Darcy, a member of British Columbia's legislature and the province's first-ever minister for mental health and addiction, is giving an opening address to over six hundred conference attendees. She's talking about the government's role in addressing the overdose crisis.

A tall man with a shock of white hair stands up and shouts, "It's not good enough, Minister."

Darcy gets quiet.

The man continues, "This is an emergency health situation without an emergency health response. Please to the government—stop gaslighting us. Meet with drug users. Give us a proper seat at the table. This is not working. It's feeling so grim right now. We met with you last year, and one of the people in that meeting is now dead . . . We are not on an emergency response footing. We are on a status quo footing. And I beg you to please change that."

Lots of applause.

The man is Garth Mullins, a journalist and activist from Vancouver. *Crackdown*, the groundbreaking podcast he hosts, centers on the experiences of people who use drugs as correspondents from the front lines of a war.[20] It considers them the most important people in this crisis, and they are also the ones doing the reporting. The podcast also centers on a healthy dose of righteous, justified anger. Anger may not always win you friends, and sometimes it will not help build alliances, but the reality is that sometimes anger comes from a place of truth. I'd heard Garth speak the day before about lukewarm government responses, about the civil disobedience of people trying to save lives. "Any attempt to address this must start with smashing white supremacy," he said. Colonization, racism, and overdose are wrapped up together. These things are, and should be, anger provoking.

As I listened to Garth, my mind turned to Ohio, where people are dying from unintentional drug overdoses, from languishing in prisons and jails, from the repercussions of being incarcerated, from living in a country that pays lip service to care. All of these things can be fixed. Sometimes anger is justified. And in Canada, it seemed to me, some people are angry. Which is an appropriate response. But it's not a response I've seen often enough in the United States.

After witnessing Garth Mullins speak out so eloquently and with such force, I texted my wife: "37 million people live in Canada. 4k overdose deaths in 2017. 12 million people in Ohio. 5,111 overdose deaths in 2017. Why are we not freaking out?"

She responds: "Because we don't believe in the social contract anymore." A few minutes pass and she texts again: "I'm not sure what that means, but it sounds smart."

She's right, though. As European Enlightenment thinkers John Locke, Jean-Jacques Rousseau, and Hugo Grotius described it, the theory of the social contract says that we give up some of our individual freedoms in order to be protected by a government that is, essentially, us. But we're not protecting each other anymore—if we ever have. There are certainly outliers— this book is full of them—but until we all recognize the crisis we're in, we're putting Band-Aids on a bullet wound. And as Bruce Alexander, Lisa

Roberts, and Spike Peachey explain, the problem is not the overdoses, it's dislocation.

When I moved about the Downtown Eastside neighborhood with Spike, he always introduced me as "Jack from Ohio," and some of the people I met would express genuine concern and sorrow for what is happening there. Coco Culbertson at the Portland Hotel Society was one of them. She told me that she studied with Bruce Alexander at Simon Fraser University and that his work has had a profound influence on her.

"I do believe that we are psychosocially disconnected," she said. "You see it everywhere you look." She called what was happening "this monster" and stumbled over what term to use. She's said *opioid crisis* and *overdose crisis*. "I think I've said all the things. I'm sick of all of them, and none of them feel appropriate, to be quite honest. It feels like genocide to me. It feels like structural genocide against a certain population, but I usually say *opioid overdose crisis* because that's what it is."

When I first exchanged emails with Gordon Casey, I was surprised to notice this line of text underneath his name and contact info: "The Brave Technology Coop is situated on unceded xʷməθkwəy̓əm (Musqueam), Skwxwú7mesh (Squamish), and Səl̓ílwətaʔ/Selilwitulh (Tsleil-Waututh) territory." It includes a link to a map of the world. You can type your location in and discover whose lands you are currently on. And indeed the Downtown Eastside, where Gordon works, has a large number of indigenous peoples (and across Canada, First Nations people have the highest rate of overdoses).[21] This was my first encounter with widespread use of "land recognition"—an acknowledgment and recognition of history, of violence, and of genocide. After attending a few lectures in Vancouver, I learned that it's considered common courtesy to say that you're about to speak on lands that are unceded, on lands that are the home to the Musqueam, Squamish, and Salish people.

What would this sound like in the United States? What would we say?

How could we acknowledge the brokenness that some of us who are so privileged, like me, simply skirt past on our daily walks? A land recognition acknowledgment is not about guilt or about living in the past. It is about living in a present in which we come to terms with the trauma of the past, acknowledge it, and use that acknowledgment to try to imagine a way forward. I am writing from Ohio. I respectfully acknowledge that I am writing on the lands of the Wyandot, Shawnee, Delaware, and Seneca-Cayuga nations, and the ancestral people who built the Octagon and Great Circle Earthworks. I acknowledge this history. I acknowledge that there is much we do not speak of. I acknowledge that we have work to do.

For all of the harm-reduction efforts I observed there, Vancouver's Downtown Eastside is no Shangri-la for drug use. It's clear that there is dislocation, as Bruce Alexander might say. The neighborhood is a tough place, a concentrated pocket of poverty and substance use disorder. And it's a neighborhood being squeezed by a cutthroat housing market, by—if I'm going to be brave enough to say it (to borrow from Allen Schwartz)—gentrification. On a July 2019 episode of *Crackdown,* Garth Mullins reported from the Downtown Eastside of the increased police presence there—especially in alleys outside overdose prevention sites—a common response when a neighborhood is being gentrified.[22] The juxtapositions are obvious. Across from the Crosstown Clinic is a hipster coffee shop full of people wearing headphones staring at laptops. I could feel it as I sat there drinking a cup of black coffee and taking notes. I stared out the floor-to-ceiling glass window at the corner of Abbot and West Hastings to the clinic, perched on a corner next to a laundry and dry cleaner.

People enter the clinic. They get their medicine. They leave. The world does not end. Then I see Spike coming out of Crosstown. I jump up from my seat and go outside to greet him. He introduces me to his friend, who launches straightaway into a story about a recent health scare. He had a high fever and felt awful. Spike told him they should go to the ER immediately. They had trouble flagging down a cab—no one would stop—until Spike stood out in the street in front of one. Then, when they made it to the hospital, the folks in the ER told them they didn't have any wheelchairs. Spike's friend has limited mobility because of multiple sclerosis. It turned out that Spike's friend had pneumonia and stayed in the hospital for weeks.

"See, this is what I was talking about," Spike tells me. "We don't have an overdose crisis. We have a stigma crisis."

Despite the bad feelings that his story engenders, Spike is in a good mood. He just got his medicine and is delighted that we ran into each other. A guy on a Harley pulls up to the light. "Wow, nice bike!" Spike says. The man on the Harley looks over at Spike, smiles, and says, "Thank you!" And then, almost in the same moment, a group of mostly blond-haired teenage boys and girls with backpacks passes by, and Spike says, "Hello! Get home safe." They barely look up. One of them sneers. Spike's face drops.

"You don't have to sneer!" Spike says to them as they wait for the light to change. "Just say, 'Have a good day!'"

A stigma crisis is one that prevents people from giving space to people who use drugs, and prevents them from hearing what those people have to say. It also prevents people who use drugs from speaking up, and then those people end up overdosing alone and it starts all over.

In the United States, the struggle for safe injection sites, for harm-reduction practices in general, is heated and challenged by the persistent beating of the drum that demonizes drug users and calls for a ramped-up war on drugs. Over the summer of 2019, in Philadelphia, activists battled in the courts for a safe injection site—and eventually won (the DOJ appealed the decision).[23] On Twitter, Charles King, a former ACT UP activist and lawyer, and current CEO of the New York nonprofit Housing Works, tagged a photo of a bus full of activists from the grassroots membership organization Voices of Community Activists & Leaders (VOCAL-NY) heading to Philadelphia to support the struggle there.

Things are coming full circle and a movement is growing—sometimes in the unlikeliest of places. Louise Vincent, the executive director the Urban Survivors Union (see chapter 7), works on an old computer sitting on a ratty desk in a squat, inconspicuous brick building with faded gray shutters on Grove Street near the corner of Glenwood in Greensboro, North Carolina. Shaded by a large oak, the building is across the street from Christ United Methodist Church and down the street from a corner store. The neighborhood is old and lush, close enough to the University of North Carolina–Greensboro and to downtown, as well as a bus line. But there's nothing fancy about the building. Louise, I suspect, wouldn't want it any other way. Inside, it looks a bit like a political campaign headquarters: posters with slogans and meeting notes cover the cinder-block walls above comfy couches, and the organization's red-black-and-yellow logo can be seen on a window.

The Urban Survivors Union—one of the most innovative, stigma-busting, knowledge-spreading activist organizations in the country—is a part of a much larger movement spreading across the United States. This movement is shifting the narrative toward a human rights approach that is most perceptible on the ground. Louise says they began with about three unions and are now at about twenty-four and growing. There are users unions in New York and New England, California and Ohio, offering support and access to health care for members and building a platform to advocate for harm reduction, building a political movement even when it's dangerous to do so. It's hard to be a proud drug user, she says, because it's criminal. "This is absolutely a war, people are traumatized," she explains. "The systems set up that are supposed to take care of us have abandoned us." People don't overdose because of drugs all the time, she says; people overdose because of poverty. She says that the battle lies in helping people see that the social determinants of health have everything to do with what's happening.

Louise has a master's degree in public health, so she can draw the connections.[24] She had a middle-class childhood but turned to drugs as a young person dealing with bipolar disorder. She says she sold drugs, but that barely kept her afloat; it was really just a way to support her habit. In 2003, she was charged with possession with intent to sell cocaine and was given treatment in lieu of prison—she says she was lucky, that in some ways her privileged background kept her from a worse sentence. And she has seen how bad it can get. In 2013, she lost her daughter to a drug over-dose and was in a hit-and-run that led to the loss of her leg. When I first spoke with her two years ago, she was one of the first people I heard say the term *human rights* in the context of the overdose crisis. After watching states ramp up charges in response to overdose deaths, she helped start Re-frame the Blame.

Louise sees such initiatives as a way for some of the most stigmatized people to speak up for themselves. To that end, the board of the Urban Survivors Union is comprised of people who have used drugs—especially recently. She points out that it would make little sense not to engage people who understand and have experienced the fentanyl risk personally.

"And if the government's not going to regulate, which they're not, or get involved in any kind of meaningful way," she adds, "then it's going to be back to what it always is—drug users taking care of each other."

"But," I tell her, "people will say, 'You can't trust them. They lie a lot.'"

"Those are drug policy problems."

"How are those drug policy problems?"

Louise launches into an explanation: "I mean, if I made cigarettes illegal today, the guys on the block are gonna do all kinds of shit for a Newport. We jack the price up, we make it difficult to get, we criminalize it, and we create all this stuff. I mean, it's very expensive to be a drug user, and then you're criminalized, and then you can't get a job, and then you're discon-nected. People do all kinds of fucked-up shit, but drugs don't make you do that. The most powerful drug I've ever used is alcohol. That's the only drug I've ever woke up from, could have possibly done something terrible [while using], and not know why I did it or how I did it. We've created a world where we've blamed drugs for so much that people would actually think if you took drugs out of it, we'd have some sort of utopia, and we wouldn't. They're just a symptom.

"I'm not fighting a war for drug user rights so people can get high. It's about human rights, it's about racial justice, it's about social justice. If we're not talking about racial justice, we're not doing our job. If we're not taking a look at all these things, if we are not deconstructing this shit right now . . ." She pauses, and then asks, "Then what's the point?"

For this to be a movement that privileges human rights, she argues, there must be space for the most marginalized: "The entire harm-reduction argument . . . is really that human life is valuable and all people should be treated with human rights, all people should be treated with dignity and respect, and we don't ever throw people away."

Louise points out that we cannot use imprisonment as a way to solve social and economic problems, or to address the lack of adequate health care. Or, as she says more straightforwardly, "Everybody has to shake their shit out and figure out this intersectional response. And once everybody does it, everybody stands their ground, this is my shit, this is your shit, and then we'll have a movement." Drug users are the perfect group to do it to because, for many of them, their lives are shaped by the justice system.

On a recent conference call that she organized, Louise cites Angela Davis's book *Freedom Is a Constant Struggle*[25] and says that the harm-reduction movement should be linked to human rights struggles around the world, that it needs to be linked to other movements for prison reform, for prison abolition. These movements, she says, are questioning the systems perpetuating the overdose crisis. And then, toward the end of the call, someone gives a shout-out to UnHarming Ohio, a nascent movement organizing people who are survivors of the drug war. The group has ten chapters around the state so far, and is working to ensure better access to naloxone. Amanda Kiger-Stoffel, one of the organizers, told me that they are working to end the war on drugs and on drug users. "We have to start naming this monster and naming it for what it is and take it out," she said, reminding me of Coco Culbertson.

A movement is growing.[26] Connections are being made. In the fall of 2019, Louise Vincent of the Urban Survivors Union tells Travis Lupick, writing for *Yes! Magazine*, "Drug-user unions are going to play a major role in ending this overdose epidemic . . . We have the knowledge and the tools to do that, we just don't have the money and the resources. But with sustainable unions across the country, we cannot be ignored any longer."[27] Louise and Jess Tilley of the New England Users Union meet with people with lived experience at a harm-reduction conference in Iowa.[28] Weeks later, Louise sounds an alarm: a syringe exchange had been shut down in Charleston, West Virginia, in 2018, and now there was growing cluster of HIV cases.[29] Activists from around the region and as far away as New York City show up to pass out harm-reduction supplies. They stand on the steps of the statehouse with signs that read, "We see you West Virginia. Overdose death is a public health failure."

They are naming the monster.

Worth Our Keep

U p in Cleveland, the opioid lawsuits in which Ohio and Licking County are plaintiffs are moving slowly under the watchful eye of U.S. district judge Dan Polster.[1] In late August 2019, Purdue Pharma offered to settle for between $10 and $12 billion for over two thousand different lawsuits against the company—a significant payout, but a far cry from the $100 billion or more many experts claim it will take to address the opioid crisis.[2] The case is visibly pitting the struggling communities most affected by this crisis against the enormous wealth of the Sackler family. The Sacklers are the nineteenth-richest family in the United States, according to *Forbes* magazine, with around $13 billion between twenty family members (and will likely remain wealthy even though Purdue filed for bankruptcy).[3] In another suit, drug makers Teva, McKesson, Cardinal Health, and AmerisourceBergen settled out of court for $260 million with Ohio's Summit and Cuyahoga Counties.[4]

The scramble for the opioid lawsuit money has already begun. Former Ohio governor John Kasich and West Virginia University president Gordon Gee have started a nonprofit to help lobby and direct the money from the lawsuits to hospitals, arguing that these caregivers will be best able to use the money effectively.[5] There's some pushback from Ohio's attorney general, Dave Yost, who suggested that this would preclude using the money for law enforcement. But the social and economic circumstances that fostered the crisis persist, as do other harms—stigma and policies and lack of adequate health care—that have made the crisis worse.[6] Possession of illicit drugs will still disrupt the lives of men and women around the state, sending them from probation to jails to prisons and back—the churn.

And so people will continue to push, nobly, persistently, to transform these systems one law, one needle, one person, one enormous rock at a time. Lisa Roberts will continue to work with what she can. Eric Lee will find another person to mentor. Lesha Farias and Allen Schwartz will keep organizing. And Trish Perry will wake up early on her day off. It's 8:00 a.m. on a Saturday, and her apartment door is wide open, her rusted-out red Ford Ranger is backed up to it. Inside, boxes cover the floors and couches, any flat surface of the cramped room. Resting on top of a large orange Rubbermaid water cooler is a copy of the Narcotics Anonymous "basic text"—the comprehensive book aimed at people seeking recovery. I can smell the coffee. Family photos, with a young, smiling Billy, frame a flat-screen TV set to a classic rock music station blaring Jimi Hendrix's "Little Wing," then Steve Miller's "Jet Airliner" and, appropriately, AC/DC's "If You Want Blood."

About fifty brown paper bags are opened up and scattered about the room. It's hard to tell what the system is or even if there is a system. I don't ask. I just watch as Trish moves and talks. She goes to a box, picks up a handful of something, and walks around dropping supplies into bags. She stuffs items (cottons, condoms, cookers, bands, alcohol swabs, and needles) into paper bags, which she then staples shut. Supplies are donated or come out of her pocket—but she can barely keep up with demand. One time at the corner, a frequent visitor suggested they set up a car wash to raise money. Trish is also distributing a lot of naloxone these days, which is a good thing. There is lot of support for naloxone, though maybe not as much as there could be, but it's still not always getting to the people who need it the most.[7] People who use drugs have been harmed by the criminal justice system and by health care, making even low-barrier online access, as exists in Licking County, a tough sell. It's a lot easier for some folks to walk up to Trish at the corner, fill out the paperwork (required for many free naloxone distribution sites), and walk away.

Sometimes people ask her what's in the harm-reduction kit. Sometimes people wanting sterile syringes talk to the wrong folks. She tries to coach them—"I go over and say, I can't help you right now. You guys have to come to me only, and you have to ask for a brown harm-reduction bag! Most of them are getting it." She talks a bit about the risk of getting arrested and wonders if the Newark police even care. "Well, I'm on private property, so I don't know," she says. Then she shrugs and exhales. "Well, it don't really matter." Trish knows that if the police did go after her, she would have a moral victory.

That there is not enough movement on harm reduction in Newark and in Licking County continues to frustrate Trish, but she persists on this sunny morning. She says she tells anyone who will listen about the corner and about naloxone—because of the stakes, though, she's careful in sharing information about syringes. At a recent work meeting, she explained what harm reduction is to her managers. Were they surprised or confused? She says she couldn't tell. Some more politically astute folks have said she should start by seeking changes on the board of health, but that frustrates Trish. She wants change now, and she acts with a zeal that irritates some.

"People don't like what I have to say about Newark sometimes," she says, and then gets distracted by her cat, who comes into the room, begs to go outside, but immediately turns around. "Make up your mind," she says. She keeps working while talking about local politics, her job, the complicated new online system for visiting inmates at the county jail, a mother who just found out her son is using heroin—she's going to meet her for coffee tomorrow—and her father, who is down in Chillicothe battling cancer. She says she feels supported, despite the busyness of her days, the frantic nature of her life. Her family supports the work she's doing. They get it. Some of them have gone down this road themselves, so they support not only her but also Billy. That, of course, is all that matters to her.

"Looking back, you see all the signs. But at the time"—she pauses to staple a bag shut—"I didn't see the signs." She says that there were a lot of half-truths, a lot of hiding, and, on her part, a lot of confusion. "I've heard every story from Billy. It used to embarrass me, but now I don't care. In the beginning, everybody has that—they care what people think."

Trish gathers all the bags and puts them into boxes and carries them into the truck. Then she starts moving other boxes—clothing mostly—and putting them into the truck. A large cooler, random bags of food, more boxes. She checks her email on a computer in the corner. She keeps moving. I get up to leave, and she grabs a box with a fondue pot in it.

"Know anybody who wants a fondue pot or a juicer? I got both of them. They give 'em to us at work, but I don't want a fondue pot."

Later that morning, I drive over to the corner with my family. The Newark Think Tank on Poverty is hosting its annual picnic across the street at the basketball courts. Eric Lee smoked about ten racks of ribs, and he wants me to stop by. He starts by marinating the ribs and adds a sweet sauce, then Vidalia onions, liquid smoke, chili powder, sometimes a hint of vinegar, brown sugar, and sometimes lemon, cooking them slowly over pecan wood chips. He also has a special blend of seasonings, Eric's Special Blend, but that's about all he'll tell me—and he won't give me portions. (And secretly, he says, he waits for his friend George to test the ribs to see if they're good.)

When we get there, the corner is hopping and Trish is telling folks to go across the street for more food. Eric is set up by the grill. I'm surprised he's even here—so much has been going on in his life. Earlier in the spring, his daughter was in a car accident with her cousin, who passed away. Eric wasn't sure if his daughter would ever walk again, but after extensive surgery and rehab, she's getting ready to start work. Now Eric is trying to support her recovery, trying to figure out how to cover her medical bills and keep her moving forward. There's no good days and bad days, Eric often says, just days. What that means in the context of his own life, he says, is that when you're struggling with addiction you tend to focus on the ten bad moments in a day, when you might have had a hundred good ones.

The accident has been another test of his resilience—another time for him to lean on his community, and maybe that explains why he's doing this today. His community has responded by helping him cover those bills—the Think Tank held a fundraiser at Allen and Lesha's house, and many others in this city have reached out to help him. When we spoke after that fundraiser, Eric said that if all someone sees in Newark is an addiction crisis, then they are small-minded. He says that since he's been through the things he has been through, and seeing his own daughter struggle, his sense of community has grown and his belief in the love and goodness of some people has grown, despite it all. He wants to see connections, collaborations that he's not seeing yet. He wants to see a rising tide—where a victory for one is a victory for all. A victory for Trish is a victory for all. A victory for the Think Tank, that's a victory for the community. And ultimately, he said, that is just about love, about spreading the love.[8]

My son is playing on the basketball court, and Eric comes over and says, "Give me that ball. Let me show you something." He starts at the top of the key, shooting with one hand. He misses. His shot is akin to Kareem Abdul-Jabbar's Skyhook, though he's not up against a seven-foot, one-inch Wilt Chamberlain, just my seven-year-old. He keeps missing—maybe seven times—and keeps saying, "Let me try one more." Until, eventually, he makes it.

Sometimes you miss, of course. When I spoke with Allen and Lesha about what happened at the city council meeting last winter—Allen calling them out, Lesha confronting the mayor—Allen wonders if that was the best approach: "Absolutely true, and they deserved it. But tactically, was it a good idea? Probably not."

And yet, he says, members of the Think Tank felt empowered by that moment of opening up the public sphere, of speaking their truths in a public forum, of being heard. "It was what we've been fighting for, for five years," Allen says. It made him think about a lot of things, about how he feels like he is constantly stifling the "expressions of anger" from Think Tank members out of fear of the consequences.

"It's the middle-class power game. So I'm reproaching myself in exactly the same way and making myself mentally unhealthy in exactly the same way." It might not have been the best thing politically, but sometimes pushing the envelope, going beyond the limits of acceptable speech, can be an important tool for a movement. This movement has successfully lobbied for political change, turned the ears of people with access to resources, and become an important collective voice in the community and beyond—Lesha has been helping to organize think tanks in Zanesville and in Perry County. The Think Tank has made inroads with social service organizations in Licking County—they know that this organization wants them to allow their clients to have more agency in effecting their own survival. And when those agencies go to the state for more resources, the people of the Think Tank are there to help and advocate. This is certainly what happened when the Mental Health and Recovery Board received funding from the state to address the overdose crisis after hearing C.J. Wills and the Think Tank ask for more support for people who use methamphetamines. Now they are working to open access to this resource. (And Congress recently passed a bill opening all funds earmarked for opioids to be used to address cocaine and meth use, as well.)[9]

But the truth is, we are just bailing out the bathtub, to borrow the metaphor that showed up at the beginning of this book. All of these interventions—the corner, the shelters, the syringe exchange—they are good projects established by good people, but they are also good examples of bailing out the water. When those people come together at a city council meeting, when they lobby for structural change, when they begin to question systems, they are beginning to address root causes and are slowly turning the spigot off.

"People don't know what that looks like," Allen says, "to turn off the spigot of poverty, to really address poverty in this town, rather than purifying it or riding it out of town or sticking it in a corner. It would really require major restructuring of the way we think and the way we do things. At the same time, the very opposite is gathering steam, and that's the development plan for Newark, which is . . . Where would that be in the metaphor? Eliminate the bathtub?"

"Or make a prettier one?" I suggest.

"Yeah, give poor people toys so they can play in the bathtub and not notice that we're all drowning."

It's not just about changing the decisions, though; it's about changing the way decisions are made. Real systemic change looks like a movement of empowered people. And there are glimmers of that here.

At the end of the summer, Allen and Lesha got a flat tire in Pennsylvania while driving home from visiting family. It caused them to miss a Think Tank leadership meeting. The meeting was held in the dimly lit fellowship hall at Holy Trinity Lutheran Church on West Main Street in Newark. Eric was there. C.J. was there. Trish was there—and so was the retired teacher and social worker Linda Mossholder. A woman named Jeanette ran the meeting, and the group discussed gaps in services that they are all seeing—especially when it comes to getting information about treatment to the most vulnerable and marginalized people in the community. They are starting to ask questions. Having a voice is not enough, they know; power is also needed. They are working on that. And so, the next day, in the very same fellowship hall, Trish and Linda, Tresa Jewell, and Nancy Welu were all invited by Newark city councilman and mayoral candidate Jeremy Blake to participate in a roundtable discussion about poverty with U.S. senator Sherrod Brown.[10] At the roundtable, they are praised for their work and listened to by one of the most powerful men in the state. It feels like a sea change.

There is momentum in Licking County, Ohio. Certainly, there have been enormous changes in the years during which I have been reporting this story—a grant from Housing and Urban Development for more affordable housing for people with disabilities, new efforts to support people who use methamphetamine, a quick-response team, greater access to medication-assisted treatment, and two new recovery houses opened up by a local social entrepreneur.[11] Across Ohio, the number of syringe service programs has tripled since 2016—from six to eighteen.[12] Other measures that could help still seem impossible. At the most recent Overdose Awareness Day rally, Sheila Humphrey-Craig set up her supervised consumption site in downtown Newark. People seemed interested, curious. But the Sparta, the diner that was once a hub of organizing and work opportunities, is now closed, and the Basket, the former office building that sits empty on the side of Highway 16, is slated to be transformed into a luxury hotel—just a mile or so from several homeless camps.[13] For some of the folks on the streets and for people with other visions for this community, the Basket represented something, an empty space to be filled with people who need shelter for whatever reason. At one point someone had suggested turning it into a recovery house.

But to a person, people are changing, moving forward. Trish's colleague Jen Kanagy is running for Newark City Council. C.J. is working hard in his new life as a homeowner and a proud and dedicated father with custody of his son. He says that lately he has been reading the Book of Psalms. The local United Way and the Ohio State Senate have honored his work.[14] Johnathon is doing well—one day at a time. The woman with dark hair and bright eyes from the prologue has found housing and had it furnished with the help of the women from Newark Homeless Outreach. The rail-thin young man with two backpacks who'd been discharged from the hospital was eventually tracked down by the Newark Addiction Recovery Initiative and went to treatment. Jeremiah, who showed me his camp in the woods, has now found an apartment with his wife. Gordon Casey and Oona Krieg's

Brave Technology Coop from Vancouver won the million-dollar Ohio Opioid Technology Challenge and will be back in Ohio to help implement their overdose prevention technology.[15] Harm Reduction Ohio is lobbying the Ohio Senate and House for better laws and, after obtaining a license to distribute naloxone, getting it into the hands of every "Trish Perry" they can find in Ohio. Trish herself has been going to board of health meetings again, continuing to advocate for an SSP. At a recent meeting, she tells me, there was interest in supporting efforts to make medication-assisted treatment more available in Licking County. Every change positive.

These people are writing a new shared story that this is Ohio, that this is a place where people can organize, can build, can renew. There is a time for loaves and fishes, but there is also a time for a sermon on the mount. While we do need direct service, we also need to push for changes in attitude and policy. Many lives depend on it. Can we end the war on drugs? The war on poor people and people of color? Can we do this thing? This summer we remembered the July 20, 1969, moon landing, when a man from Ohio walked down a ladder outside what amounted to a tin can and took a "giant leap for mankind." They said it could not be done. But we did it. And now they say that we cannot save lives. But we are doing so. They say that another world is not possible. I do not believe them.

Addressing overdose deaths and substance use disorder through the justice system is not effective. The overdose crisis has exposed the already apparent gaps in health care in this country, as well as the ever-growing burdens of inequality. And the research is clear that those on the margins are affected the most. In the short term, we know what works to reduce overdose deaths and to address substance use disorder: a public health approach focused on harm reduction—easy access to naloxone, fentanyl-testing strips, drug checking, safe injection sites, treatment on demand, low-barrier access to medication-assisted treatment, housing, and stigma reduction.[16]

Oh, and love. We need a lot more of that.

We should be open, too, to the idea that recovery happens in all sorts of ways for all kinds of folks, and we should therefore work even for those solutions that might make us uncomfortable.

Such was the message of a young minister named Blyth Barnow on a rainy night in late August at the United Methodist Church for All People on Parsons Avenue in Columbus, Ohio. The church is in a storefront, a well-lit room with maybe thirty people gathered, along with a slew of reporters from *The Columbus Dispatch* and local TV stations. I sit down as they're beginning the service. Blyth stands behind an altar adorned with a cross, a vase of black-eyed Susans, a banner that reads "Harm Reduction Saves," and a basket overflowing with naloxone donated by Harm Reduction Ohio. She opens her address by saying that when we talk about overdose we often talk about death and not about life. This event, she says, is about saving lives. In that vein, she explains that the media is here because "too often when the media is reporting on overdoses, the same sad, awful, dehumanizing, disrespectful pictures get looped over and over again, and we want to be able to tell a new, different, and more vibrant story."

She asks people to light a candle in honor of someone who has died from an overdose and who may not have had access to the medical care they needed—this is part of grappling with death before addressing the hope and promise of resurrection, she explains. People file up front, men and women, young and old, and light votive candles, placing them on the altar as they say the name of their loved one aloud:

Ralph
Christina
Adrianne
Billy
Terrance

Paul

Rosemary

Linda

Blyth then lights a candle for those we've lost and do not know.

Dylan Stanley, who long ago spoke at the Licking County Library to educate the community about syringe exchange, steps forward to read Lucille Clifton's poem "Won't You Celebrate with Me." This poem about the resilience of a black woman in a hostile world concludes: "come celebrate / with me that everyday / something has tried to kill me / and has failed." The audience is then challenged to be a "resurrection people," and two women step up front to sing "I'm Gonna Live So God Can Use Me." The pianist picks up the tune, a man on a djembe joins in, and the space is filled with music and energy and determination: "I'm gonna live so God can use me, anywhere, Lord, anytime!" We begin to clap. Over in the corner, a man starts dancing, clapping in rhythm. I'm reminded of Francis Weller's comment that grief is wild, feral, as the candles flicker in the front of the room and the man in the corner becomes a kind of dynamo, filled with some kind of momentum or force.

And then we pray. And then we sing. And we are invited into the circle, into community with one another. "Love lights up our world," say the banners on the walls of this room. We are reminded of Jesus's admonition to the apostles in Matthew 10:8: "Heal the sick, raise the dead, cleanse those who have leprosy, drive out demons. Freely you have received; freely give." That passage continues with Jesus telling his followers not to carry anything with them, but to accept food and support from those they meet and not to feel guilty about accepting that support "for the worker is worth his keep." If you do the work, he's saying to them, you will be rewarded by and with the community you create.

Blyth Barnow then begins her sermon by telling a personal story, a story about someone she lost to an opioid overdose when she was twenty years old.

At her friend's funeral, in a large church in northeastern Ohio, the pastor said that her friend could have avoided hell—that only the altar could save people who use drugs. But she knew then and she knows now that she and her friend had been saving each other for years. That even when people gave up on them, they stayed together and supported each other. The comments of that pastor, she said, did not come from the gospel. "Shame can never be the work of the gospel because it is death-dealing and not life-giving."

I'm sitting there thinking about Billy, who is now at Belmont Correctional Institution in St. Clairsville, in a part of the prison full of men with mostly low-level felonies, many of them related to drug use. He is in a place that does not affirm life, does not give life, only postpones it. He calls me on Fridays, and we talk about what's happening inside (which is not much), what he does (reads, watches TV), and what he wants to do next (get out of the justice system, as far away as possible). I tell him I've been reading through the journals he shared with me. I tell him I think he's too hard on himself sometimes.

He says, "Yeah, that's what they try to get you to do in treatment—to make it about you."

I say, "But all of this trouble is about policy. It's not you. It's us."

Blyth transfixes everyone in the room as she takes the Christian metaphor of resurrection, of new life, to its logical and ambitious conclusion, as she takes the story of a man who cared for and accepted the outcast, the vulnerable, and applies it to the present. She asks: Why is it that we do not save the people who can be saved, like the seventy-two thousand people who died from a fatal drug overdose in the United States in 2017? For her, it is both a spiritual and a political problem. Every overdose is a policy failure—and yet we know the solution. For starters, that solution includes harm reduction, an approach she says is rooted in justice and human rights. "Theologically put," she says, harm reduction "is the recognition of what is divine in yourself and others. It is the unconditional love of God, the love of the neighbor, the work of the gospel." And for Blyth, the work of the gospel is to spread naloxone far and wide, to support community distribution, to remove regulations that prohibit access—like in Ohio.

She then says, "The overdose crisis is not new to poor communities or communities of color." There is specific work that needs to be done in this moment when overdose is increasing among black men more than any group. We need to talk about how racism has shaped not only the war on drugs but also our popular understandings of drug use. "White supremacy has used this lie to devastate communities of color while simultaneously abandoning many white communities," she says. "Because the truth is that white supremacy has never been concerned with the well-being of white people. It has only ever been concerned with the concentration of white power. Which is why it makes all these demands on behalf of white children and then allows them to die without access to naloxone. People who use drugs, people of color, poor people, LGBTQ people do not help to advance white power, and so they have always been met with punishment, isolation, and death. We have to be honest and recognize that part of the reason that we are here today, having ignored overdose in the past, is because this current overdose crisis that has touched the halls of white, affluent power has proven itself politically useful."

The prevailing policies erupted out of the fear, ignorance, and racism fueled by the crack epidemic of the 1980s and '90s, which disrupted and destroyed so many lives. "Had we intervened then," she says, "we might not have gotten here. Harm reduction requires the tough work of reclaiming dignity, and white supremacy is a collective wound to our dignity. Ignoring it leaves us all at risk."

After her friend's death, she says, she was angry that he was gone. She blamed him, herself, his parents, she blamed the people who left him while he was overdosing, one of whom died of an overdose ten years later. She realized then that it wasn't bad choices but bad policies that led to these people's deaths. They didn't need to die. They didn't have naloxone because they didn't know what it was and they didn't want to get caught with it. If policies had treated her friend and those in his circle like human beings, they would still be here. That is our work, to be people focused on resurrection, to "claim our legacy as an Easter people in this Good Friday world."

Then, using the naloxone kits donated by Harm Reduction Ohio, Blyth teaches everyone in the audience how to recognize an overdose and how to reverse one. Afterward, over coffee and cookies, we fill out paperwork, shake hands, introduce ourselves to one another, grab a few naloxone kits, and walk out into the rain, back to our communities, our homes. There is work to be done. And we are the workers, worth our keep.

Postscript

On November 5, 2019, Trish's underground syringe access program was brought out into the light of day by a short video posted online by CNN.[1] Shortly afterward, stories ran in *The Newark Advocate* and *The Columbus Dispatch*. After this media coverage, Licking County's health commissioner, Joe Ebel, released a statement:

> It has come to our attention that Patricia Perry appears to be operating a syringe distribution program without board of health approval as required under Ohio state law—ORC 3707.57. For this reason, the health department has suspended our partnership with Ms. Perry regarding the distribution of naloxone. The health department will continue to provide naloxone through the health department website, at distribution events, and through our other local partner organizations.

After all the attention, Trish was worried that she might be arrested. But she was more worried that this decision would limit access to naloxone in the county—especially among people who use drugs.

Data analysis by a team of researchers from Denison University shows that more than 87 percent of people who died of an unintentional drug overdose in Ohio from July 2016 till June 2018 did not receive naloxone.[2] By the time first responders arrive, it is very often too late. Of the 13 percent who did receive naloxone, less than 1 percent had it administered by bystanders. In other words, more people could be saved from an opioid overdose death if more people had naloxone—especially people who use drugs.

But then folks started donating supplies to Trish—in part because of the CNN story, in part because of the decision to no longer give her naloxone. One night she came home from work to a box full of Neosporin on her doorstep. A note attached read: "For the harm-reduction kits." Trish kept on doing her work—including handing out sterile syringes.

Billy was released from prison just before Christmas 2019 and was sent to a community control facility in Lancaster. He will eventually be able to work and get his truck back. He's looking forward to spending time with his family, helping Harm Reduction Ohio, and drinking real coffee again.

A bipartisan bill sponsored by Ohio's U.S. senator Rob Portman will give states more flexibility to use dollars earmarked to address the opioid crisis to also address methamphetamine and cocaine use. Ohio Senate Bill 3 would turn some drug possession charges from felonies to misdemeanors. It has the support of Americans for Prosperity and the ACLU, but is getting pushback from the Ohio Prosecuting Attorney's Association and the Buckeye Sheriff's Association.

The Newark Think Tank on Poverty has been hosting a series of workshops about the Green New Deal, trying to push people to think big, imagining what a "new deal" would look like for a city like Newark. And after a long summer of discussion, there is a clear plan for a warming shelter this winter.

And in early January 2020, at a public forum of the Licking County Taskforce on Homelessness, consultants discussed a number of solutions offered during focus-group meetings. Trish and Dennis and Peggy were sitting at a table behind me. Allen Schwartz came in late and was sitting at the back of the packed room. One focus was "Substance Use Treatment and Mental Health Services"; the discussion included mention of a syringe exchange. One of the consultants noted offhandedly that a syringe exchange program was attempted last year but "it didn't quite get off the ground in part because of a lack of public support."

Trish muttered out loud, "So they say."

Dennis (who recently reported on his website a possible rise in overdose numbers for 2019) raised his hand and suggested that the report not be worded that way, that in fact there was a lot of public support for it and that in all the public forums there has been little open opposition. There's some murmuring around the room. "How do people get on the board of health?" a woman asked. Someone else proposed a separate meeting to discuss it. The issue isn't going away. The workers keep showing up.

And then the coronavirus pandemic spread across the globe, across Ohio, a fierce, uncompromising shadow. On March 20, the day after flash flooding destroyed roads and homes throughout Licking County, the department of health announced the first case of COVID-19 in the county. Sorrow on top of sorrow. The pandemic revealed gaps in our safety net and our health-care system—things that the folks on the front lines of the overdose crisis have shouted about for years.

Wealthy people seemed to have immediate access to testing while poor and working-class people floundered or just kept working in grocery stores, warehouses, or delivery trucks. As of this writing, the national unemployment rate is 14.7 percent. And in the first eight weeks of the pandemic, Ohio has reported 1,169,694 jobless claims, more than the total of those filed during the past three years. The effects of unemployment were visible almost immediately in Newark. *The Newark Advocate* reported that in April 2019, the Newark Salvation Army served 5,957 meals, but in April 2020, they served 13,864.

According to the Marshall Project, as of May 13, there were 25,239 COVID-19 cases in state and federal prisons, with 4,449 cases in Ohio prisons. By mid-May in Belmont Correctional Institution, where Billy served time in 2019, ninety-five inmates and seventy-three staff members had tested positive for COVID-19. Two inmates had died.

For some people, the pandemic has exacerbated isolation, disruption, and dislocation—and this has made life more complicated for people with substance use disorder. Some people may have lost access to MAT. Federal guidelines have relaxed the amount of MAT drugs that can be prescribed, and doctors are allowed to use telehealth appointments for meeting with patients, but some are still struggling to get access to this health care. Now more people could be using alone or using again after not using for some time. Overdose rates appear to be on the rise. Licking County's neighbor Franklin County has reported a 50 percent increase in overdoses in the first months of 2020 compared to 2019 and significant spikes during the pandemic.

In some ways, this is a moment that the people in this book have been preparing for because as soon as the pandemic hit, all the people I've been writing about stepped up. Allen Schwartz has attended several online trainings to figure out how to organize when you can't meet people face-to-face. Lesha and others with the Think Tank have organized a mutual aid group; a Justice Café, billed as "a virtual night out for people in recovery" and a way for people to stay connected; and a newsletter called "People, Pandemic, and Poverty," with some of the stories written by C.J. The Crossroads Crusaders, Newark Homeless Outreach, and John's Helping Hands have volunteered to open up the showers at the high school football field every Wednesday for people who are homeless. And Harm Reduction Ohio, at the request of the Ohio Department of Health, is mailing out naloxone to people who request it from their website. So far they've sent naloxone to eighty-six of Ohio's eighty-eight counties.

For her part, Trish is still going to the corner, though food is being handed out in paper bags, everyone is asked to stand six feet apart in a line as they move from table to table, and all the volunteers are wearing masks and gloves. Harm-reduction kits, which were once kept out of sight, are now out in the open and are running out quickly every Saturday. Trish recently gave out fifty kits in forty-two minutes. Each kit contains a pack of ten syringes, naloxone, and information about safe use during the pandemic.

"We're thinking about how to still be there and give, and not jeopardize anybody," Trish tells me. "I feel bad. There ain't nothing to tell [unhoused people]. There's nothing to tell them; they're just out there, lost people."

Reporting the story of the overdose crisis in my community for years now, I never imagined a disaster like this, but I did imagine that one day we would have to reckon with our health-care system and with capitalism in this country. And here we are. Maybe, as many have said, we are on the cusp of something better. Maybe this pandemic will force us to think about how we can build a more just world for everyone now before it is too late.

I do have hope for another world. But as activist DeRay Mckesson writes, "Hope is not magic. Hope is work."

To do that work we will need a shared vision that fronts community concerns and needs before those of the individual, that centers sacrifice for the greater good. It will require not just grassroots reform efforts but vast changes to the systems that have left so many destitute.

Now we've been tasked with taking care of each other by wearing a mask. A mask can reduce the risks to yourself and to others and signal that these are serious times. But it's more than that—wearing a mask is about acknowledging that you live in a communal society and that everyone in that society matters. Every single person. The person in front of you, the person behind you, and the person next to you.

Acknowledgments

I respectfully acknowledge that this book was written on the lands of the Wyandot, Shawnee, Delaware, and Seneca-Cayuga nations, and of the ancestral people who built the earthworks.

I have enormous respect for all the people in this book. Thank you for making my world a bigger place and for giving me hope. Reporting and writing about people can lead to feelings of connection and even friendship. I fully acknowledge that's what happened for me, and I knew going into this project that for someone who wears his heart on his sleeve, keeping a safe distance would become harder the deeper I got into the story. The people I was writing about became people I cared for deeply.

Many people who were not mentioned, though they played a role in this narrative, include the many first responders, social services folks, and active and engaged citizens, like Kandice Hairston and Wendy Tarr, who have given their time to meet with me and teach me. To Linda Seville, Jayson Hysell, and Elicia Sandlin, among others from the Newark Homeless Outreach team who are at the corner every Saturday, thank you.

Many thank-yous to my friend Sarah Schaff, who watched this story develop from the beginning and who was a constant cheerleader and intrepid researcher.

Thank you to the many folks in Newark who shared information, let me attend meetings, and, in general, tolerated my presence—this is a very long list for sure. I want to thank especially Deb Dingus, Jeremy Blake, and Kay Spergel. Thank you to all the inspiring activists and organizers in Ohio who spent time with me in Dayton, Portsmouth, Columbus, Canton, and of course Newark. This includes but isn't limited to Carole Robinson, Sheila Humphrey-Craig, and Amanda Kiger-Stoffel. Thank you to all the folks in Vancouver who spent time with me, especially Gordon Casey, Oona Krieg, and Spike Peachey. And thanks to all the people who helped me research in New York City, especially Tino Fuentes, who has saved and is saving so many lives. A shout-out to those in the harm-reduction community on Twitter who have taught me so much by sharing ideas and research. Thank you to Zachary Siegel, Maia Szalavitz, Abraham Gutman, Sheila Vakharia, Kim Sue, and many others. Zach and Sheila, thank you for reading drafts— you are both doing the work.

Thank you to Jack Herrera for your incredible fact-checking skills (I could not have done this without you), and to Heather Shaw for your last-minute reading.

My colleagues in the Denison University Department of English and in the Narrative Journalism program have been listening to me talk about this story for some time. Thank you for your patience, advice, and eyes. Thanks go to Margot Singer and Mike Croley, for the first read and for listening to me talk about this project for years; Doug Swift, for teaching me to be a more patient storyteller; Jessica Nelson, for being an empathetic collaborator; and James Weaver, Linda Krumholz, Beth Lossing, Peter Grandbois, Dennis Read, and Maggie Messitt. So many other supporters, researchers, writers, and editors from Denison (and beyond) made this happen, people like Kunal Ray, Amy Elliott, Paul Tullis, Meg Galipault, Ron Abram,

Kerry Penland, Kellon Patey, Shanti Basu, Liz Anastasiadis, Drew Balduff, Kelli Van Wasshenova, Susan Kennedy, and, for the many discussions about substance abuse disorder, Cody Brooks. Thank you to the journalists from the Between Coasts forums for inspiration and solidarity. A grant from the Denison University Research Foundation helped fund research for some of the chapters in this book.

I appreciate and care for all of you at the United Church of Granville, including (but not limited to!) Linda Mossholder, Caroline Cook, Julie Mulroy, Janet Greene, David Greene, Jerry Griffin, Cliff Houston, and Dwight Davidson. Shalom.

Thank you to Elise Capron at Dijkstra Literary Agency and Dan Smetanka, my awesome editor at Counterpoint. Many thank-yous to the team who helped make this book: Dan Lopez, Jordan Koluch, and Janet Renard.

There are many other people who helped me along the way as I wrote this book—including folks who helped with sunshine requests or who connected me to sources. If I've left you off this list, I apologize.

Thank you to good friends like Marcus Boroughs and the Blue Grass, Virginia, crew.

Lastly, thank you to Ceciel, my children, and my family (especially the best chef and reader, Gene Shaw) for all the love, laughter, and tolerance. I love y'all. Writing this has reminded me of how important y'all are.

This book is based in part on previously published work: "A Year in Heart of the Addiction Crisis in Rust Belt America," *Pacific Standard*, December/January 2018/2019; "What the Addiction Crisis Looks Like to First Responders," *Pacific Standard*, January 25, 2019; "How a Former USA Today Reporter Became a Leading Voice for Needle Exchanges in Ohio," *Pacific Standard,* January 15, 2019; "Overdose and Punishment," *The New Republic*, September 2018; "An Ohio Community Confronts the Opioid Crisis Head On," *Bill Moyers and Company*, September 22, 2017;

and "Fighting for Seats at the Table: A Poor People's Movement in a Rust-belt Town," *Truthout*, July 24, 2016. I appreciate the superb work of the editors and fact-checkers who helped make these stories happen and pushed me along the path to writing this book: Nicholas Jackson, Ted Ross, Sasha Belenky, Miguel Salazar, Max Ufberg, Kate Wheeling, Ben Rowen, Maya Dusenbery, Alana Yu-lan Price, and John Light.

A Note About Sources

This book is based on hours and hours of reporting that began in spring 2016: going to the corner; to meetings; to coffee, breakfast, lunch, and dinner; to ride-alongs, firehouses, forums, rallies, conferences, and church services. It started at the Sparta over coffee with Allen Schwartz and Lesha Farias, and, I think, continues. I am grateful to all the people who let me listen in or who sat down with me. I am grateful for all the conversations and look forward to more. At community meetings, I often saw the same people again and again, and those are the people, the ones who are committed and impressive, that I ended up writing about. Some of those people's names do not appear in the book itself, but I acknowledge their assistance and the offering of their time and energies here.

I was present at most of the recent events described here. If not, I relied on reporting and other sources. For readers who want to learn more, I offer extensive citations from the local newspaper of record, *The Newark Advocate*, to reinforce my own account. I do this as a reminder that local journalism matters—especially when trying to understand issues of national import. I appreciate all the reporters doing this work in Licking County and beyond. In addition to the local paper, there is an extensive library of videos from Newark City Council meetings freely available on YouTube. This is a testament to the importance of open access to records, a cornerstone of any functioning democracy.

Thank you to Julie Mulroy and Jerry Griffin for helping me to identify the trees that appear in this book, to Olivia Biggs for responding to my many requests, and to Jeff Gill for helping me track down many sources.

Notes

Prologue: The Corner

1. Naloxone is an "opioid antagonist," which means it can bind to opioid receptors and block the effects of other opioids. It can be given by intranasal spray, intramuscularly, subcutaneously, or intravenously.

2. Indeed, in recent years there has been a notable increase in people going to food pantries in central Ohio as incomes are stagnating, making it hard for people to pay for housing, health care, and childcare. See Karen Kasler, "Food Pantries Serving More Customers, with Bad Economic Signs Ahead," WOSU Public Media, September 3, 2019, radio.wosu.org/post/food -pantries-serving-more-customers-bad-economic-signs-ahead#stream/0.

3. Joe Ebel, "Hepatitis A Cases on the Rise in Licking County," *Newark Advocate*, March 2, 2019, www.newarkadvocate.com/story/news/2019/03/02 /joe-ebel-hepatitis-cases-rise-licking-county/2979528002.

4. Kent Mallett, "Ohio Magazine Selects Newark One of Ohio's Best Hometowns," *Newark Advocate*, July 25, 2019, www.newarkadvocate.com/story /news/2019/07/25/ohio-magazine-selects-newark-one-ohios-best-hometowns /1808298001.

5. Mara Kilgore, "Newark Think Tank on Poverty to Host Up to P.A.R. Community Workshop," *Newark Advocate*, April 29, 2019.

6. Jeff Brand, "The Opioid Epidemic as Collective Trauma: An Introduction to the Crisis," *Group* 42, no. 4 (Winter 2018): 291–309.

7. Ibid., 300.

8. Ibid., 301.

9. Ibid.

10. Ibid., 303.

11. Ibid., 304.

12. Ibid.

13. See "Harm Reduction," Drug Policy Alliance, www.drugpolicy.org/issues /harm-reduction.

14. U.S. Centers for Disease Control and Prevention, "U.S. Drug Overdose Deaths Continue to Rise; Increase Fueled by Synthetic Opioids," press release, March 28, 2018, www.cdc.gov/media/releases/2018/p0329-drug-overdose -deaths.html.

15. U.S. Centers for Disease Control and Prevention, "Drug Overdose Deaths," www.cdc.gov/drugoverdose/data/statedeaths.html.

16. Abby Goodnough, Josh Katz, and Margot Sanger-Katz, "Drug Overdose Deaths Drop in U.S. for First Time Since 1990," *New York Times*, July 17, 2019, www.nytimes.com/interactive/2019/07/17/upshot/drug-overdose-deaths -fall.html; and U.S. Centers for Disease Control and Prevention, "NCSH Releases Provisional Drug Overdose Death Data and Several New Reports," Statcast, week of July 15, 2019, www.cdc.gov/nchs/pressroom/podcasts /20190718/20190718.htm.

17. I found conflicting numbers for deaths in 1995, but it seems to be between 48,000 and 50,876. See Dennis H. Osmond, "Epidemiology of HIV/AIDS in the United States," HIV InSite, University of California, San Francisco, March 2003, hivinsite.ucsf.edu/InSite?page=kb-01-03; and "The HIV/AIDS Epidemic in the United States: The Basics," KFF.org, March 25, 2019, www .kff.org/hivaids/fact-sheet/the-hivaids-epidemic-in-the-united-states-the -basics/#footnote-391348-14. Coincidentally, 1995 was also the year that the National Academy of Sciences concluded that syringe exchange programs are effective at preventing infectious disease.

18. Between 1999 and 2017, more than 700,000 people in the United States died from a drug overdose. See U.S. Centers for Disease Control and Prevention, "Understand the Epidemic," December 19, 2018, www.cdc.gov/drugoverdose /epidemic/index.html.

19. Ohio Department of Health, "Drug Overdose," October 23, 2019, odh.ohio .gov/wps/portal/gov/odh/know-our-programs/violence-injury-prevention -program/Drug-overdose.

20. O. Trent Hall et al., "Years of Life Lost Due to Opioid Overdose in Ohio: Temporal and Geographic Patterns of Excess Mortality," *Journal of Addiction Medicine*, October 7, 2019, journals.lww.com/journaladdictionmedicine /Abstract/publishahead/Years_of_Life_Lost_due_to_Opioid_Overdose_in _Ohio_.99325.aspx.

21. I'm reporting numbers from the Licking County Coroner, though there is some discrepancy between those numbers and those reported by the Ohio Department of Health. See "Drug Overdose Death Review," Licking County Health Department, 2018, www.lickingcohealth.org/documents /hed/2018DrugOverdoseDeaths.pdf.

22. Ohio Department of Health, "2017 Ohio Drug Overdose Data: General Findings," odh.ohio.gov/wps/wcm/connect/gov/5deb684e-4667-4836-862b -cb5eb59acbd3/2017_OhioDrugOverdoseReport.pdf?MOD=AJPERES &CONVERT_TO=url&CACHEID=ROOTWORKSPACE.Z18 _M1HGGIK0N0JO00QO9DDDDM3000.

23. Mark Rembert et al., "Taking Measure of Ohio's Opioid Crisis," Ohio State University, C. William Swank Program in Rural-Urban Policy, October 2017, aede.osu.edu/sites/aede/files/publication_files/Swank%20-%20Taking %20Measure%20of%20Ohios%20Opioid%20Crisis.pdf, 1.

24. Kent Mallett, "Licking County Continues to Set Records for Children in Its Care," *Newark Advocate*, April 13, 2018, www.newark advocate.com/story/news/2018/04/13/licking-county-continues-set-records -children-its-care/511504002.

25. Rembert et al., "Taking Measure of Ohio's Opioid Crisis," 1. These numbers refer specifically to medication-assisted treatment, the gold standard for addiction treatment.

26. Bethany Bruner, "Drug Treatment Available, but with a Wait," *Newark Advocate*, April 16, 2016, www.newarkadvocate.com/story/news/crime/high -in-ohio/2016/04/16/drug-treatment-available-but-wait/32580723.

27. Licking County Health Department, "Drug Overdose Death Review."

28. There is ongoing research into a medication-assisted treatment option for methamphetamine use disorder. See Andrea Dukakis, "A Medication to Treat Meth Addiction? Some Take a New Look at Naltrexone," National

Public Radio, November 7, 2019, www.npr.org/sections/health-shots/2019
/11/07/776135642/a-medication-to-treat-meth-addiction-some-take-a-new
-look-at-naltrexone?fbclid=IwAR3HDQhsMxFWA7h5iU0nn5Kjf0cmtwVn
BjHyz2AYa8OzV88c_1k6W0WcrvY.

29. "Keith Brown NYS Senate Joint Task Force Hearing," YouTube, posted
by Cortney Lovell, November 19, 2019, www.youtube.com/watch?v
=LXJq7-QKnS0&feature=youtu.be.

30. Walt Whitman, "Notes Left Over," in *Whitman: Poetry and Prose* (New York:
Library of America, 1996), 1099.

31. "Use of Drugs," United Nations Office on Drugs and Crime, Statistics and
Data, dataunodc.un.org/drugs/prevalence_map_2017.

Chapter 1: Rusted Belts and Think Tanks

1. "2016 Ohio Presidential Election Results," *Politico*, www.politico.com
/2016-election/results/map/president/ohio/.

2. Dave Ghose, "The Longaberger Basket Case," *Columbus Monthly*, April 19,
2017; and "Big Basket Building in Ohio to Be Sold," BBC News, July 14, 2016.

3. Laura Newpoff, "Iconic Longaberger Basket Building Headed Toward Fore-
closure," *Columbus Business First*, March 17, 2017, www.bizjournals.com
/columbus/news/2017/03/17/iconic-longaberger-basket-building-headed
-toward.html.

4. See E. M. P. Brister, *Centennial History of the City of Newark and Licking
County Ohio*, vols. 1 and 2 (Chicago-Columbus: S. J. Clarke Publishing,
1909); Chance Brockway, *Images of America: Newark* (Chicago: Acadia Publishing, 2004); and Gordon R. Kingery, *A Beginning: Licking County, Ohio—
Land of Legend* (Newark, OH: Spencer-Walker Press, 1967).

5. Bradley Lepper, *The Newark Earthworks: A Wonder of the Ancient World* (Columbus: Ohio Historical Society, 2002).

6. "Asset Limited, Income Constrained, Employed (ALICE) Report: Ohio," United
for ALICE, Summer 2017, www.unitedforalice.org/national-comparison.

7. Affordable housing is a growing issue throughout the central Ohio region.
See "All Sides with Ann Fisher: Affordable Housing and Homelessness in
Columbus," WOSU Public Media, January 23, 2019, radio.wosu.org/post
/affordable-housing-and-homelessness-columbus#stream/0.

8. Gabriele Eimontaite, "Let's Talk about the Plight of Housing Instability in
Licking County," *Newark Advocate*, May 24, 2018.

9. "Ohio Unemployment Rates: October 2019 (Not Seasonally Adjusted)," Ohio Department of Job and Family Services, ohiolmi.com/portals/206/LAUS /Archive/2019/ColorRateMap1019.pdf; and "Unemployment Rate in Licking County, OH," Economic Research, Federal Reserve Bank of St. Louis, fred.stlouisfed.org/series/OHLICK0URN. See also Kent Mallett, "County Employment, Workforce Hit High," *Newark Advocate*, June 21, 2016, www .newarkadvocate.com/story/news/local/2016/06/21/county-employment -labor-force-reach-all-time-highs/86184696; and Kent Mallett, "Licking County Unemployment Rate Hits Record Low of 2.8 Percent," *Newark Advocate*, May 21, 2019, www.newarkadvocate.com/story/news/2019/05/21 /licking-county-unemployment-rate-record-low-2-8-percent-april/375710 7002.

10. Kent Mallett, "Amazon Seeks to Hire Thousands for New Etna Facility," *Newark Advocate*, July 8, 2016, www.newarkadvocate.com/story/news/2016/07/08 /amazon-seeks-hire-thousands-new-etna-facility/86871454. There's also some concern that Amazon may not be paying its fair share. See Mya Frazier, "Amazon Is Getting a Good Deal in Ohio, Maybe Too Good," *Bloomberg Businessweek,* October 26, 2017, www.bloomberg.com/news/articles/2017-10-26 /amazon-is-getting-a-good-deal-in-ohio-maybe-too-good.

11. Mark Rembert et al., "Taking Measure of Ohio's Opioid Crisis," Ohio State University, C. William Swank Program in Rural-Urban Policy, October 2017, aede.osu.edu/sites/aede/files/publication_files/Swank%20-%20Taking %20Measure%20of%20Ohios%20Opioid%20Crisis.pdf, 12.

12. Ashleigh Thornton, "2018 Overdose Fatality Review Data Overview Presentation," Licking County Health Department. Note: This presentation was compiled with the help of LCHD epidemiologist Adam Masters, Licking County deputy coroner Dr. Jeff Lee, members of the Licking County Overdose Fatality Review Board, and Licking County health commissioner Joe Ebel.

13. "Alternative Measures of Labor Utilization, Ohio—2018," Bureau of Labor Statistics, Midwest Information Office, April 26, 2019, www.bls.gov/regions /midwest/news-release/laborunderutilization_ohio.htm.

14. See Brian Alexander, *Glass House: The 1% Economy and the Shattering of the All-American Town* (New York: St. Martin's, 2017), which explores the effects of unfettered free-market capitalism (specifically private equity firms) on Lancaster, Ohio.

15. Kent Mallett, "Intersection Opening Completes Downtown Project," *Newark Advocate*, September 11, 2018.

16. Sheridan Hendrix, "Licking County Shows Off Renovated Courthouse," *Columbus Dispatch*, September 17, 2018.

17. "Newark City, Ohio, Quickfacts," U.S. Census Bureau, www.census.gov /quickfacts/fact/table/newarkcityohio/AGE295218.

18. For conditions at Amazon, see David Jamieson, "The Life and Death of an Amazon Warehouse Temp," *Huffington Post*, highline.huffingtonpost.com /articles/en/life-and-death-amazon-temp.

19. Rich Exner, "Ohio Tax Changes Under Gov. John Kasich Leave Villages, Cities Scrambling to Cope with Less (Database)," *Cleveland Plain Dealer*, March 9, 2016.

20. To watch the organization's early activism, watch *Up River*, directed by Doug Swift (Wild Iris Films, 2015).

21. "Wasted Assets: The Cost of Excluding Ohioans with a Record from Work," Policy Matters Ohio, December 18, 2018, www.policymatters ohio.org/research-policy/fair-economy/work-wages/wasted-assets-the-cost -of-excluding-ohioans-with-a-record-from-work.

22. "Fair Hiring," Ohio Justice and Policy Center, www.ohiojpc.org/what-we-do /policy/fair-hiring; and Eric Lyttle, "Newark Posed to Join Entities Dropping Felon Box," *Columbus Dispatch*, July 13, 2015, www.dispatch.com/content /stories/local/2015/07/13/newark-poised-to-join-entities-dropping-felon-box.html.

Chapter 2: The Cavalry's Not Coming

1. Terry DeMio, Dan Horn, and Kevin Grasha, "Ohio, Kentucky Doctors Among 60 Charged in Pain Pill Bust Acted 'Like Drug Dealers,'" *Cincinnati Enquirer*, April 17, 2019.

2. Jan Hoffman, "Groundwork Is Laid for Opioids Settlement That Would Touch Every Corner of the U.S.," *New York Times*, June 14, 2019, www .nytimes.com/2019/06/14/health/opioids-lawsuit-settlement.html.

3. Beth Macy, *Dopesick: Dealers, Doctors, and the Drug Company That Addicted America* (New York: Little, Brown, and Company, 2018); and Sam Quinones, *Dreamland: The True Tale of America's Opiate Epidemic* (New York: Bloomsbury, 2015).

4. For an excellent account of one "pill mill," see Philip Eil, "The Pill Mill That Ravaged Portsmouth," *Cincinnati Magazine*, July 5, 2017.

5. "Drilling into the DEA's Pain Pill Database," *Washington Post*, July 21, 2019, www .washingtonpost.com/graphics/2019/investigations/dea-pain-pill-database/.

6. Aaron Marshall, "Gov. John Kasich Announces Help for County Ravaged by Prescription Drug Abuse," *Cleveland Plain Dealer*, February 21, 2011, www .cleveland.com/open/2011/02/gov_john_kasich_announces_help.html.

7. Sabrina Tavernese, "Ohio County Losing Its Young to Painkillers' Grip," *New York Times,* April 19, 2011.

8. Ashton Marra, "New Federal Data Confirms What We Already Know: Opioid Distributions Inundated Appalachia," *100 Days in Appalachia*, July 19, 2019, www.100daysinappalachia.com/2019/07/19/new-federal-data-confirms -what-we-already-know-opioid-distributions-inundated-appalachia.

9. "Mortality," Ohio Public Health Information Warehouse, Ohio Department of Health, dataset, publicapps.odh.ohio.gov/EDW/DataBrowser/Browse /Mortality; and "Ohio 2018 Overdose Rates," Harm Reduction Ohio, www.harmreductionohio.org/details-on-ohio-overdose-deaths-in-2018-who -died-where.

10. Nabarun Dasgupta, Leo Beletsky, and Daniel Ciccarone, "Opioid Crisis: No Easy Fix to Its Social and Economic Determinants," *American Journal of Public Health* 108, no. 2 (2018): 182–86.

11. Zachary Siegel, "The Opioid Crisis Is About More Than Corporate Greed," *New Republic*, July 30, 2019.

12. See also "Ex-DEA Agent: Opioid Crisis Fueled by Drug Industry and Congress," *60 Minutes*, CBS News, June 17, 2018. The subtitle for the online version of the story says it all: "Whistleblower Joe Rannazzisi says drug distributors pumped opioids into U.S. communities—knowing that people were dying—and says industry lobbyists and Congress derailed the DEA's efforts to stop it."

13. "Opioid Overdose Crisis," National Institute on Drug Abuse, January 2019, www.drugabuse.gov/drugs-abuse/opioids/opioid-overdose-crisis; Kevin E. Vowles et al., "Rates of Opioid Misuse, Abuse, and Addiction in Chronic Pain: A Systematic Review and Data Synthesis," *PAIN*, Volume 156.4 (April 2015): 569–576.

14. Gabor Maté, *In the Realm of Hungry Ghosts: Close Encounters with Addiction* (Berkeley, CA: North Atlantic Books, 2008), 142.

15. Lee N. Robins et al., "Vietnam Veterans Three Years After Vietnam: How Our Study Changed Our View of Heroin," *American Journal on Addictions* 19, no. 3 (2010): 203–11.

16. "Addiction," *Diagnostic and Statistical Manual of Mental Disorders*, 5th ed. (Washington, DC: American Psychiatric Association, 2013).

17. "Definition of Addiction," American Society of Addiction Medicine, September 15, 2019, www.asam.org/resources/definition-of-addiction.

18. L. Bevilacqua and D. Goldman, "Genes and Addictions," *Clinical Pharmacology and Therapeutics* 85, no. 4 (April 2009): 359–61.

19. Maia Szalavitz, *Unbroken Brain: A Revolutionary New Way of Understanding Addiction* (New York: St. Martin's Press, 2016), 36.

20. Jeni L. Burnette et al., "Mindsets of Addiction: Implications for Treatment Intentions," *Journal of Social and Clinical Psychology* 38, no. 5 (2019): 367; and Abraham Gutman, "Framing Addiction as a Disease: Research Shows That Message Might Backfire," *Philadelphia Inquirer*, July 17, 2019.

21. Szalavitz, *Unbroken Brain*, 164, 142–44.

22. Marc Lewis, *Biology of Desire: Why Addiction Is Not a Disease* (New York: Public Affairs, 2016).

23. George F. Koob and Jay Schulkin, "Addiction and Stress: An Allostatic View," *Neuroscience and Biobehavioral Reviews* 106 (November 2018): 245–62.

24. See Maté, *In the Realm of Hungry Ghosts*.

25. Szalavitz, *Unbroken Brain*, 135.

26. Bruce K. Alexander, *The Globalization of Addiction: A Study in Poverty of the Spirit* (New York: Oxford University Press, 2008), 173–206. See also Carl Hart, *High Price: A Neuroscientist's Journey of Self-Discovery That Challenges Everything You Know About Drugs and Society* (New York: Harper Perennial, 2014).

27. See Bruce K. Alexander, Robert B. Coambs, and Patricia F. Hadaway, "The Effect of Housing and Gender on Morphine Self-Administration in Rats," *Psychopharmacology* 58, no. 2 (1978): 175–79; and Szalavitz, *Unbroken Brain*, 132–35.

28. From a recent study on methamphetamine: "Social housing of females protects against the risk of enhanced motivation to self-administer drugs. Understanding how a positive social environment can reduce the susceptibility to drug abuse and examining the differences between high and low risk subpopulations, may provide important insight in the underlying neurobiology of addiction-vulnerability." See Christel Westenbroek et al., "Effect of Social Housing and Oxytocin on the Motivation to Self-Administer Methamphetamine in Female Rats," *Physiology and Behavior* 203 (2019): 16.

29. Alexander, *The Globalization of Addiction*, 59.

30. Ibid., 58.

31. Ibid., 59–60.

32. Ibid., 48.

33. Ibid., 69

34. Ibid., 60.

35. Ibid., 62.

36. Ibid.

37. Ibid., 64.

38. Zachary Siegel, "*Euphoria* Doesn't Have a Drug Problem," *Vulture*, August 6, 2019.

39. Overdose rates have been especially high in Native American communities as well. Melodie Edwards, "Lack of Health Funding Led to Opioid Crisis on Reservations," Wyoming Public Media, April 16, 2018, www.wyomingpublic media.org/post/lack-health-funding-led-opioid-crisis-reservations#stream/0.

40. Katherine McLean, " 'There's Nothing Here': Deindustrialization as Risk Environment for Overdose," *International Journal of Drug Policy* 29 (March 29, 2016): 19–26.

41. Ibid., 19.

42. Ibid., 20.

43. Ibid., 24.

44. Alex S. Vitale, *The End of Policing* (New York: Verso, 2017), 153.

45. There is plenty of research underscoring this assertion. People who are homeless are more likely to overdose; see John R. Marshall et al., "Socioeconomic and Geographical Disparities in Prescription and Illicit Opioid-Related Overdose Deaths in Orange County, California, from 2010–2014," *Substance Abuse* 40, no. 1 (2018): 80–86.

    But those who are on the margins are also at a greater risk of dying. Overdose deaths rise when unemployment increases; Alex Hollingsworth, Christopher J. Ruhm, and Kosali Simon, in "Macroeconomic Conditions and Opioid Abuse," *Journal of Health Economics* 56 (2017): 222–33, note that "opioid deaths and ED visits are predicted to rise when county unemployment rates temporarily increase" (223). See also Christopher S. Carpenter et al., "Economic Conditions, Illicit Drug Use, and Substance Use Disorders in the United States," *Journal of Health Economics* 52 (2017): 63–73.

    Ezequiel Brown and George L. Wehby, in "Economic Conditions and

Drug and Opioid Overdose Deaths," *Medical Care Research and Review* 76, no. 4 (August 2019): 462–77, note the links between a rise in overdose death and housing price drops: "A drop in median house prices by about $70,000 as observed during the Great Recession could potentially contribute to nearly 25% rise in opioid death rates with larger effects among males, non-Hispanic Whites, and younger adults" (12). There is also a link between property values and risky behaviors that lead to overdose deaths (14). Brown and Wehby suggest shoring up funding to prevent overdose in times of economic crisis.

In counties with more blue-collar and service jobs and other economic disadvantages, drug mortality rates are higher; see Shannon M. Monnat et al., "Using Census Data to Understand County-Level Differences in Overall Drug Mortality and Opioid-Related Mortality by Opioid Type," *American Journal of Public Health* 109, no. 8 (2019): 1084–91.

Gene M. Heyman, Nico McVicar, and Hiram Brownell, in "Evidence That Social-Economic Factors Play an Important Role in Drug Overdose Deaths," *International Journal on Drug Policy* 74 (December 2019): 274–84, report that "social-economic factors play a critical role" in overdose specifically and that "variation in the supply of legal opioids is highly correlated with variation in social capital and work force participation." They argue for state-level interventions that extend schooling and address other socioeconomic factors: "When we are talking about the overdose epidemic, we are not just talking about changes in the supply of drugs, we are also talking about the decline in social-economic conditions in the United States."

There is also a relationship between poverty and incarceration and drug use disorder. Elias Nosrati et al., in "Economic Decline, Incarceration, and Mortality from Drug Use Disorders in the USA Between 1983 and 2014: An Observational Analysis," *Lancet Public Health* 4, no. 7 (July 2019): 326–33, conclude: "Reduced household income and high incarceration rates are associated with poor health. The rapid expansion of the prison and jail population in the USA over the past four decades might have contributed to the increasing number of deaths from drug use disorders" (326).

Amy S. B. Bohnert et al., in "Policing and Risk of Overdose Mortality in Urban Neighborhoods," *Drug and Alcohol Dependence* 113 (2011): 62–68, assert that greater police activity, especially "broken windows" policing, "may be an important determinant of drug overdose mortality." This can be particularly problematic in racially and economically marginalized communities.

Acknowledging the myriad challenges faced by the LGBTQ+ community in North America, Ehsasn Moazen-Zadeh et al., in "A Call for Action on Overdose Among LGBTQ People in North America," *Lancet Psychiatry* 6, no. 9 (2019): 725–26, call for greater research and resources for working with this particular population. They note, too, that public health professionals must equip themselves.

See also Dasgupta, Beletsky, and Ciccarone, "Opioid Crisis"; Dave Liddell, "Poverty Is the Root of Scotland's Fatal Drug Overdose Crisis," The Poverty Alliance, August 1, 2019, www.povertyalliance.org/blog-poverty-is-the-root-of-scotlands-fatal-drug-overdose-crisis; and Cara L. Frankenfeld and Timothy F. Leslie, "County-Level Socioeconomic Factors and Residential Racial, Hispanic, Poverty, and Unemployment Segregation Associated with Drug Overdose Deaths in the United States, 2013–2017," *Annals of Epidemiology* 35 (July 2019): 12–19.

46. Scott Higham, Sari Horwitz, and Steven Rich, "Internal Drug Company Emails Show Indifference to Opioid Epidemic," *Washington Post*, July 19, 2019.

47. Sara Randazzo and Jared S. Hopkins, "OxyContin-Maker Owner Maligned Opioid Addicts, Suit Says," *Wall Street Journal*, March 29, 2019, www.wsj.com/articles/purdue-pharma-owner-maligned-opioid-addicts-suit-says-11553899968.

48. Portsmouth City Council Meeting, agenda, March 28, 2011, portsmouthoh.org/sites/default/files/03-28-11.pdf.

49. Lisa Roberts, "Waging the War Against the Devil in Scioto County: A Grassroots Response to Prescription Drug Abuse in a Rural Community," Portsmouth City Health Department, www.deadiversion.usdoj.gov/mtgs/drug_chemical/2012/roberts.pdf.

50. "Senate Passes Bill to Curb 'Pill Mills,' " *Columbus Dispatch*, May 18, 2011.

51. See S. C. Brighthaupt et al., "Effect of Pill Mill Laws on Opioid Overdose Deaths in Ohio & Tennessee: A Mixed-Methods Case Study," *Preventive Medicine* 126 (2019): 4, who write: "Pill mill law enactment had no effects on overall, prescription opioid, heroin, or synthetic opioid overdose deaths in Ohio or Tennessee. Interview results suggest that both states engaged in robust enforcement and implementation of the law. A multi-pronged policy approach, including but not limited to pill mill laws, may be required to effectively address opioid overdose deaths."

52. Daniel Ciccarone, "The Triple Wave Epidemic: Supply and Demand Drivers

of the US Opioid Overdose Crisis," *International Journal of Drug Policy* 71 (2019): 183–88.

53. "Drug Overdose Deaths," U.S. Centers for Disease Control and Prevention, June 27, 2019, www.cdc.gov/drugoverdose/data/statedeaths.html.

54. An ER physician and toxicology expert named Ryan Marino asserts, "Policymakers seem to have taken this urban legend to heart, and are using it as an excuse to divert resources away from evidence-based and lifesaving interventions (like naloxone)"; see Zachary A. Siegel and Maia Szalavitz, "Media Frame: Fentanyl Panic Is Worsening the Overdose Crisis," *The Appeal*, July 16, 2019, theappeal.org/media-frame-fentanyl-panic-is-worsening-the-overdose-crisis. See also Elizabeth Brico, "A Dangerous Fentanyl Myth Lives On," *Columbia Journalism Review*, April 11, 2019.

55. "2016 Ohio Drug Overdose Data," Ohio Department of Health, odh .ohio.gov/wps/wcm/connect/gov/d174de32-5703-4ef2-ad0c-804f9aa5f0de /2016_OhioDrugOverdoseReport.pdf?MOD=AJPERES&CONVERT _TO=url&CACHEID=ROOTWORKSPACE.Z18_M1HGGIK0N0JO00 QO9DDDDM3000-d174de32-5703-4ef2-ad0c-804f9aa5f0de-miTFA2Q.

56. Dasgupta, Beletsky, and Ciccarone, in their article "Opioid Crisis," assert, "The accepted wisdom about the US overdose crisis singles out prescribing as the causative vector. Although drug supply is a key factor, we posit that the crisis is fundamentally fueled by economic and social upheaval, its etiology closely linked to the role of opioids as a refuge from physical and psychological trauma, concentrated disadvantage, isolation and hopelessness" (182). In other words, it wasn't overprescribing. They add, "The emphasis on prescribing volume may be a manifestation of subconscious racial bias that frames the famously White opioid crisis as inadvertently induced by physicians; this stands in direct contrast with previous drug panics perceived to afflict minorities, whose drug use was considered a moral failing" (184).

57. Medication-assisted treatment (MAT) for opioid use disorder comes in many forms and is considered one of the most effective forms of treatment. Methadone is perhaps the most well-known medication used in MAT—it's a synthetic opioid agonist that is typically taken at a clinic. Naltrexone, sold under the brand name Vivitrol, is an extended-release drug that can be taken as a monthly injection. Suboxone (a combination of buprenorphine and naloxone) is a partial antagonist that has a ceiling effect. A study by led by Harvard professor Dr. Sarah E. Wakeman found that "treatment with buprenorphine or methadone was as-

sociated with reductions in overdose and serious opioid-related acute care use compared with other treatments." S. E. Wakeman, M. R. Larochelle, O. Ameli, et al. "Comparative Effectiveness of Different Treatment Pathways for Opioid Use Disorder," *JAMA Network Open.* 2020;3(2):e1920622. jamanetwork.com /journals/jamanetworkopen/fullarticle/2760032.

58.   In 1995, France made it easier for physicians to prescribe buprenorphine— with no extra training or licensing—and more people were able to access treatment. According to Olga Khazan, in "How France Cut Heroin Over- doses by 79 Percent in 4 Years and the United States could, too," *The Atlantic,* April 16, 2018, "Within four years, overdose deaths declined by 79 percent."

59.   "Naloxone Access and Good Samaritan Law in Ohio," Network for Pub- lic Health Law, static1.squarespace.com/static/5b896c3cfcf7fd71ad6a0d47 /t/5d5c465ea7a2bf0001bcf52f/1566328415214/Ohio-OD-law-fact-sheet -8_30_18-FINAL.pdf.

60.   Abby Spears, "Emerging Technologies: Utilizing Data and Geomapping to Identify Health Disparities," (Re)Covering Appalachia, Shawnee State Uni- versity, Portsmouth, Ohio, November 1, 2019.

61.   Samantha Artiga and Elizabeth Hinton, in "Beyond Health Care: The Role of Social Determinants in Promoting Health and Health Equity," Kaiser Family Foundation, www.kff.org/disparities-policy/issue-brief/beyond-health-care -the-role-of-social-determinants-in-promoting-health-and-health-equity, write: "Social determinants of health include factors like socioeconomic status, education, neighborhood and physical environment, employment, and social support networks, as well as access to health care. Addressing so- cial determinants of health is important for improving health and reducing long-standing disparities in health and health care."

Dasgupta, Beletsky, and Ciccarone, in their article "Opioid Crisis," write: "The social determinants lens lays bare the urgency of integrating clin- ical care with efforts to improve patients' structural environment" (185).

Chapter 3: Hope Shot

1.   Doug Swift talks to Eric about this in his documentary *Up River* (Wild Iris Films, 2015).

2.   "U.S. Correctional Population Declined for the Ninth Consecutive Year," U.S. Department of Justice, Office of Justice Programs, press release, April 26, 2018, www.bjs.gov/content/pub/press/cpus16pr.pdf; and Michelle Al-

exander, *The New Jim Crow: Mass Incarceration in the Age of Colorblindness* (New York: The New Press, 2010).

3. But the war on drugs has long been used as a tool to harass and control others. Alex S. Vitale, in *The End of Policing* (New York: Verso, 2017), points to opium's link to laborers from China in the nineteenth century: "The prohibition of opium gave police a tool to justify constant harassment and tight social regulation of this 'suspect' population" (131). He also discusses how the drug was largely ignored until upper- and middle-class white women started using it. Years later, and in the same vein, he notes, marijuana was associated with black culture and led to a kind of "moral panic" among white people (132). A search of any historical newspaper database reveals the racist tropes that fueled this panic. For example, "Use of Cocaine Is Increasing at an Alarming Rate Drug Stores Downtown Are Daily Overrun by Confirmed Fiends," *St. Louis Republic*, September 2, 1897; "Cocaine Is Terrible. Use of the Drug Is Growing Constantly Among Negroes," *Fort Worth Morning Register*, September 3, 1899; "Cocaine Drug and Fiend. These Be Interesting Facts," *Charlotte Observer*, September 29, 1906; "Specter Among Negroes—Cocaine: America's Worst Drug Habit Has Made Great Inroads with More," *Daily Herald*, July 20, 1909; and "Chinese Laundries Sell Deadly Opium . . . ," *Columbus Daily Enquirer*, November 21, 1909, all via *Readex: America's Historical Newspapers*.

4. Issac J. Bailey writes, in "Why Didn't My Drug-Affected Family Get Any Sympathy?" *Politico*, June 10, 2018, "Contrast all of this coverage with the coverage of crack addicts in the 1980s and 1990s. The photos from that era weren't of innocent children being harmed; it was of U.S. marshals pointing pistols in the faces of drug addicts at crack houses, of black men in handcuffs, of crack smokers passed out on sidewalks. There were few childhood photos and shots of crying mothers."

5. John Gramlich, "The Gap Between the Number of Blacks and Whites in Prison Is Shrinking," Pew Research Center, April 30, 2019, www .pewresearch.org/fact-tank/2019/04/30/shrinking-gap-between-number-of -blacks-and-whites-in-prison.

6. "Ohio Profile," Prison Policy Initiative, www.prisonpolicy.org/profiles /OH.html. Consider, too, how this is playing out within this current crisis: Panama Jackson, "This Is America: Save a White Drug Addict, Jail a

Black One," *The Root*, May 10, 2018, verysmartbrothas.theroot.com/this
-is-america-save-a-white-drug-addict-jail-a-black-1825923681.

7. Marica Ferri, Laura Amato, and Marina Davoli, "Alcoholics Anonymous and
   Other 12-Step Programmes for Alcohol Dependence," *Cochrane Database of
   Systematic Reviews* 3 (July 19, 2006): CD005032.

8. "With Sobering Science, Doctor Debunks 12-Step Recovery," *All Things
   Considered*, National Public Radio, March 23, 2014. See also Lance Dodes
   and Zachary Dodes, *The Sober Truth: Debunking the Bad Science Behind 12-
   Step Programs and the Rehab Industry* (Boston: Beacon, 2014).

9. "With Sobering Science, Doctor Debunks 12-Step Recovery."

10. Ibid.

11. Maia Szalavitz, *Unbroken Brain: A Revolutionary New Way of Understanding
    Addiction* (New York: St. Martin's Press, 2016), 219.

12. Ibid. For more on drug courts and substance use disorder, see Marianne
    Møllmann and Christine Mehta, "Neither Justice nor Treatment: Drug
    Courts in the United States," Physicians for Human Rights, June 2017, phr
    .org/wp-content/uploads/2017/06/phr_drugcourts_report_singlepages.pdf.

13. To be sure, there is a range of opinion on medication-assisted treatment
    among the many twelve-step organizations that exist. There are also, increas-
    ingly, recovery groups specifically for people using medication-assisted treat-
    ment. See, for example, Jillian Bauer-Reese, "There's a New 12-Step Group:
    Medication-Assisted Recovery Anonymous," *Slate,* April 17, 2018, slate.com
    /technology/2018/04/theres-a-new-12-step-group-for-people-in-recovery
    -who-are-prescribed-medications-like-methadone.html.

14. Annette Mendola and Richard L. Gibson, "Addiction, 12-Step Programs,
    and Evidentiary Standards for Ethically and Clinically Sound Treatment
    Recommendations: What Should Clinicians Do?" *AMA Journal of Ethics* 18,
    no. 6 (June 2016): 647.

15. John-Kåre Vederhus and Øistein Kristensen, in "High Effectiveness of Self-
    Help Programs After Drug Addiction Therapy," *BMC Psychiatry* 6, no. 1
    (2006): 35, suggest that self-help groups can be useful "as a supplement to
    drug addiction treatment."

16. House Bill 56, Committee Activity, Ohio Legislature, 133rd Assembly, 2015,
    www.legislature.ohio.gov/legislation/legislation-committee-documents?id
    =GA131-HB-56.

17. James I. Charlton, *Nothing About Us Without Us: Disability Oppression and Empowerment* (Berkeley: University of California Press, 2000).

Corey Davis, Traci Green, and Leo Beletsky, in "Action, Not Rhetoric, Needed to Reverse the Opioid Overdose Epidemic," *Journal of Law, Medicine, and Ethics* 45, no. S1 (2017): 20–23, note that it took the work of activists to get any effective change during the HIV/AIDS crisis: "Structural change to address both the causes and effects of the epidemic is urgently needed. In the case of HIV/AIDS, failure to deploy non-judgmental, evidence-based interventions was directly responsible for the preventable deaths of hundreds of thousands of Americans. Improvement, when it came, was championed not by officials but by activists such as ACT UP. We are now faced with the choice of whether to learn from that mistake—or repeat it" (22).

Chapter 4: Semicolons

1. Dennis Cauchon, "Fentanyl-Laced Cocaine Is Ohio's Newest Killer—But We Can Combat This Scourge," *Cleveland Plain Dealer*, January 19, 2018.

2. Billy designed this tattoo and says he was inspired by Project Semicolon. See projectsemicolon.com/about-project-semicolon/.

3. Patricia Perry, "Letter to the Editor," *Newark Advocate*, November 22, 2011.

Chapter 5: Swimming Upstream

1. Colin Dwyer, "Ohio Sues 5 Major Drug Companies for 'Fueling Drug Epidemic,'" National Public Radio, May 31, 2017.

2. Julie Hirschfeld Davis, "Trump Declares Opioid Crisis a 'Health Emergency' but Requests No Funds," *New York Times*, October 26, 2017, www.nytimes.com/2017/10/26/us/politics/trump-opioid-crisis.html.

3. Mike DeWine, "Recovery Ohio," DeWine/Husted for Ohio, campaign website, October 31, 2017, www.mikedewine.com.

4. See, for example, "GOP Lieutenant Governor Wants to End Ohio Medicaid Expansion," Associated Press State Wire: Ohio, September 19, 2017; and "Policy Matters Weighs In on State Budget Sent to Governor Kasich," Policy Matters Ohio, June 30, 2017, www.policymattersohio.org/press-room/2017/06/30/ohios-medicaid-expansion-must-be-protected.

5. Bethany Bruner, "Three Arrested with Ties to Mexican Cartel," *Newark Advocate*, July 12, 2017.

6. Alex S. Vitale, *The End of Policing* (New York: Verso, 2017), 129.

7. Gabor Maté, *In the Realm of Hungry Ghosts: Close Encounters with Addiction* (Berkeley, CA: North Atlantic Books, 2008), 165, 197–210.
8. Ibid., 39.

Chapter 6: Systems of Care

1. Rob Wells, "Rally in Newark Draws Attention to Opioid Crisis, Recovery," ABC 6, November 26, 2017, abc6onyourside.com/on-your-side/fighting-back /rally-in-newark-draws-attention-to-opioid-crisis.
2. "Definition of Recovery-Oriented Systems of Care," Selected Papers of William L. White, www.williamwhitepapers.com/pr/CSAT%20ROSC%20 Definition.pdf.
3. Increased "social capital" also protects communities against drug overdose. See Michael J. Zoorab and Jason L. Salemi, "Bowling Alone, Dying Together: The Role of Social Capital in Mitigating the Drug Overdose Epidemic in the United States," *Drug and Alcohol Dependence* 173 (April 2017): 1–9; and Jan Sundquist et al., "Neighborhood Linking Social Capital as a Predictor of Drug Abuse: A Swedish National Cohort Study," *Addictive Behaviors* 63 (2016): 37–44.
4. Bruce K. Alexander, The *Globalization of Addiction: A Study in Poverty of the Spirit* (New York: Oxford University Press, 2008), 340.
5. Anne Case and Angus Deaton, "Mortality and Morbidity in the 21st Century," *Brookings Papers on Economic Activity* (Spring 2017): 397–476.
6. Mark Rembert et al., "Taking Measure of Ohio's Opioid Crisis," Ohio State University, C. William Swank Program in Rural-Urban Policy, October 2017, aede.osu.edu/sites/aede/files/publication_files/Swank%20-%20Taking %20Measure%20of%20Ohios%20Opioid%20Crisis.pdf, 10, and footnotes in chapter 2.
7. Life expectancy in this part of Licking County is perhaps the lowest in the country. "Licking County Community Health Assessment," www.licking cohealth.org/data/index.html.

Chapter 7: None of Us Are Bad People

1. This chapter is based on my article "Overdose and Punishment," *The New Republic*, September 10, 2018, and relies on interviews with Lindsay LaSalle, Clifford Murphy, Kathie Kane-Willis, Leo Beletsky, and Louise Vincent, as well as the transcripts for *State of Ohio v. Thomas A. Kosto*, 2017, Case No.

16, CR 00069, and *State of Ohio v. Thomas A. Kosto*, 2018, Court of Appeals Case No. 17-CA-54. For introductions to the issue of "drug-induced homicide," see Zachary A. Siegel and Leo Beletsky, "Charging 'Dealers' with Homicide: Explained," *The Appeal*, November 2, 2018, theappeal.org/charging-dealers-with-homicide-explained; and "An Overdose Death Is Not Murder: Why Drug-Induced Homicide Laws Are Counterproductive and Inhumane," Drug Policy Alliance, November 2017, www.drugpolicy.org/sites/default/files/dpa_drug_induced_homicide_report_0.pdf.

2. "Sentencing Reform through a Stronger SB 3," Policy Matters Ohio, May 13, 2019, www.policymattersohio.org/research-policy/quality-ohio/corrections/sentencing-reform-through-a-stronger-sb-3.

3. "Drug Induced Homicide Laws," Prescription Drug Abuse Policy System, with Health in Justice Action Lab and Legal Science, January 1, 2019, www.pdaps.org/datasets/drug-induced-homicide-1529945480-1549313265-1559075032.

4. "An Overdose Death Is Not Murder."

5. Rosa Goldensohn, "The Shared Drugs," *New York Times*, May 25, 2018, www.nytimes.com/2018/05/25/us/drug-overdose-prosecution-crime.html.

6. "Use of Guidelines and Specific Offense Characteristics," U.S. Sentencing Commission, 2017, www.ussc.gov/sites/default/files/pdf/research-and-publications/federal-sentencing-statistics/guideline-application-frequencies/2017/Use_of_SOC_Offender_Based.pdf.

7. "Remarks by President Trump on Tax Reform," Whitehouse.gov, February 5, 2018, www.whitehouse.gov/briefings-statements/remarks-president-trump-tax-reform-3.

8. Jamie Ducharme, "Trump Said China Doesn't Have a Drug Problem. The Data Tells a Different Story," *Time*, February 15, 2019, time.com/5530597/trump-china-drug-problem.

9. Adrian Chen, "What Trump Sees in Philippine President Rodrigo Duterte," *The New Yorker*, May 2, 2017, www.newyorker.com/news/news-desk/what-trump-sees-in-philippine-president-rodrigo-duterte.

10. "Attorney General Sessions Issues Memo to U.S. Attorneys on the Use of Capital Punishment in Drug-Related Prosecutions," U.S. Department of Justice, March 21, 2018, www.justice.gov/opa/pr/attorney-general-sessions-issues-memo-us-attorneys-use-capital-punishment-drug-related.

11. Megan Mitchell, "Middletown Considers 3 Strike Policy on Responding to

Overdoses," WLWT 5, June 23, 2017, www.wlwt.com/article/middletown
-considers-3-strike-policy-on-responding-to-overdoses/10215284.

12. "Drug-Induced Homicide," Health in Justice Action Lab, Northeastern University School of Law, 2018, www.healthinjustice.org/drug-induced-homicide.

13. Between 2016 and 2019, five people were charged in Licking County.

14. *State of Ohio v. Thomas A. Kosto*, 2017, Case No. 16, CR 00069.

15. Bethany Bruner, "Jury Convicts Man in Overdose Death," *Newark Advocate*, June 30, 2017, www.newarkadvocate.com/story/news/crime/2017/06/30
/jury-convicts-man-heroin-overdose-death/439388001.

16. Ibid.

17. "Charged with Manslaughter; A Doctor Arrested and Accused of Culpable Ne-
glect," *New York Times*, April 25, 1885, www.nytimes.com/1885/04/25/archives
/charged-with-manslaughter-a-doctor-arrested-and-accused-of-culpable.html.

18. "Harrison Narcotics Tax Act, 1914," National Alliance of Advocates for Buprenorphine Treatment, www.naabt.org/documents/Harrison_Narcotics
_Tax_Act_1914.pdf; and "Three Held in Death of Boy from Overdose,"
Washington Times, April 17, 1916, chroniclingamerica.loc.gov/lccn/sn8402
6749/1916-04-17/ed-1/seq-1.

19. Emanuel Perlmutter, "Two Indicted for Homicide in Girl's Death by Heroin," *New York Times*, February 26, 1970, www.nytimes.com/1970/02/26
/archives/two-indicted-for-homicide-in-girls-death-by-heroin-2-indicted-for
.html.

20. Radley Balko, "America's Drug War: 30 Years of Rampaging Wildebeest,"
Washington Post, October 28, 2016, www.washingtonpost.com/news/the
-watch/wp/2016/10/28/americas-drug-war-30-years-of-rampaging-wildebeest.

21. Sue Ann Forrest, "HB 474/SB 375—Death by Distribution," North Carolina Medical Society, July 9, 2019, www.ncmedsoc.org/hb-474-death-by
-distribution. See also Michelle Lou, "Under New North Carolina Law,
Drug Dealers Could Be Charged with Second-Degree Murder," CNN,
July 9, 2019, www.cnn.com/2019/07/09/us/north-carolina-hb-474-death-by
-distribution-trnd/index.html; and Session Law 2019-83, House Bill 474,
General Assembly of North Carolina, Session 2019, www.ncleg.gov/Sessions
/2019/Bills/House/PDF/H474v6.pdf.

22. "More Imprisonment Does Not Reduce State Drug Problems," Pew Charitable Trusts, March 8, 2018, www.pewtrusts.org/en/research-and-analysis

/issue-briefs/2018/03/more-imprisonment-does-not-reduce-state-drug
-problems#4-drug-imprisonment-varies-widel.

23. Peter Wagner and Wendy Sawyer, "Mass Incarceration: The Whole Pie 2018," Prison Policy Initiative, March 14, 2018, www.prisonpolicy.org/reports /pie2018.html.

24. Stephanie Schmitz Bechteler and Kathleen Kane-Willis, "Whitewashed: The African American Opioid Epidemic," Chicago Urban League, Research and Policy Center, November 2017.

25. Jackie Borchardt, "Ohio '911 Good Samaritan' Law Granting Immunity for Overdose Calls Signed by Gov. John Kasich," Cleveland.com, June 13, 2016, www.cleveland.com/open/2016/06/ohio_911_good_samaritan_law _gr.html; and "Drug Overdose and Ohio's Good Samaritan Law," Ohio-START: Sobriety, Treatment & Reducing Trauma Program, The Ohio State University, College of Social Work, October 4, 2019, u.osu.edu/ohiostart /2019/10/04/drug-overdose-and-ohios-good-samaritan-law.

26. Amanda D. Latimore and Rachel S. Bergstein, "'Caught with a Body' yet Protected by Law? Calling 911 for Opioid Overdose in the Context of the Good Samaritan Law," *International Journal of Drug Policy* 50 (December 2017): 82–89.

27. Illinois Controlled Substances Act, 720 ILCS 570, www.ilga.gov/legislation /ilcs/ilcs5.asp?ActID=1941&ChapterID=53.

28. "Statewide Narcotics Action Plan," New Jersey Division of Criminal Justice, issued January 1988, revised March 1993, www.state.nj.us/lps/dcj/agguide /snap93.htm.

29. "No. 54. An Act Relating to Selling or Dispensing Illegal Drugs," Vermont General Assembly, H. 206, www.leg.state.vt.us/docs/legdoc.cfm?URL =/docs/2004/acts/ACT054.htm.

30. Jim Edwards, "Making Friends into Felons," *New Jersey Law Journal*, September 9, 2002, 1.

31. Joe Gyan Jr., "Denham Springs Man Serving Life Term in Fatal Heroin Overdose Seeks Relief from State High Court," *The Advocate*, May 1, 2019, www.theadvocate.com/baton_rouge/news/courts/article_3380e782-6b81 -11e9-abe3-f39a445d2d42.html.

32. Lindsay Bever, "She Shot Up Her Father with Heroin: Now He's Dead and She's in Prison," *Washington Post*, January 11, 2017, www.washingtonpost

.com/news/to-your-health/wp/2017/01/11/she-shot-up-her-father-with
-heroin-now-hes-dead-and-shes-in-prison.

33. Stephanie Grady, " 'It's Been Used More and More,' but Is Wisconsin's Len
Bias Law an Effective Deterrent to Opioid Abuse?" Fox 6 Now, November
21, 2016, fox6now.com/2016/11/21/its-been-used-more-and-more-but-is
-wisconsins-len-bias-law-an-effective-deterrent-to-opioid-abuse.

34. Brian Polcyn and Stephen Davis, "High-Level Drug Dealers Rarely Charged
with Drug-Related Homicides as Wisconsin Death Toll Reaches 10K,"
Fox 6 Now, February 9, 2017, fox6now.com/2017/02/09/high-level-drug
-dealers-are-rarely-charged-with-drug-related-homicides-as-wisconsin
-death-toll-reaches-10000.

35. Bethany Bruner, "Manslaughter Conviction in Overdose Death Overturned
on Appeal," *Newark Advocate*, May 22, 2018, www.newarkadvocate.com
/story/news/crime/2018/05/22/manslaughter-conviction-overdose-death
-overturned-appeal/628426002.

36. Bethany Bruner, "After Appeal, Man Resentenced for Heroin Possession in OD Case," *Newark Advocate*, July 3, 2018, www.newarkadvocate
.com/story/news/crime/2018/07/03/after-appeal-man-resentenced-heroin
-possession-od-case/755031002.

37. Joel Brinkley, "Anti-Drug Law: Words, Deeds, Political Expediency,"
New York Times, October 27, 1986, www.nytimes.com/1986/10/27/us
/anti-drug-law-words-deeds-political-expediency.html.

38. Ibid.

39. Rita Rubin, "Surgeon General Urges Expanded Availability of Naloxone,"
JAMA 319, no. 20 (2018): 2068, doi.org/10.1001/jama.2018.6254.

40. For starters, see Michelle Alexander, *The New Jim Crow: Mass Incarceration
in the Age of Colorblindness* (New York: The New Press, 2010); and Michael
F. Walther, "Insanity: Four Decades of U.S. Counterdrug Strategy," Strategic
Studies Institute, U.S. Army War College, December 27, 2012.

41. In an email exchange, Gutman told me he was appropriating Dan Riffle's
"Every billionaire is a policy failure."

42. Maia Szalavitz, "These Drug Users Don't Want Their Dealer Prosecuted
if They OD," *Vice*, August 20, 2018, www.vice.com/en_us/article/kzyk7n
/these-drug-users-dont-want-their-dealer-prosecuted-if-they-od.

43. According to a 2012 study, 87.5 percent of people who said they sold drugs in

the past year also said they used drugs in the past year. And 41.3 percent of people who said they sold drugs in the past year reported that they met criteria for a substance use disorder. See "Results from the 2012 National Survey on Drug Use and Health: Summary of National Findings," U.S. Department of Health and Human Services, Substance Abuse and Mental Health Services Administration (SAMHSA), September 2013, www.samhsa.gov/data/sites /default/files/NSDUHresults2012/NSDUHresults2012.pdf.

44. Description based on "Emergency Room Report," Pike County Sheriff's Office, Ohio Uniform Incident Report, 14-357, August 15, 2014.

Chapter 8: The Churn

1. "Newark: Exploring Community Solutions to the Addiction Crisis," Your Voice Ohio, April 2018, yourvoiceohio.org/wp-content/uploads/2018/05 /Your-Voice-Ohio-Newark-Report.pdf.

2. These are some of the responses found in their report.

3. Kate Dengg, "Addiction Town Hall: We're Coming Together to Solve a Problem," *Newark Advocate*, June 1, 2018, www.newarkadvocate.com/story/news /local/2018/06/01/city-schools-think-tank-host-addiction-forum/659116002.

4. Andy Chow, "Issue 1, Explained: What to Know About Ohio's Drug Sentencing Amendment," WOSU Public Media, October 18, 2018, radio .wosu.org/post/issue-1-explained-what-know-about-ohios-drug-sentencing -amendment#stream/0.

5. "Downtown Newark Association General Membership Meeting," meeting minutes, May 7, 2019.

6. "Downtown Newark Association General Membership Meeting," meeting minutes, September 4, 2018.

7. Wendy Sawyer and Peter Wagner, "Mass Incarceration: The Whole Pie 2019," Prison Policy Initiative, March 19, 2019, www.prisonpolicy.org /reports/pie2019.html.

Chapter 9: Any Positive Change

1. "Syringe Services Programs Fact Sheet," U.S. Centers for Disease Control and Prevention, May 23, 2019, www.cdc.gov/ssp/syringe-services-programs -factsheet.html; and Jennifer J. Carroll, Traci C. Green, and Rita K. Noonan, "Evidence-Based Strategies for Preventing Opioid Overdose: What's Working in the United States," U.S. Centers for Disease Control and Prevention,

National Center for Injury Prevention and Control, 2018, www.cdc.gov /drugoverdose/pdf/pubs/2018-evidence-based-strategies.pdf.

2. Carroll, Green, and Noonan, "Evidence-Based Strategies for Preventing Opioid Overdose," 27.

3. Legalized syringe exchanges had dramatically reduced possible HIV cases in Baltimore and Philadelphia. See Monica S. Ruiz et al., "Using Interrupted Time Series Analysis to Measure the Impact of Legalized Syringe Exchange on HIV Diagnoses in Baltimore and Philadelphia," *Journal of Acquired Immune Deficiency Syndrome* 82, suppl. 2 (December 1, 2019): S148–S54; and Victoria Knight, "Needle Exchanges Find New Champions Among Republicans," *USA Today*, May 8, 2019, www.usatoday.com/story/news/nation/2019/05/08 /needle-exchange-programs-more-accepted-republican-states/1139672001.

4. Joe Ebel, "Syringe Exchanges Are an Evidence-Based Public Health Intervention," *Newark Advocate*, November 10, 2018, www.newarkadvocate.com /story/news/2018/11/10/syringe-exchanges-evidence-based-public-health -intervention/1905865002.

5. "Persons Living with Diagnosed HIV Infection Reported in Licking County," Ohio Department of Health, June 30, 2019, odh.ohio.gov; "Ohio Hepatitis B Cases 2015–2018," Demographic Breakdown of Ohio, odh.ohio.gov; "Ohio Hepatitis C Cases 2014–2018," Demographic Breakdown of Ohio, odh.ohio.gov.

6. Dennis Cauchon, "For Many on 9/11, Survival Was No Accident," *USA Today*, December 19, 2011.

7. "Kasich Administration Blocks Ohio's Cash-Strapped Syringe Programs from Getting Federal Funds," Harm Reduction Ohio, June 25, 2018, www .harmreductionohio.org/kasich-administration-blocks-ohios-cash-strapped -syringe-programs-from-getting-federal-funds; and JoAnne Viviano, "Ohio Wants to Use Federal Grant Money for Needle-Exchange Programs," *Alliance Review*, July 22, 2018, www.the-review.com/news/20180722/ohio -wants-to-use-federal-grant-money-for-needle-exchange-programs.

8. According to the Harm Reduction Coalition, "Overamping means a lot of things to a lot of people. Sometimes it is physical, when our bodies don't feel right. Other times it is psychological, like paranoia, anxiety or psychosis—or a mixture of the two. It's complicated because sometimes one person will consider something overamping, and the other person actually considers it just part of the high, or maybe even enjoys a feeling that someone else hates."

Harm Reduction Coaltion. harmreduction.org/issues/overdose-prevention /overview/stimulant-overamping-basics/what-is-overamping.

9. Maia Szalavitz, "Dan Bigg Is a Harm Reduction Pioneer and His Overdose Doesn't Change That," *Vice*, October 24, 2018, www.vice.com/en_us /article/7x3yag/dan-bigg-overdose-harm-reduction.

10. Michael A. Irvine, Margot Kuo, Jane A. Buxton, Robert Balshaw, Michael Otterstatter, Laura Macdougall, M-J Milloy, et al. "Modelling the Combined Impact of Interventions in Averting Deaths During a Synthetic-Opioid Overdose Epidemic," *Addiction* 114, no. 9 (2019): 1602–1613; Rebecca B. Naumann, Christine Piette Durrance, Shabbar I. Ranapurwala, Anna E. Austin, Scott Proescholdbell, Robert Childs, Stephen W. Marshall, Susan Kansagra, and Meghan E. Shanahan. "Impact of a Community-Based Naloxone Distribution Program on Opioid Overdose Death Rates," *Drug and Alcohol Dependence* 204, (2019): 107536.

11. For a thorough read on harm reduction best practices, read Sheila P. Vakharia and Jeannie Little, "Starting Where the Client Is: Harm Reduction Guidelines for Clinical Social Work Practice," *Clinical Social Work Journal* 45, no. 1 (2017): 65–76.

12. Maia Szalavitz, *Unbroken Brain: A Revolutionary New Way of Understanding Addiction* (New York: St. Martin's Press, 2016), 241.

13. Ibid.

14. Lesly-Marie Buer, "Overdosing in Appalachia," *Boston Review*, July 8, 2019.

15. "3707.57 Bloodborne Infectious Disease Prevention Programs," Ohio Revised Code, codes.ohio.gov/orc/3707.57. See also Ohio Revised Code 3709 for an explanation of the role of a board of health in Ohio.

16. "Newark FED Up Rally," *Newark Advocate*, August 30, 2018, www.newark advocate.com/media/cinematic/gallery/1153608002/newark-fed-up-rally.

17. Dennis Cauchon, "Needle Exchange Programs Save Money, Lives," *Newark Advocate*, September 9, 2018.

Chapter 10: The Foot of the Mountain

1. Brian Alexander, "The Ghost Bosses," *The Atlantic*, March 13, 2017, www .theatlantic.com/business/archive/2017/03/lancaster-ohio-glass-house/519351.

2. Brian Alexander, *Glass House: The 1% Economy and the Shattering of the All-American Town* (New York: St. Martin's, 2017).

3. Brian Alexander, "What America Is Losing as Its Small Towns Struggle," *The Atlantic*, October 18, 2017.

4. Meghan Mongillo, "'Do You Know Who Murdered Us?': Progress Made but More Info Sought in Pike Co. Massacre," Local 12 News, WKRC, April 13, 2017, local12.com/news/local/do-you-know-who-murdered-us-progress -made-but-more-info-sought-in-pike-co-massacre.

5. "Prison and Jail Incarceration Rates Decreased by More Than 10% from 2007 to 2017," U.S. Department of Justice, press release, April 25, 2019, www.bjs.gov/content/pub/press/p17ji17pr.pdf.

6. Craig McDonald, "County Officials United in Strong Opposition to Issue 1," *Newark Advocate*, October 8, 2018.

7. Chengyuan Zhou et al., "The Costs and Benefits of Day Reporting Centers: A New Model of Adult Probation in Allegheny County," Allegheny County Department of Human Services, September 2014, www.alleghenycountyanalytics .us/wp-content/uploads/2016/06/The-Costs-and-Benefits-of-Day-Reporting -Centers-A-New-Model-of-Adult-Probation-in-Allegheny-County.pdf.

8. According to Douglas J. Boyle et al., in "An Evaluation of Day Reporting Centers for Parolees: Outcomes of a Randomized Trial," *Criminology & Public Policy* 12, no. 1 (2013): 119–43, "The data show that DRC participants were more likely to be arrested and convicted for a new offense in the short term compared to the Control group. DRC participants' median time to new arrest was 99 days shorter than Control group parolees; however, this difference was not significant. No differences were found between the groups in the long term."

9. Day reporting is, in some ways, akin to a drug court relying on "police as gatekeepers." See Alex S. Vitale, *The End of Policing* (New York: Verso, 2017), 145.

10. The Licking County Board of Health is comprised of eleven members, though one seat (from the city of Pataskala) was unfilled as of this writing. All of the board members are appointed, and Ohio law (Ohio Revised Code 3709) says that only one must be a physician. Of the ten members on the board at the time of this writing, there was one physician, two nurses, one chiropractor, and one paramedic. See "Board of Health," Licking County Health Department, www.lickingcohealth.org/admin/board.html.

11. Albert Camus, *The Myth of Sisyphus and Other Essays*, trans. Justin O'Brien (New York: Knopf, 1955), 121.

12. Ibid., 123.

Chapter 11: The Person Next to You

1. See brave.coop to learn more about their Be Safe community app and the Brave Button.

2. Gordon was referring to Eli Beer, "The Fastest Ambulance? A Motorcycle," TED Talk, April 2013, www.ted.com/talks/eli_beer_the_fastest_ambulance_a_motorcycle.

3. "Ohio Opioid Technology Challenge," Ohio Development Services Agency, development.ohio.gov/bs_thirdfrontier/ootc.htm.

4. Often people do not have access to MAT (which cut the risk of overdose in half) while inside. Or they are given naltrexone (Vivitrol), which requires compliance. Shabbar I. Ranapurwala et al., "Opioid Overdose Mortality Among Former North Carolina Inmates: 2000–2015," *American Journal of Public Health* 108, no. 9 (September 2018): 1207–13.

5. See, for example, this sticker available for $4.98 plus shipping: "Shoot Your Local Heroin Dealer," Amazon.com, www.amazon.com/Shoot-Your-Local-Heroin-Dealer/dp/B07N46Y1R2.

6. Rhea W. Boyd, "Despair doesn't kill, defending whiteness does," *The Lancet*, Volume 395, Issue 10218 (January 2020): 105–6.

7. Katherine McLean, "'There's Nothing Here': Deindustrialization as Risk Environment for Overdose," *International Journal of Drug Policy* 29 (March 29, 2016): 25.

8. Ibid., 26.

9. Lynn Hunt, *Inventing Human Rights: A History* (New York: Norton, 2007), 20.

10. This is not an original thought, for sure, but see Jack Shuler, *Calling Out Liberty: The Stono Rebellion of 1739 and the Universal Struggle for Human Rights* (Jackson: University of Mississippi Press, 2009).

11. Hunt, *Inventing Human Rights*, 20.

12. "Newark City Committee, Dec 17, 2018," YouTube, posted by Newark City Council, December 17, 2018, www.youtube.com/watch?v=vCMDlbEeY5I.

13. "Syringe Services Programs Fact Sheet," U.S. Centers for Disease Control and Prevention, May 23, 2019, www.cdc.gov/ssp/syringe-services-programs-factsheet.html.

Chapter 12: Punk Rock Harm Reduction

1. Peter Baker, "Trump Declares National Emergency, and Provokes a Constitutional Clash," *New York Times*, February 15, 2019, www.nytimes.com/2019/02/15/us/politics/national-emergency-trump.html.

2. Kaitlin Shroeder, "Opioid Battle in Region Getting Boost from Big Data," *Dayton Daily News*, February 10, 2019, www.daytondailynews.com/news/local/opioid-battle-region-getting-boost-from-big-data/2jIma9Pyc69A8l nT2l0jaO. See also Katie Wedell, "Ohio City Attempts to Shed 'Overdose Capital of the Nation' Title," *Dayton Daily News*, June 24, 2018.

3. Abby Goodnough, "This City's Overdose Deaths Have Plunged. Can Others Learn from It?" *New York Times*, November 25, 2018, www.nytimes.com/2018/11/25/health/opioid-overdose-deaths-dayton.html.

4. Erin Welch, "A Community of Recovery: Dayton, Ohio's Compassionate, Collective Approach to the Opioid Crisis," Center for American Progress, January 10, 2019, www.americanprogress.org/issues/criminal-justice/reports/2019/01/10/464889/a-community-of-recovery.

5. Julie O'Donnell et al., "Notes from the Field: Overdose Deaths with Carfentanil and Other Fentanyl Analogs Detected—10 States, July 2016–June 2017," *Morbidity and Mortality Weekly Report* 67, no. 27 (July 13, 2018): 767–68, dx.doi.org/10.15585/mmwr.mm6727a4.

6. Chris Harris, "Spirit Airlines Pilot and Wife Found Dead by Kids Had Overdosed on Cocaine and Animal Tranquilizer," *People*, May 31, 2017, people.com/crime/spirit-airlines-pilot-wife-found-dead-children-overdosed-cocaine-animal-tranquilizer.

7. "Carfentanil: A Dangerous New Factor in the U.S. Opioid Crisis," U.S. Drug Enforcement Administration, Officer Safety Alert, www.justice.gov/usao-edky/file/898991/download.

8. O'Donnell et al., "Notes from the Field: Overdose Deaths with Carfentanil and Other Fentanyl Analogs Detected." See also Dennis Cauchon, "Ohio's Carfentanil Death Rate 21 Times Higher—Yes, 2000%!—Than in Other States," Harm Reduction Ohio, August 6, 2018.

9. Corky Siemaszko, "Too Many Bodies in the Morgue so Coroner Gets Death Trailer, " *NBC News*, March 14, 2017.

10. Jon E. Zibbell et al., "Association of Law Enforcement Seizures of Heroin, Fentanyl, and Carfentanil with Opioid Overdose Deaths in Ohio, 2014–2017," *JAMA Network Open* 2, no. 11 (November 1, 2019): e1914666.

11. Dennis Cauchon, "Special Report: Carfentanil's Deadly Role in Ohio Drug Overdose Deaths," Harm Reduction Ohio, www.harmreductionohio.org/special-report-carfentanils-deadly-role-in-ohio-drug-overdose-deaths.

12. Ibid.

13. Richard C. Cowan, "How the Narcs Created Crack," *National Review Magazine*, December 5, 1986, 26–31.

14. Johann Hari, *Chasing the Scream: The First and Last Days of the War on Drugs* (New York: Bloomsbury, 2015), 230.

15. Cauchon, "Special Report."

16. Goodnough, "This City's Overdose Deaths Have Plunged. Can Others Learn from It?"

17. Ibid.

18. "Senate Passes Landmark Opioid Reforms, Including Portman's STOP Act," press release, Rob Portman, U.S. Senator for Ohio, October 3, 2018, www.portman.senate.gov/newsroom/press-releases/senate-passes-landmark-opioid-reforms-including-portmans-stop-act.

19. Wedell, "Ohio City Attempts to Shed 'Overdose Capital of the Nation' Title."

20. "GBD Results Tool," Global Health Data Exchange, ghdx.healthdata.org/gbd-results-tool.

21. "Top Employers in the Dayton Area," Dayton.com, February 27, 2015, www.dayton.com/business/employment/top-employers-the-dayton-area/58X4L6ox8z15TNIiRpgWZI; and Samuel R. Staley, "Dayton Ohio: The Rise, Fall, and Stagnation of a Former Industrial Juggernaut," *New Geography*, August 4, 2008.

Chapter 13: Rainbows and Unicorns

1. Masha Gessen, "Nan Goldin Leads a Protest at the Guggenheim Against the Sackler Family," *The New Yorker*, February 10, 2019, www.newyorker.com/news/our-columnists/nan-goldin-leads-a-protest-at-the-guggenheim-against-the-sackler-family.

2. According to Jennifer J. Carroll, Traci C. Green, and Rita K. Noonan, in "Evidence-Based Strategies for Preventing Opioid Overdose: What's Working in the United States," U.S. Centers for Disease Control and Prevention, National Center for Injury Prevention and Control, 2018, www.cdc.gov/drugoverdose/pdf/pubs/2018-evidence-based-strategies.pdf, "Programs with one-for-one exchange policies, for example, allow participants only as many syringes as the number of used syringes they return, thus undercutting the program's own effectiveness. When no limits are set on the number of syringes distributed, participants are more likely to have clean syringes on hand when they need them, and they can provide syringes to many more people

than can attend the program themselves, thus multiplying the program's effectiveness. This also increases participants' incentive to visit the program and interact with staff and counselors" (26).

3. Joe Ebel, "Syringe Exchanges Are an Evidence-Based Public Health Intervention," *Newark Advocate*, November 10, 2018, www.newark advocate.com/story/news/2018/11/10/syringe-exchanges-evidence-based -public-health-intervention/1905865002.

4. Gregg S. Gonsalves and Forrest W. Crawford, "Dynamics of the HIV Outbreak and Response in Scott County, Indiana, 2011–15: A Modeling Study," *Lancet HIV* 5, no. 10 (October 2018): e569–e577; and Steven W. Thrasher, "Mike Pence Is Still to Blame for an HIV Outbreak in Indiana—but for New Reasons," *The Nation*, October 4, 2018, www.thenation.com/article/mike -pence-is-still-to-blame-for-an-hiv-outbreak-in-indiana-but-for-new-reasons.

5. See Gonsalves and Crawford, "Dynamics of the HIV Outbreak and Response in Scott County, Indiana, 2011–15."

6. Ellsworth M. Campbell et al., "Detailed Transmission Network Analysis of a Large Opiate-Driven Outbreak of HIV Infection in the United States," *Journal of Infectious Diseases* 216, no. 9 (November 27, 2017): 1053–62.

7. Kent Mallett, "Licking County Board of Health Votes Against Needle Exchange Program," *Newark Advocate*, February 20, 2019, www.newark advocate.com/story/news/2019/02/20/licking-county-board-health-votes -against-needle-exchange-program/2927840002.

8. The Advocate Editorial Board, "Our View: Licking County Health Board's Needle Exchange Vote Was Cowardly," *Newark Advocate*, February 22, 2019.

9. Sheridan Hendrix, "Licking County Balks at Volunteer's Needle Exchanges," *Columbus Dispatch*, November 23, 2019; and Sheridan Hendrix, "Advocates Blast Licking County Health Board's Decision to Ban Needle-Exchange Programs," *Columbus Dispatch*, March 19, 2019.

10. Will Stone, "Phoenix's Underground Needle Exchange Offers Lifeline for Opioid Users," KJZZ, August 31, 2017, science.kjzz.org/content/527188 /phoenixs-underground-needle-exchange-offers-lifeline-opioid-users; and Stephanie Innes, "Shot in the Dark: Phoenix Area Needle Exchange Could End Due to Low Funding, Politics," *Arizona Republic*, July 22, 2019, www .azcentral.com/story/news/local/arizona-health/2019/07/22/shot-dark-needle -exchange-could-close-due-low-funding/1719306001.

11. Katarina Sostaric, "Underground Needle Exchange Helps Iowans Who Inject Drugs," Iowa Public Radio, January 25, 2018, www.iowapublicradio.org/post /underground-needle-exchange-helps-iowans-who-inject-drugs#stream/0.

12. Kent Mallett, "Critics Confront Licking County Health Board on Needle Exchange Rejection," *Newark Advocate*, March 20, 2019.

13. The Advocate Editorial Board, "Our View: Licking County Health Board's Needle Exchange Vote Was Cowardly," *Newark Advocate*, February 22, 2019.

14. See Hendrix, "Advocates Blast Licking County Health Board's Decision to Ban Needle-Exchange Programs."

15. Bryant Somerville, "Licking County Residents Address Health Board, Defend Desire for Needle Exchange Program," 10TV WBNS, March 19, 2019, www.10tv.com/article/licking-county-residents-address-health-board -defend-desire-needle-exchange-program-2019-apr.

16. Christine B. Hanhardt, " 'Dead Addicts Don't Recover': ACT UP's Needle Exchange and the Subjects of Queer Activists History," *GLQ: A Journal of Lesbian and Gay Studies* 24, no. 4 (October 2018): 428.

17. William A. Schwartz, "Drug Addicts with Dirty Needles," *The Nation*, June 20, 1987, 843–46.

18. Daliah Heller and Denise Paone, "Access to Sterile Syringes for Injecting Drug Users in New York City: Politics and Perception (1984–2010)," *Substance Use and Misuse* 46 (2011): 140–49.

19. "Up in Arms Over Needle Exchange," video, Gay Men's Health Crisis, 1988, Gay Men's Health Crisis Records, Manuscripts and Archives Division, New York Public Library.

20. "Possessing Drug Abuse Instruments," Ohio Revised Code 2925.12, codes .ohio.gov/orc/2925.12.

    Syringe programs are covered by "Bloodborne Infectious Disease Prevention Programs," Ohio Revised Code 3707.57, codes.ohio.gov/orc/3707.57.

21. Dennis Hevesi, "Dave Purchase Dies at 73; Led Early Needle Exchange," *New York Times*, January 27, 2013.

22. Benjamin Shepard, *Community Projects as Social Activism: From Direct Action to Direct Services* (Los Angeles: Sage, 2015), 139.

23. Bruce Lambert, "Drug Group to Offer Free Needles to Combat AIDS in New York City," *New York Times*, January 8, 1988.

24. Bruce Lambert, "10 Seized in Demonstrations as They Offer New Needles,"

New York Times, March 7, 1990; and "ACT UP Capsule History: 1990," ACT UP Historical Archive, actupny.org/documents/cron-90.html.

25. Shepard, *Community Projects as Social Activism*, 139–44; and "Needle Exchange Trial," video, Royal S. Marks AIDS Activist Video Collection, 1983–2000, Manuscripts and Archives Division, New York Public Library.

26. Evelyn Nieves, "Judge Acquits Four of Distributing Needles in an Effort to Curb AIDS," *New York Times*, November 8, 1991.

Chapter 14: Beyond Rat Park

1. For the results of some of this library research, see Bruce K. Alexander, *The Globalization of Addiction: A Study in Poverty of the Spirit* (New York: Oxford University Press, 2008), 207–39.

2. According to Steven H. Woolf and Heidi Schoomaker, in "Life Expectancy and Mortality Rates in the United States, 1959–2017," *JAMA* 322, no. 20 (November 26, 2019): 1996–2016, doi.org/10.1001/jama.2019.16932, "The largest relative increases in midlife mortality rates occurred in New England (New Hampshire, 23.3%; Maine, 20.7%; Vermont, 19.9%) and the Ohio Valley (West Virginia, 23.0%; Ohio, 21.6%; Indiana, 14.8%; Kentucky, 14.7%). The increase in midlife mortality during 2010–2017 was associated with an estimated 33,307 excess US deaths, 32.8% of which occurred in 4 Ohio Valley states."

3. Some salient points from "Suicide Deaths Increased by 45% Among All Ohioans and by 56% Among Youth Ages 10–24 from 2007–2018," Ohio Department of Health, November 13, 2019, odh.ohio.gov/wps/portal/gov /odh/media-center/odh-news-releases/ohio-suicide-demographics-trends -report: "From 2007 to 2018 the number of suicide deaths increased nearly 45% in Ohio. Suicide rates are highest among white, non-Hispanic males. From 2007 to 2018 the number of suicides among youth ages 10–24 increased by 56%, and the suicide rate increased by 64%. In 2018, 271 of Ohio's suicide deaths were in this age group. From 2014 to 2018 the suicide rate among black non-Hispanic males increased nearly 54%."

4. "Newark Teen Sentenced for Accidentally Killing Friend," 10TV, WBNS, December 16, 2009, www.10tv.com/article/newark-teen-sentenced-accidentally -shooting-killing-friend.

5. George Orwell, *Down and Out in Paris and London* (New York: Harcourt, 1933), 180–81.

6. Ibid., 182–84.

7. Ibid., 184–85.

8. Tim McKee, "The Geography of Sorrow: Francis Weller on Navigating Our Losses," *The Sun*, October 2015, thesunmagazine.org/issues/478/the -geography-of-sorrow.

Chapter 15: Moments of Recognition

1. Barbara Lazear Ascher, "On Compassion," in *The Habit of Loving* (New York: Random House, 1986).

2. Kent Mallett, "Homelessness Appears to Be a Growing Problem in Licking County," *Newark Advocate*, February 17, 2019.

3. Ibid.

4. " 'It's a Long Hard Ride': The Faces of Newark's Homeless," *Newark Advocate*, February 17, 2019.

5. "Newark City Council Mar 4 2019," YouTube, posted by Newark City Council, March 4, 2019, www.youtube.com/watch?v=kqvLnC2MagA&t=1081s.

6. Ibid., at 29:42–30:07.

7. Michaela Sumner, "Newark Defends Police, Parks Actions in Homeless Camp Removal," *Newark Advocate*, March 5, 2019, www.newarkadvocate .com/story/news/local/2019/03/05/newark-official-defends-police-parks -actions-homeless-camp-removal/3065712002. More recently in central Ohio, camps were demolished in Columbus. See Rita Price, "Homeless Struggle After Makeshift Camps Demolished," *Columbus Dispatch*, December 17, 2019.

8. Field Case Report, Newark Police Department, Case #2019-00005334, February 27, 2019.

9. Alex S. Vitale, *The End of Policing* (New York: Verso, 2017), 91.

10. Ibid., 92.

11. Ibid.; and Bidish Sarma and Jessica Brand, "The Criminalization of Homelessness: Explained," *The Appeal*, June 29, 2018.

12. "Housing Not Handcuffs, 2019: Ending the Criminalization of Homelessness in U.S. Cities," National Law Center on Homelessness and Poverty, December 2019.

13. "Newark City Council Mar 18 2019," YouTube, posted by Newark City Council, March 18, 2019, www.youtube.com/watch?v=MwJvf1fTIdo.

14. Sheridan Hendrix, "Newark Council Confronted About City's Treatment of Homeless," *Columbus Dispatch*, March 18, 2019, www.dispatch.com /news/20190318/newark-council-confronted-about-citys-treatment-of -homeless; and Kent Mallett, "Residents Express Outrage at Removal of Homeless Camps to Newark City Council," *Newark Advocate*, March 19, 2019.

15. "Newark City Council Apr 15 2019," YouTube, posted by Newark City Council, April 15, 2019, www.youtube.com/watch?v=SMLYnI6nbHU.

16. Kent Mallett, "Mayor Confronted on Homeless Issue After Council Meeting," *Newark Advocate*, April 17, 2019, www.newarkadvocate.com/story /news/2019/04/17/newark-mayor-confronted-homeless-issue-after-council -meeting/3482707002.

17. Michaela Sumner, "Community-Based Group Aims to Reduce Chronic Homelessness in Licking County," *Newark Advocate*, May 23, 2019.

18. Naomi Klein, "Reclaiming the Commons," in *A Movement of Movements: Is Another World Really Possible?* ed. Tom Mertes (New York: Verso, 2004), 227.

19. Ibid., 228.

20. According to Gabor Maté, in his TED talk "The Power of Addiction and the Addiction of Power," TEDxRio, October 9, 2012, www.youtube.com /watch?time_continue=1&v=66cYcSak6nE&feature=emb_title, "Let's not look to the people in power to change things. Because the people in power, I'm afraid to say, are very often some of the emptiest people in the world and they're not going to change things for us. We have to find that light within ourselves, that light within communities."

Chapter 16: Corners

1. "Licking County Health Department: The Stigma of Addiction," video, Flicker-lit Productions, 2019, posted on Vimeo, vimeo.com/337444434.

2. "Agenda for HRO's 'Family Matters' Conference on Saturday, April 6," Harm Reduction Ohio, March 29, 2019.

3. "The Granville Riot: Granville's Reaction to the 1836 Abolitionist Convention Held at the Bancroft Barn on North Street," *The Historical Times: Newsletter of the Granville, Ohio, Historical Society* 12, no. 3 (Summer 1998), static.squarespace.com/static/5054b15de4b02b42cb2ebd87/5054b1c0e 4b02aa16c339410/5054b1c0e4b02aa16c339413/1339881980031.

4. Kent Mallett, "Residents Rally Against Move of Gazebo from Courthouse Square," *Newark Advocate*, October 3, 2017.

5. Kent Mallett, "Commissioners Won't Light Courthouse in LGBTQ Rainbow Colors for Pride Event," *Newark Advocate*, April 20, 2018, www.newark advocate.com/story/news/2018/04/20/commissioners-wont-light-courthouse -lgbtq-rainbow-colors-pride-event/532882002.

6. Sara Tobias, "People's Pride Lights Courthouse," *Newark Advocate*, June 9, 2018, www.newarkadvocate.com/story/news/local/2018/06/09/peoples-pride -lights-courthouse/687268002.

7. Jack Shuler, *The Thirteenth Turn: A History of the Noose* (New York: Public Affairs, 2014), 183–95.

8. See Johann Hari, *Chasing the Scream: The First and Last Days of the War on Drugs* (New York: Bloomsbury, 2015).

9. For a quick discussion of this, see David Emery and Kim Lacapria, "Did the U.S. Government Purposely Poison 10,000 Americans During Prohibition?" Snopes.com, May 12, 2017, www.snopes.com/fact-check/government -poison-10000-americans.

10. *State of Ohio v. Billy R. McCall*, Case No. 18 CR 490, Second Stage Revocation Hearing, Transcript of Proceedings Before the Honorable Thomas Marcelain, July 18, 2019.

11. Jails and prisons increase a person's risk of death, especially for those people with substance use disorders. See Elias Nosrati et al., "Economic Decline, Incarceration, and Mortality from Drug Use Disorders in the USA Between 1983 and 2014: An Observational Analysis," *Lancet Public Health* 4, no. 7 (July 2019): e326–e333.

12. *State of Ohio v. Billy R. McCall*, 2017, Case No. CR 00709.

13. Elizabeth L. C. Merrall et al., "Meta-Analysis of Drug-Related Deaths Soon After Release from Prison," *Addiction* 105, no. 9 (2010): 1545–54.

14. "HRO Syringe Program Advocacy Director Billy McCall Sentenced to Prison for Addiction to Heroin," Harm Reduction Ohio, July 18, 2019, www .harmreductionohio.org/hro-syringe-program-advocacy-director-billy -mccall-sentenced-to-prison-for-addiction-to-heroin.

Chapter 17: "Every Overdose Is a Policy Failure"

1. "Drug Overdose Deaths," U.S. Centers for Disease Control and Prevention, June 27, 2019, www.cdc.gov/drugoverdose/data/statedeaths.html.

2. Travis Lupick, "Is Vancouver's Downtown Eastside Still the 'Poorest Postal Code'

in Canada?" *Georgia Straight*, April 8, 2019, www.straight.com/news/1225081 /vancouvers-downtown-eastside-still-poorest-postal-code-canada.

3. Nurses and Nurse Practitioners of BC, "B.C. Honours Excellence in Nursing," press release, GlobeNewswire, December 17, 2018, www.globenewswire .com/news-release/2018/12/17/1668231/0/en/B-C-Honours-Excellence-in -Nursing.html.

4. Travis Lupick, *Fighting for Space: How a Group of Drug Users Transformed One City's Struggle with Addiction* (Vancouver: Arsenal, 2017). Note: This book should be the starting point for anyone wanting to understand this movement. It is a force.

5. Bud Osborn, "1000 Crosses in Oppenheimer Park," video, posted at Vimeo by Liz Evans, vimeo.com/94463923.

6. "Insite User Statistics," Vancouver Coastal Health, July 2019, www.vch.ca /public-health/harm-reduction/supervised-consumption-sites/insite-user -statistics.

7. Ibid. The following statistics are listed:
    - 189,837 visits by 5,436 individuals
    - An average of 337 injection room visits per day
    - 1,466 overdose interventions
    - 3,725 clinical treatment interventions (such as wound care, pregnancy tests)
    - Substances reported used were opioids (62% of instances), stimulant (19% of instances), and mixed (19% of instances)

8. Elana Gordon, "In Vancouver, People Who Use Drugs Are Supervising Injections and Reversing Overdoses," *The World*, Public Radio International, September 24, 2018, www.pri.org/stories/2018-09-24/vancouver-people-who -use-drugs-are-supervising-injections-and-reversing-overdoses.

9. "Overdose Prevention Sites," Portland Hotel Society, www.phs.ca/project /overdose-prevention-sites.

10. "Providence Crosstown Clinic," Providence Health Care, www.providence healthcare.org/hospitals-residences/providence-crosstown-clinic.

11. Spike, "How Legal Prescription Heroin Saved Me: One Participant of a Groundbreaking Vancouver Health Experiment Tells His Story," *The Tyee*, February 8, 2016, thetyee.ca/Opinion/2016/02/08/Legal-Prescription -Heroin; and "How Crosstown Clinic Helped a Vancouver City Council Candidate Get His Life Back," *Daily Scan*, September 17, 2018, thedailyscan .providencehealthcare.org/2018/09/crosstown-and-spike.

12. Eugenia Oviedo-Joekes et al., "Diacetylmorphine versus Methadone for the Treatment of Opioid Addiction," *New England Journal of Medicine* 361, no. 8 (August 2009): 777–86.

13. The program at Crosstown even has an independent peer-run group connected to the HAT program. See Susan Boyd, Dave Murray, and Donald MacPherson, "Telling our Stories: Heroin-Assisted Treatment and SNAP Activism in the Downtown Eastside of Vancouver," *Harm Reduction Journal* 14, no. 1 (May 2017): 27–14.

14. See Franziska Güttinger et al., "Evaluating Long-Term Effects of Heroin-Assisted Treatment: The Results of a 6-Year Follow-Up," *European Addiction Research* 9, no. 2 (May 2003): 73–79. For an overview of early HAT programs, see Benedikt Fischer et al., "Heroin-Assisted Treatment (HAT) a Decade Later: A Brief Update on Science and Politics," *Journal of Urban Health* 84, no. 4 (July 2007): 552–62.

15. BC Substance Use Conference, May 23–25, 2019, www.bccsu.ca/event/bc -substance-use-conference-2019/.

16. Geoff Bardwell, Evan Wood, and Rupinder Brar, "Fentanyl Assisted Treatment: A Possible Role in the Opioid Overdose Epidemic?" *Substance Abuse Treatment, Prevention, and Policy* 14, no. 1 (2019): 1–3; Taylor Fleming, Alison Barker, et al., "Stimulant Safe Supply: A Potential Opportunity to Respond to the Overdose Epidemic," *Harm Reduction Journal* 17, 6 (2020).

17. "Safe Supply Concept Document," Canadian Association of People Who Use Drugs, February 2019.

18. See, for example, John L. McKnight and John P. Kretzmann, "Mapping Community Capacity," revised ed., Institute for Policy Research, Northwestern University, 1996, web.archive.org/web/20161011224806/http://www .abcdinstitute.org/docs/MappingCapacity.pdf.

19. "Episode 3: Unsanctioned," *Crackdown*, crackdownpod.com/podcast/episode -3-unsanctioned.

20. *Crackdown*, crackdownpod.com.

21. Ten years ago, an article in *The Globe and Mail* asserted that 14 percent of the people in the Downtown Eastside were indigenous. See Patrick Brethour, "Exclusive Demographic Picture," *Globe and Mail*, February 13, 2009.

22. "Episode 7: Stand Down," *Crackdown*, podcast, July 31, 2019, crackdownpod .com/podcast/episode-7-stand-down; and Alexandra B. Collins et al., "Policing Space in the Overdose Crisis: A Rapid Ethnographic Study of the Impact

of Law Enforcement Practices on the Effectiveness of Overdose Prevention Sites," *International Journal of Drug Policy* 73 (November 2019): 199–207.

23. E. J. Dickson, "Philadelphia May Become the First City to Open Safe Injection Sites," *Rolling Stone*, September 5, 2019, www.rollingstone.com /culture/culture-news/philadelphia-safe-injection-sites-880346; and Bobby Allyn, "Judge Rules Planned Supervised Injection Site Does Not Violate Federal Drug Laws," National Public Radio, October 2, 2019, www.npr .org/2019/10/02/766500743/judge-rules-plan-for-safehouse-drug-injection -site-in-philadelphia-can-go-forwar.

24. "Louise's Story," Drug Policy Alliance, www.drugpolicy.org/drugsellers /louise; and Louise Vincent, "The Rage of Overdose Grief Makes It All Too Easy to Misdirect Blame," *Filter*, December 5, 2018, filtermag.org /the-rage-of-overdose-grief-makes-it-all-too-easy-to-misdirect-blame.

25. Angela Y. Davis, *Freedom Is a Constant Struggle: Ferguson, Palestine, and the Foundations of a Movement* (Chicago: Haymarket Books, 2015).

26. "Episode 18: Drug User Unions—The Rebirth of Harm Reduction," *Narcotica*, podcast, podcasts.apple.com/us/podcast/narcotica-podcast/id1390336378?i =1000437419170.

27. Travis Lupick, "How Drug Users Are Fighting Back Against America's War on Drugs," *Yes! Magazine*, December 10, 2019.

28. Zachary Siegel, "The Struggle of Death, Hope and Harm Reduction in the Midwest," *Filter*, October 7, 2019, filtermag.org/death-harm-reduction-midwest.

29. Colin Miller, "On a Mission to Show Up for Drug Users in West Virginia," *Filter*, October 22, 2019, filtermag.org/drug-users-west-virginia.

Chapter 18: Worth Our Keep

1. "17-2804 - In Re: National Prescription Opiate Litigation," GovInfo, www .govinfo.gov/app/details/USCOURTS-ohnd-1_17-md-02804/USCOURTS -ohnd-1_17-md-02804-0/summary.

2. Laura Strickler, "Purdue Pharma Offers $10–12 Billion to Settle Opioid Claims," *NBC News*, August 27, 2019, www.nbcnews.com/news/us-news /purdue-pharma-offers-10-12-billion-settle-opioid-claims-n1046526.

3. As of early 2020. "America's Richest Families," *Forbes*, www.forbes.com /families/list/#tab:overall; Tom Maloney, Jef Feeley, and Bloomberg, "Sacklers to Remain Billionaire Family If Purdue Settles Opioid Lawsuits," *Fortune*, August 28, 2019, fortune.com/2019/08/28/sackler-family-billionaires

-opioid-crisis-lawsuits; and Mike Spector, "OxyContin Maker Purdue Pharma Files for Bankruptcy Protection," *Reuters*, September 15, 2019, www .reuters.com/article/us-purdue-pharma-bankruptcy-idUSKBN1W1058.

4. Jan Hoffman, "$260 Million Opioid Settlement Reached at Last Minute with Big Drug Companies," *New York Times*, October 21, 2019, www .nytimes.com/2019/10/21/health/opioid-settlement.html.

5. Andy Chow, "Kasich Fears Potential Opioid Settlement Could Be Frittered Away," Statehouse News Bureau, August 22, 2019.

6. One positive intervention would be for more money to get in the hands of community-based harm-reduction programs. See Maia Szalavitz, "The Bankruptcy Money from the Makers of Oxycontin Might Actually Save Lives," *Vice*, October 24, 2019, www.vice.com/en_us/article/kz4y7x/purdue-pharma -oxycontin-bankruptcy-could-fund-harm-reduction-and-save-lives.

7. Some suggest that naloxone should be readily available over the counter. See Corey S. Davis and Derek Carr, "Over the Counter Naloxone Needed to Save Lives in the United States," *Preventive Medicine* 130 (November 2019): 105932.

8. Johann Hari, in *Chasing the Scream: The First and Last Days of the War on Drugs* (New York: Bloomsbury, 2015), says it well when writing about a few of the issues this book addresses: "If you are alone, you are vulnerable to addiction, and if you are alone, you are vulnerable to the drug war. But if you take the first step and find others who agree with you—if you make connection—you lose your vulnerability, and you start to win" (297).

9. Ricardo Alonso-Zaldivar, "Feds to let states tap opioid funds for meth, cocaine surge," Associated Press News, January 21, 2020, apnews.com /d71e1848689d214595387169cd946f39.

10. "Jeremy Blake with Sherrod Brown," YouTube, posted by Adam Rhodes, September 16, 2019, www.youtube.com/watch?v=7sKKzhUGXYo&feature =youtu.be.

11. Shanti Basu, "Success of Newark Recovery Home for Women Leads to New Option for Men," *Newark Advocate*, December 8, 2019, www .newarkadvocate.com/story/news/local/2019/12/08/success-newark-recovery -home-women-leads-new-option-men/4302691002.

12. Sam Sobul, "Ohio Syringe Services Program Profiles," The Center for Community Solutions, May 2019, www.communitysolutions.com/wp-content

/uploads/2019/05/IssueBrief_Ohio-Syringe-Services-Program-Profiles_SSobul_updated-05202019.pdf.

13. Kent Mallett, "Former Longaberger Building to Open for Business Again as Luxury Hotel," *Newark Advocate*, October 21, 2019, www.newarkadvocate.com/story/news/2019/10/21/former-longaberger-basket-building-open-business-again/4057557002.

14. Kent Mallett, "United Way's Hope Award Winner: From Homeless to Helping Others," *Newark Advocate*, May 3, 2018, www.newarkadvocate.com/story/news/2018/05/03/united-ways-hope-award-winner-homeless-helping-others/576494002.

15. Clare Roth, "Ohio Opioid Technology Challenges Awards $1 Million to Four Projects," WOSU Public Media, August 27, 2019, radio.wosu.org/post/ohio-opioid-technology-challenges-awards-1-million-four-projects#stream/0.

16. This will require a significant amount of momentum and money—some estimate at least $100 billion. See Nabarun Dasgupta, Leo Beletsky, and Daniel Ciccarone, "Opioid Crisis: No Easy Fix to Its Social and Economic Determinants," *American Journal of Public Health* 108, no. 2 (2018): 184; and Daniel Ciccarone, "The Triple Wave Epidemic: Supply and Demand Drivers of the US Opioid Overdose Crisis," *International Journal of Drug Policy* 71 (2019): 186.

Postscript

1. "She's Saving Lives by Giving Clean Needles to Opioid Addicts," CNN, November 5, 2019, www.facebook.com/watch/?v=559631781455570.

2. Lin Ma, Lam Tran, and David White, "A Summary of the State Unintentional Drug Overdose Reporting Surveillance Dataset in Ohio, 2016–2018," under review. This research is based on analysis of the National Center for Injury Prevention and Control, State Unintentional Drug Overdose Reporting Surveillance (SUDORS) dataset for Ohio, 2016–2018, retrieved July 20, 2019, Ohio Department of Health. Work on this dataset can be found here: personal.denison.edu/~whiteda/research.html.

JACK SHULER is the author of three books, including *The Thirteenth Turn: A History of the Noose*. His writing has appeared in *The New Republic, Pacific Standard, The Christian Science Monitor, 100 Days in Appalachia*, and *Los Angeles Times*, among other publications. He is chair of the narrative journalism program at Denison University. He lives in Ohio. Find out more at jackshulerauthor.com.